# SUPERPOWER RIVALRY AND THIRD WORLD RADICALISM

# SUPERPOWER RIVALRY &3rd WORLD RADICALISM:

## THE IDEA OF NATIONAL LIBERATION

S. Neil MacFarlane

**THE JOHNS HOPKINS UNIVERSITY PRESS**
Baltimore, Maryland

© 1985 S. Neil MacFarlane

First published in the United States of America, 1985, by
The Johns Hopkins University Press
Baltimore, Maryland 21218

First published in Great Britain by
Croom Helm Ltd

Library of Congress Cataloging in Publication Data

MacFarlane, S. Neil.
    Superpower rivalry and Thirld World radicalism.

    Bibliography: p. 216
    Includes index.
    1. Nationalism.  2. National liberation movements.
3. World politics — 1945-     . I. Title.
JC311.M255   1985     320.5'4     84-43081
ISBN 0-8018-2671-3


Printed and bound in Great Britain

# CONTENTS

# ACKNOWLEDGEMENTS

The author is indebted to Professor Hedley Bull and Doctor Richard Kindersley, both of the University of Oxford, for their suggestions at various stages of this study. He is also grateful to the Social Sciences and Humanities Research Council of Canada, the Olin Foundation, and the Canadian Department of National Defence for financial support. The International Institute for Strategic Studies, Harvard University's Center for International Affairs, and the University of British Columbia's Institute of International Relations provided a congenial working environment in which to write the book. Lastly, the author wishes to express his gratitude to his wife, to whom this book is dedicated, for her advice, stamina and patience.

# SUPERPOWER RIVALRY AND THIRD WORLD RADICALISM

# 1 INTRODUCTION

> In its individual and concrete expressions, nationalism carries
> a different meaning with different peoples and at different
> ages. But an understanding of nationalism can be gained only
> by comparing similar developments among different peoples;
> only a universal history of nationalism will enable the student
> to see each individual case in its proper perspective and in its
> conditional nature.[1]

Perhaps the most significant development in international politics since
the Second World War has been the disappearance of the overseas
colonial empires of the European powers and the emergence from their
ashes of a host of new members of the system of states. This may be
attributed to a number of factors: the exhaustion of the colonial
powers in two world wars; the rise of two superpowers on the edges of
Europe, both of which were committed to some form of self-determination for colonial peoples (with the exception of subject peoples within
their own borders); and the growing preoccupation of European publics
and their governments with considerations of economic well-being and
social welfare at home rather than imperial power and prestige abroad.

Yet any explanation of the decline of European and, more broadly,
Western power in the Third World[2] which failed to take into account
indigenous Asian, African and Latin American forces would be incom-
plete and distorted. Among these forces, the most significant was the
anti-colonialism of new elites in colonial societies.

In the 1950s and early 1960s, the struggle of subject peoples against
colonial rule took the form of peaceful agitation, followed by the grant
of independence. This pattern was dominant in such cases as India and
Ceylon, and in many of the British and French colonies in sub-Saharan
Africa. In a number of cases where insurgencies against colonial rule
occurred (for example, Kenya, Malaya, Madagascar and the Cam-
eroons), the colonial power accompanied or followed its defeat of the
rebels with concessions leading ultimately to independence.

But during this period, there was another pattern of struggle in the
Third World, one typified by the appearance of national revolutionary
movements — groups engaged in struggle against foreign rulers or
against indigenous regimes deemed to be dependent upon and sub-
servient to outsiders and indifferent to the basic needs of the populations these regimes purported to serve.[3] Such movements were

1

prominent, for example, in the Chinese revolution which culminated in the establishment of communist power in 1949, in the struggle of the Vietnamese against the French and, subsequently, in the Indochinese conflict of 1956-75, in the Algerian war, in civil violence in Latin America from the mid-1950s to the present, and in the convulsions which have beset Southern Africa since the early 1960s. All of these struggles have been waged by indigenous movements and their external allies in the name of 'national liberation'. The movements prominent in them have all to varying degrees attempted to elaborate 'doctrines of national liberation'.[4] The growing salience in the 1970s of this kind of struggle in Africa in particular, as the continent's colonial problem narrowed to territories governed by states peculiarly resistant to the self-determination of subject peoples, led some to conclude that there had occurred a qualitative transition from an era of decolonization to one of national liberation.

The anti-Western rhetoric and, often, actions of national liberation movements, the close links which many of them have forged with the Soviet Union,[5] and the emergence of a number of states formed and led by them to positions of influence in the nonaligned movement and in the group of states agitating for a reform of the international economic order, make the phenomenon of national liberation in the Third World and its ideological underpinnings matters of serious concern for Western policy-makers.

For these reasons, a clearer understanding of the idea of national liberation and of its implications for the internal and external policies of states formed by national liberation movements would be of considerable utility. It is the purpose of this analysis to provide such an understanding. With this in mind, the following chapters address a number of questions. Does there exist an idea of national liberation which is widely shared by national revolutionary movements in the Third World? How does this idea fit into the wider current of Third World nationalism? What are the historical, intellectual, and experiential roots of doctrines of national liberation? How does the idea of national liberation relate to European nationalism, to the principle of self-determination, and to marxist-leninist thought concerning social and political change in the Third World? To what degree and in what ways is the idea of national liberation consistent with Soviet and Western conceptions of political development in the Third World? What practical implications does the spread of doctrines of national liberation have for the internal and external behaviour of states formed by national liberation movements, for Soviet and Western interests in the Third World, and for the structure of the international system?

Before beginning the analysis, two critical assumptions should be spelled out. First, man's ideas, and the political programmes in which these are sometimes expressed, are related to practical reality in two ways. They reflect the concrete problems with which men are trying to cope, and they influence the behaviour of those who hold them. As the term is used here, a political ideology is a system of ideas, comprehending basic ethical commitments and a vision of a better world towards which we should strive. Particularly in the case of revolutionary ideologies,[6] these constitute a basis for criticism of things as they are. Beyond this, such a system of ideas includes fundamental methodological and analytical assumptions which constitute the intellectual prism through which the world is perceived.[7] At a less profound level they provide a political programme, designed to move the society in question from where it is to where it should be.[8]

Historical and political reality may impinge upon theory at a number of levels. It is in response to this reality that men define their basic commitments. It is under the constraints of this reality that they translate basic commitments into strategy and tactics. It is as a consequence of historical experience that they recast strategies and tactics, and, when necessary, adjust the perceptual filters which an ideology provides. Finally, continued frustration in political activity may ultimately cause actors to moderate, postpone, or abandon their basic commitments.

Theory, on the other hand, may affect practice in determining the ultimate objectives and basic direction of a movement, in providing its methodology, and in that it embodies the strategic and tactical principles upon which specific actions are based.

It is not being maintained here that the practice of radical political movements is guided solely by the ideology which its members embrace. Self-interest — the quest for power, prestige, or property — or personal eccentricity may account in large part for the actions of national revolutionaries. Ideology provides in such cases a justification for action and a veneer of legitimacy and respectability in the search for support inside and beyond borders. But to exclude entirely the possibility that ideology influences behaviour — to hold doctrine to be irrelevant in explaining actions and the mistakes of political movements — is to maintain that there is no relation between belief and action and between strategy and policy. Even if one were to accept such improbable assertions, the study of ideology would remain important, given the significance of ideology in mobilizing support among elites, if not among the mass of the population,[9] in securing external support, and in legitimizing party rule.

The second assumption concerns methodological problems in determining what doctrine really is. The statements a group issues or the thoughts which its thinkers set to paper are not absolutely reliable, for they are often adjusted to appeal to specific audiences whose support is being sought.[10] In this sense, the public utterances of a political figure may represent not what he thinks or the cause he embraces, but what he wants a particular audience to hear.[11] The tone and substance of a speech by the leader of a liberation movement to a Soviet party congress at which he is making an appeal for material support are likely to differ substantially from statements he might make to a meeting of American churchmen or at indoctrination sessions for party cadres.

It is frequently suggested in response to this problem that it is the actions of a group, rather than its programmes or theories, which are indicative of its beliefs and commitments. But actions, *a priori*, may not be very reliable indicators of real desires either. A man with no desire to kill may yet be coerced into murdering another. To take a more pertinent example, when a government dependent on Soviet support consistently backs the Soviet line on Afghanistan and Kampuchea in the United Nations, this does not necessarily mean that it shares the Soviet viewpoint. It may wish however, to avoid the loss of Soviet aid.

In a similar vein, a group may act in a certain way, not because such a course of action is its preferred alternative, but because its range of choice is severely restricted. The action chosen is the one which is most palatable in these circumstances. Many revolutionaries choose violence after much soul-searching, not because they like the taste of blood, but because they perceive it to be the only alternative to continued oppression. Analogously, Angola and Mozambique welcome foreign direct investment in their economies not because their commitment to socialism is mere rhetoric, but largely because the only alternative to such involvement is stagnation and privation. Purely socialist development is not an available option, in the prevailing circumstances.

Finally, even if one discounted completely the utility of stated commitments and objectives of political movements as evidence of beliefs — a step which for reasons noted above seems somewhat extreme — the statements of political movements may none the less have considerable historical impact. However insincere they may be, they contribute to a strengthening and spread of hitherto often little known and little accepted concepts. Barrington Moore noted with regard to the example cited above (note 10) that despite the hypocrisy of those propounding the rights of man and the social contract in defence of their own privileges, 'the conceptions of the inviolability of property and freedom of the individual received a powerful impetus from this concrete historical situation'.[12]

In summary, neither statements nor actions are unambiguous indicators of commitment. As such, judgement must be exercised in evaluating their value as evidence. Statements made in some contexts (for example material prepared for the indoctrination of cadres, or congress and politburo resolutions which result from internal debate and which are intended for the guidance of party activists) are more reliable than ones made in others (for example, those designed to acquire the support of those outside the movement). Positions which remain constant over substantial periods of time are more useful here than those which oscillate wildly in response to external pressures. Doctrinal statements and actions vary with the doctrine and policy of critical allies more certainly reflect basic values than do those which conform strictly to the outsiders' position. Theory and practice are of greater significance as indications of real objectives when they coincide than when they diverge. The second assumption is, therefore, that a movement's ideology may be determined with reasonable accuracy by careful attention to its stated doctrine and its actions, and to the relation between the two in the context of the external constraints under which the movements must operate.

The argument of this book may be summarized as follows. First, there exists − despite the great variety in historical circumstance and ideological commitment among national revolutionary movements in Asia, Africa, and Latin America − a widely shared idea of national liberation. National liberation, as defined by Third World revolutionary movements, comprises four elements: political independence; freedom from external economic control; social revolution aimed at removing indigenous oppression based on tradition and/or that stemming from the implantation of structures of exploitation by the colonial power; and, finally, cultural regeneration with a view to restoring the dignity and self-respect of subject peoples and destroying those aspects of the cultural legacy of imperialism and the pre-colonial heritage which stand in the way of the creation of a 'new man'. The outcome of the process is a socialist society. It is generally maintained that the process is not complete without the satisfaction of all four of these conditions.

The idea of national liberation entertained by those involved in armed revolution does not differ in essentials from the objectives outlined by prominent nationalist figures, such as Nehru, Sekou Toure, Nkrumah and Nyerere, who eschewed violence and who sought decolonization through negotiation rather than through force. This common ground between what might be loosely called militants and moderates or revolutionaries and reformists reflects a number of ubiquitous characteristics of the experience of Western domination.

Moreover, the idea reflects a shared intellectual heritage. It is a blend of marxist universalism, of nationalist particularism as it developed in Europe in the eighteenth and nineteenth centuries, and of the liberal conception of self-determination.

Fourth, while drawing from these sources, the idea of national liberation is distinct from earlier forms of nationalism in its inclusion of economic and social revolutionary tasks in the definition of the concept itself.[13] For the same reason, it goes well beyond the conception of national self-determination developed by liberal statesmen and thinkers in the nineteenth and early twentieth centuries in Europe and North America. It differs substantially from orthodox marxism-leninism in its refusal to subordinate national to class objectives and in its emphasis on the national rather than the global context in which revolutionary change is to occur.

Fifth, the idea of national liberation is far more closely compatible with the Soviet than it is with the Western conception of political and social development in the Third World. This creates an ideological affinity between the Soviet Union and the socialist camp on the one hand and revolutionary nationalist movements in the Third World on the other. This in turn gives the Soviet Union a number of advantages in its dealings with these movements and with the states which these movements have come to govern. However, the unwillingness of such movements to accept submergence within a global process of revolution or subordination to the international objectives of any external actor, an unwillingness which reflects the concern of revolutionary nationalist elites to defend and increase their own power, tightly circumscribes this affinity. Ideological incompatibilities between Soviet and Third World conceptions of national liberation — largely the result of this particularism — have contributed to a significant number of set-backs for Soviet foreign policy in Asia, Africa, and Latin America. This particularism also limits the prospects for broadly based co-operation among radical nationalist forces in the Third World.

Finally, the maximalist character of the idea of national liberation and of the economic, social, and cultural programmes which it entails, coupled with the inadequacy of economic and human resources at the disposal of national liberation movements once they take power, encourages the concentration of political and economic power in the hands of the state and of the vanguard at its centre. In general, this discourages political pluralism and may impede economic development by forcing it into modes for which the population is ill adapted and to which they are resistant.

The substantiation of these arguments takes the following form. Chapters 2 and 3 discuss the marxist, nationalist, and liberal roots of doctrines of national liberation. Chapter 4 outlines the idea of national liberation as it has been elaborated in theory and practice by a wide variety of movements in the Third World which have taken up arms in order to secure independence or what they perceive to be social justice. It then compares these doctrines with the perspectives of a sample of Asian and African nationalists who did not employ force as a means of achieving their ends. Chapters 5 and 6 contrast Soviet and Western conceptions of Third World revolution and political change with the ideas developed in Chapter 4. Chapter 7 concludes with a consideration of the implications of the analysis for the domestic and foreign policies of new states, and for the interests of East and West in the Third World.

## Notes

1. Hans Kohn, *The Idea of Nationalism*, New York, Collier, 1967, p. 120.
2. For the purposes of this analysis, the Third World includes Asia (including the non-Russian areas of Soviet Asia, but excluding Japan), Africa, Latin America, the Caribbean, and Oceania, excluding Australia and New Zealand. Attempts to define the Third World in exclusively geographical, political, or economic terms all result in anomalies. Perhaps the only real substance in what is, despite its inadequacies, quite a useful category lies in a sense of victimization by and a desire for redress from Europe and North America which has been, or is shared by elites in all of the regions mentioned above.
3. One might also characterize these groups as radical movements, in that they repudiate the very essence of existing political and social relations, seek to replace them with their own alternative vision of society, and display a willingness to work outside the political system, by whatever means at their disposal, to replace the present with their desired future. On the definition of radicalism, see R. C. Tucker, *The Marxian Revolutionary Idea*, New York, Norton, 1969, pp. 181-5. For the distinction between radical and reformist movements, see ibid., pp. 185-8.
4. For the purposes of this analysis, a doctrine is a political programme enunciating a set of objectives, providing strategies and tactics designed to attain these objectives, and defining attitudes to be adopted *vis-a-vis* political forces outside the movement.
5. On this point Jennifer Whitaker has noted that the ideological affinity between left wing national liberation movements and the Soviet Union has created opportunities for the latter to expand its influence in Africa (J. S. Whitaker, 'U.S. Policy toward Africa' in J. S. Whitaker, ed., *The U.S. and Africa: Vital Interests*,

New York, New York University Press, 1978, pp. 213, 226. S. Hosmer and
T. Wolfe (*Soviet Policy and Practice toward Third World Conflicts*, Lexington:
D.C. Heath, 1982, pp. 165, 177) also take the view that Third World 'radicalism'
works to the Soviet advantage. D. Zagoria ('Into the Breach: New Soviet Alliances
in the Third World', *Foreign Affairs*, Spring 1979, pp. 733-43) characterizes
Angola's MPLA as a pro-Soviet communist party, and views the coming to power
of such 'communist' regimes in South Vietnam, Ethiopia, Angola, South Yemen,
Kampuchea, etc., as an important alteration of the Soviet-American balance of
power.

6. I.e., those advocating action outside the institutionalized political system in
order to effect fundamental change in social relations.

7. The above corresponds to some degree to Karl Mannheim's notion of 'total
ideology', elaborated in *Ideology and Utopia*, London, Routledge and Kegan Paul,
1936, Chapter 3; and to F. Schurmann's 'pure ideology', as explained in *Ideology
and Organization in Communist China*, 2nd ed, Berkeley, University of California
Press, 1971, pp. 21-3. For discussion of ideology as an intellectual prism through
which Soviet analysts and political writers perceive the world around them, see
V. Aspaturian, 'Soviet Foreign Policy' in R. Macridis, ed., *Foreign Policy and
World Politics*, Englewood Cliffs, Prentice Hall, 1976, p. 171; and W. Zimmerman,
*Soviet Perspectives on International Relations*, Princeton, Princeton University
Press, 1969, pp. 6-7. For a discussion of the relationship between American
doctrine and policy concerning the Third World, see R. Packenham, *Liberal
America and the Third World*, Princeton, Princeton University Press, 1973,
pp. xviii-xx.

8. This resembles Schurmann's 'practical ideology' (Schurmann, *Ideology and
Organization*, pp. 21-3). For an illuminating discussion of the historical development of the concept of ideology, see G. Lichtheim, *The Concept of Ideology and
Other Essays*, New York, Random House, 1967, pp. 3-46. Admittedly, few of the
movements considered here developed bodies of writing which constituted systematic and consistent theoretical wholes corresponding to this description here.
But, in general, their writings do contain, often in rudimentary form, such basic
commitments, methodological assumptions, and statements of strategy and
tactics.

9. Joel Migdal argues convincingly that to the extent that the mass of the rural
population is involved in revolutionary activity in the less developed countries,
this is a result of desperation stemming from prolonged economic crisis rather
than revolutionary consciousness. J. Migdal, *Peasants, Politics and Revolution:
Pressures toward Political and Social Change in the Thirld World*, Princeton,
Princeton University Press, 1974, pp. 228-51. See also B. Moore, *The Social
Origins of Dictatorship and Democracy*, Boston, Beacon, 1967, p.70; and T.R.
Gurr, *Why Men Rebel*, Princeton, Princeton University Press, 1970, pp. 103-5.
Gurr notes, however, that:

> The articulation of nationalist ideologies in colonial territories of Asia and
> Africa in the first half of the 20th Century evidently strengthened preexisting
> desires for political independence among the colonial bourgeoisie, at the same
> time that it inspired quite a new set of expectations among other groups.
> (Ibid., p. 68)

10. This is an old problem. Barrington Moore (*Social Origins*, pp. 60-1), for
example, cites Voltaire's disgust in the eighteenth century with the use by the
French nobility and *bourgeois de robe* of concepts such as 'the natural rights of
man, freedom of the individual and political liberty, even the social contract' to
oppose the king's attempts to abolish the sale of hereditary offices and the

venality of justice.

11. For an argument along these lines, see C. Clapham, 'The Context of African Political Thought', *Journal of Modern African Studies*, VIII (1970), no. 1, pp. 1, 3, 4.

12. Moore, *Social Origins*, p. 61.

13. A qualified exception being made here for the economic nationalism of Friedrich List (see Chapter 2).

# 2 EUROPEAN NATIONALISM AND THE LIBERAL CONCEPTION OF NATIONAL SELF-DETERMINATION

In a number of important respects, as shall be seen in Chapter 4, Third World revolutionary nationalism draws upon developments in Western and particularly European thought and politics from the seventeenth to the early twentieth century. The first milestone which should be noted is the emergence of the modern state in seventeenth-century absolutist France — the consolidation of power in the hands of a central government and the emasculation or elimination of competing power centres within the country's borders. This process created one element of the diad which is the nation-state. A contemporaneous development in European thought, resulting from the experience of the wars of religion and the disastrous consequences of close association between state and faith, was the elaboration by Bodin in particular of the theory of state sovereignty. This divorced rulership from divine sanction and replaced the universal *respublica christiana* with a secular international society of equals.

A third and somewhat later development was the shift during the Enlightenment in the locus of sovereignty from the prince to the people and in the basis of legitimacy from dynastic inheritance to popular consent. The roots of the principle of popular sovereignty — that communities are formed by the free choice of self-determining individuals and that the 'sovereign is formed entirely of the individuals who compose it'[1] — lie in the Protestant community of Geneva in the writings of Calvin's successor Theodore de Beze[2] and in England's Puritan revolution. It found its most coherent expression in Rousseau's *Social Contract*[3] and in the theory and, to some extent, political and legal practice of the French Revolution.

Popular sovereignty rests on the assumption that the people, being in relevant senses equal to one another, have a right to an equal say in the determination of their fate, a right to self-determination. They are subjects, rather than objects, of history. It follows that they have a right to decide whether to form a community, what political institutions that community should have, and who should preside over those institutions. The nation, from this perspective, is not a natural phenomenon, but rather the product of the decision of a group of individuals to come together to form a community. Nationalism — in the sense of a feeling of identification with and loyalty to the group which allows the individual to subordinate his own wants to the broader group interest — is the 'spiritual cement' which binds the 'autonomous individual into the partnership of the community'.[4]

However, during the nineteenth century, and in particular in connection with developments in German romantic thought, the principles of popular sovereignty and the right of communities to self-determination took on an increasingly cultural dimension. Perhaps the most important contributor to this trend was Gustav Herder, who viewed the nation — a group possessing a common culture, language, and historical tradition — as a natural phenomenon, and held that the potential of the individual human being could be realized fully only within the context of the nation.[5] His focus, unlike Rousseau's, was not on individual but on national assertion, on the cultivation of the nation and its uniqueness rather than that of the individual, on the national collective rather than the members of it.[6]

This is not to say that there was no universal strain in this body of thought. Indeed, the ultimate objective was the fullest development of humanity as a whole. Yet this goal was attainable not through the transcendence of nationality, but through its cultivation. As Ergang put it:

> Although Herder's idea was universal, this universal ideal did not tend to minimize national differences; on the contrary, Herder's weltanschauung accentuated the national peculiarities, for the development of the national peculiarities was the *sine qua non* of the development of humanity at large.[7]

Schleiermacher and Schlegel took this line of thought one step further. They argued that the highest form of statehood was the nation-state, as it was the only means of developing the inherent gifts of the nation.[8] From here, it was an easy step to the view that, in situations where nations did not possess states, they had a right to establish them at the expense of 'foreign' rulers. This thinking influenced heavily the development of nationalism among subject peoples in the Austro-Hungarian Empire, and in Italy.[9] Elsewhere, it coloured English liberal discussions of self-government. One finds J.S. Mill, for example, asserting in *On Representative Government*:

> When the sentiment of nationality exists in any force, there is a *prima facie* case for uniting all the members of the nationality under

the same government a government to themselves apart. This is merely saying that the question of government ought to be decided by the governed.[10]

The right to self-determination is perceived here to pertain to culturally distinct nationalities, apparently because it is assumed that individuals prefer to live in national communities.

By the early part of this century, it was widely accepted that humanity was naturally divided into nations, that the nation-state was the only legitimate form of government; and, at least in liberal circles, that the principle of self-determination, 'that each nation has a right to constitute an independent state and determine its own government',[11] applied to European nations which formed the large multinational empires of Central and Eastern Europe. In 1919, at the Versailles conference, this principle, and the associated vision of a world order based on it, were endorsed by the victorious Entente powers,[12] though it is questionable to what degree this endorsement determined the character of the peace settlement.

To the argument concerning the rights of nations was added one pertaining to the optimal structure of the international system. Waltz encapsulated the view that an international system based upon nation-states would minimize the incidence of conflict in the following way: 'If each nationality were a separate nation, then each nation would be satisfied with its lot and wars would forever cease.'[13]

At this time, the principle of self-determination began to extend beyond Europe to include the colonial possessions of the great powers. A recognition of the eventual applicability of the right of national self-determination to colonial peoples arguably was implicit in the mandate system established in the peace settlement for the administration of erstwhile German colonies. During the Second World War, Roosevelt's pressure on the British to acquiesce in the ultimate independence of the Asian colonies reflected this trend, though it was by no means devoid of self-interest.[14]

Despite the pre-eminence within it of political and cultural dimensions, Western liberal and nationalist thought had significant economic and social aspects as well. Notions of economic independence are to some extent implicit in the seventeenth and eighteenth century mercantilist recognition that wealth was a critical determinant of national power and in their attempts to control economic activity in such a way as to maximize the wealth of the state.[15] They emerge more clearly in the work of Alexander Hamilton, who stressed the necessity of a broad manufacturing base if the independence of the new American republic were to be assured:

> Not only the wealth, but the independence and security of a country, appear to be materially connected with the prosperity of manufactures. Every nation, with a view to those great objects, ought to endeavour to possess within itself all the essentials of national supply.[16]

Given later developments in the theory of imperialism, it is important to note that it was not 'exploitation' or 'oppression' which was the basis of his plea for self-sufficiency. Self-sufficiency was, in his view, necessary for national prosperity and security. He was by no means opposed to the use of foreign resources in the quest for it. Indeed, Hamilton favoured the involvement of foreign capital in the creation of a strong national economy.[17] This contrasts rather starkly with post-Lenin radical thought on the impact of foreign involvement in less developed economies.

Friedrich List's work was animated by a similar strain of economic nationalism. Indeed List was heavily influenced by Hamilton and by other American economic nationalists such as Matthew Carey during his prolonged residence in America. For List, the overriding priority was the preservation, consolidation, and development of the nation.[18] The means by which this was to be achieved, in the case of Germany, was the restriction of foreign trade in order to foster the emergence of a national industrial base. The creation of an integrated and balanced national economy was essential if the independence and safety of the nation were to be assured. He warned that:

> History is not without examples of entire nations having perished, because they knew not and seized not the critical moment for the solution of the great problem of securing their moral, economical, and political independence.[19]

This economic strain in nationalist doctrine prefigures the later stress on economic independence in Third World doctrines of national liberation. However, the emphasis in European and American economic nationalism lay not so much on the necessity of escaping foreign economic control and oppression as it did on ensuring national prosperity through balanced economic development.

The social dimension has a similar, if not greater, longevity in

European nationalist thought. The Czech Hussites combined religious and anti-German sentiment with a demand for social justice for the poor. The rise of doctrines of popular sovereignty in Switzerland, France, and elsewhere in the eighteenth century combined a concern to establish the political rights of common people with attacks on privilege and wealth. In the United States, Jefferson coupled his commitment to individual liberty with a dislike of privilege and of the class stratification of urban society.[20]

Somewhat later, the Italian nationalist Mazzini also displayed sympathy for the emancipation of the poor from 'unjust social conditions', arguing that national consolidation and independence were prerequisites for effectively addressing social issues. In his view, 'political freedom' was a lie for 'those who from want of education, instruction, opportunities, and time cannot exercise their rights'.[21] Indeed, there is much truth in Hugh Seton-Watson's assertion that successful national movements almost without exception have adopted programmes of social (and particularly agrarian) reform designed to expand their base of popular support beyond the middle class by mobilizing the support of peasants and workers.[22]

But the fact that nationalist intellectuals embraced social as well as political objectives does not imply that social reform was an integral part of early forms of nationalism.[23] Nineteenth and early-twentieth-century nationalism and the related principle of national self-determination concerned above all else the structure of the international system and the character, rights, and interests of nations as collective entities within that system, rather than the allocation of resources among individuals and groups within nations. This was true also of the principal anti-colonial struggles of the nineteenth century.[24] The preeminently political character of these nationalisms distinguishes them, as shall be seen in Chapter 4, from Third World radical doctrines of national liberation, in which social revolution is an *integral* part of the very concept of national liberation. As Hans Kohn once observed, in the twentieth century a new revolutionary dimension has been added to nationalism: 'Nationalism has also become a social revolutionary movement, demanding equal educational opportunities for all members of the national group and the active promotion of the welfare of the socially underprivileged classes.'[25] He went on to assert that the first major nationalist revolution putting equal emphasis on this social revolutionary aspect was the Mexican Revolution of 1910-17. This set the pattern for the later development of nationalism in the Third World.[26] What occurred was a merger of certain aspects of the nationalist and socialist traditions. It is to this latter tradition which we now turn.

## Notes

1. J.-J. Rousseau, *The Social Contract*, Harmondsworth, Penguin, 1976, p. 63. See also ibid., p. 69.

2. Who wrote, for example that: 'les peuples auxqels Dieu a plu se laisser gouverner ou par un prince, ou par quelques seigneurs choisis, sont plus anciens que leurs magistrats, et, par consequent, le peuple n'est pas cree pour les magistrats, mais au contraire les magistrats pour le peuple.' Theodore de Beze, *Du Droit des Magistrats sur Leurs Sujets*, cited in Kohn, *The Idea of Nationalism*, p. 137.

3. Rousseau, *The Social Contract, passim*. See also E. Renan, 'What Is a Nation' (1882) in A. Zimmern, ed., *Modern Political Doctrines*, London, Oxford University Press, 1939, p. 193.

4. Kohn, *The Idea of Nationalism*, pp. 226, 249.

5. R. Ergang, *Herder and the Foundations of German Nationalism*, NY, Columbia University Press, 1931, pp. 239, 247, 252.

6. Ibid., pp. 98, 111-12, 249.

7. Ibid., pp. 99-100. For a similar perspective in the work of the Italian nationalist Mazzini, see J. Mazzini, *The Duties of Man and Other Essays*, London, Dent and Sons, 1936, p. 49.

8. Ergang, *Herder*, p. 256.

9. Mazzini, *The Duties of Man and Other Essays*, pp. 121, 127-36, 176, 234-5.

10. J.S. Mill, *On Representative Government* (1861) in J.S. Mill, *Three Essays*, London, Oxford University Press, 1975, p. 381.

11. A. Cobban, *The Nation State and National Self-Determination*, London, Collins, 1969, p. 39.

12. R. Hofstadter, 'Woodrow Wilson' in R. Hofstadter, *The American Political Tradition*, NY, Vintage, 1973, p. 356.

13. K. Waltz, *Man, The State, and War*, NY, Columbia University Press, 1959, p. 143. See also Kohn, *The Idea of Nationalism*, p. 257.

14. R. Hofstadter, 'Franklin Roosevelt: The Patrician as Opportunist' in Hofstadter, *The American Political Tradition*, pp. 454-5.

15. Kohn, *The Idea of Nationalism*, p. 200.

16. A. Hamilton, 'Manufactures' (1791) in *Hamilton's Works*, Vol. 3, p. 239.

17. Ibid., pp. 224-5.

18. F. List, *The National System of Political Economy*, Philadelphia, Lippincott, 1856, pp. 61, 71.

19. Ibid., pp. 72, 82, 489.

20. Kohn, *Idea of Nationalism*, pp. 109, 264, 308, 383, 533.

21. Mazzini, *The Duties of Man and OtherEssays*, pp. 53, 99.

22. H. Seton-Watson, *Nations and States*, London, Methuen, 1977, p. 439.

23. Nor, for that matter, does the fact that the French Revolution, was radically social revolutionary in character suggest that social demands were integral to European *nationalism*. This revolution, though it had a nationalist aspect, was not essentially a national revolution as we would understand this concept. It was not a struggle against *foreign oppression*.

24. Cf., for example, mainstream independence movements in Latin America in the early nineteenth century. Although there were a number of slave and tenant revolts in the region (for example, the 1795 Coro revolt in Venezuela) which combined the objectives of independence and republican government with a desire to transform the social system by unseating the white landowning elite, it is

the judgement of Jorge Dominguez that in the Latin American struggle against colonial rule, 'there was a very selective and limited merger of traditional ideas [for example, resistance to secularism, limitation of political participation through property qualification] with one new and necessary idea: political independence. This led to rule by the native elites alone or in alliance with military leaders.' J. Dominguez, *Insurrection or Loyalty: The Breakdown of the Spanish American Empire*, Cambridge, Harvard University Press, 1980, pp. 57, 179-80, 239-40.

    25. H. Kohn, 'Nationalism', *International Encyclopedia of the Social Sciences*, Vol. 7, London, Macmillan, 1968, p. 64.

    26. Ibid., p. 64.

# 3 MARX, ENGELS AND LENIN ON NATIONAL LIBERATION

## Marx and Engels on Nationalism and Colonial Revolution

Marx and Engels had little to say about the colonies and colonial revolution. Their focus was on the development of capitalism and on the proletarian revolution in the industrial economies of Western Europe. That said, a number of aspects of their work — not only their comments on non-European societies, but also their consideration of the human condition and the nature and significance of revolution — had considerable influence upon political thought in the Third World. Their writings on these subjects also informed Soviet doctrine on anti-colonial revolution to a substantial degree, as shall be seen in Chapter 5.

Several issues should be addressed in the attempt to understand the relationship between the writings of early marxists and later discussions of the problem of anti-colonial revolution in the Third World. What did Marx and Engels perceive to be the character of the problems to be resolved by revolution? What was the nature of revolution itself? What were their views on revolutionary activity outside of Europe and North America? What was their perspective on the national particularism evident both in the loyalties of many revolutionary activists and in the adaptation of theory in specific historical, economic, and cultural circumstances? What kinds of revolutionary strategies did they recommend outside of Europe? These are all complex issues worthy of extensive treatment. This account, however, is selective, focusing on elements which later came to be reflected in, or which contrasted markedly with, later ideas about revolution in Asia, Africa, and Latin America.

With regard to Marx's and Engel's view of the nature of human development, from which stems their conception of revolution, it suffices here to stress their focus on socio-economic factors. It was the division of labour, and the class structures that grew out of the successive manifestations of that division, which prevented all men from realizing their creative potential as human beings.[1] A basic aspect of all presocialist divisions of labour was the exploitation by those who controlled the means of production of those who lacked these means, the appropriation of the surplus wealth created by human labour. Satisfying human needs necessitated profound socio-economic change. In this sense, while political revolution was important, not only was it derivative (in that it grew out of changes in the relationship between forces and means of production), but it was secondary, the essence of revolutionary change being socio-economic. The fundamental characteristics of this change in the capitalist epoch were elimination of exploitation and class polarization through the expropriation by the proletariat of the means of production, and the restoration thereby to the worker of control over his labour.

Marx and Engels were of the view that only proletarian revolution in highly developed industrial economies could bring an end to exploitation and the foundation of socialist society. While revolutions at earlier stages in history — such as the bourgeois revolution which replaced feudal with capitalist relations of production — were constructive, in that they moved history forward towards the millenium, such revolutions merely replaced lower forms of appropriation and exploitation with higher ones, one form of oppression and class society with another. The essence of the problem — man's alienation from his product and hence from himself — remained and in fact grew more severe with each successive stage of historical transformation. This conception of history affected profoundly their perception of colonialism and of revolution in the areas under its sway.

In the first place, if the proletarian socialist revolution were possible only in industrial economies that were the product of capitalist development, then the introduction of capitalism into the non-European world through colonial penetration and rule was desirable from the point of view of the peoples of the non-European world themselves. This sentiment is evident in Marx's comments in the *Communist Manifesto* on the creation during the capitalist stage of a world market: 'The bourgeoisie, by the rapid improvement of all instruments of production draws all, even the most barbaric, nations into civilization.'[2]

In an article on India written in 1853 he averred that British conquest and rule were constructive in historical terms, shattering the earlier stagnant 'Asiatic mode of production', unifying the country, integrating India into the capitalist economy, and, through infrastructural development, laying the basis for progress in India.[3] Asian society, prior to Western penetration, lay stagnantly outside of history, lacking the preconditions for revolutionary transformation. Colonialism, an external agent, brought Asia into history by destroying the structure of the traditional mode of production, and laying the base for further

revolutionary development. As such, in India, 'whatever else the crimes
of England, she was the unconscious tool of history in bringing about
the revolution'.[4]

Colonialism was desirable in Marx's view, not only in terms of its
impact on the prospects for progress in colonial areas, but for the
related reason that the demise of capitalism through proletarian revolution could not arrive until capitalism had encompassed the whole
world, until it had been universalized.[5] This positive assessment of
colonialism distinguishes him from many twentieth-century writers on
national liberation or on 'dependencia', who place exclusive emphasis
on the destructive economic, psychological, and social impact of
colonial rule.

In the second place, their conception of historical development
implied that revolution in the colonies could not be socialist in
character (as there existed no large industrial proletariat) and could be
of no more than secondary importance in the overall struggle against
capitalism. The crucial battles of the proletarian revolution were to be
fought in Europe.

It followed that if revolution were to break out in Europe before the
rest of the world had been raised to European levels of capitalist indus-
trialism, the European proletariat would have to lead the less advanced
peoples forward in a relationship which can only be described as tutelage. This line of thinking is evident in Marx's views on the possibility
of non-capitalist development in pre-capitalist agrarian societies. With
reference to Russia, he held that such a path of development was possi-
ible, but only if the Russia agrarian revolution received the assistance of
the Western proletariat, victorious in its own revolution.[6] Engels was
even more blunt in a letter to Kautsky in which he stated that those
colonies remaining at a primitive stage of development would have to
be taken over by the proletariat of the metropolitan countries and led
as quickly as possible towards independence.[7]

The problem of what to do with the colonies in the event of metropolitan socialist revolution much exercised the Second International in
the early years of this century. In particular, there developed among
'revisionists' such as Bernstein, van Kol, and David a doctrine of
socialist colonialism which would appear to have been an extension of
Engels' line of argument cited above. Bernstein argued at the Stuttgart Congress (1907), for example, that 'the colonies are there and need
to be taken care of and I consider that a certain tutelage of the civilized peoples over the uncivilized peoples is a necessity.' Such a view,
despite its altruistic trappings, stemmed largely from the assumption

that exploitation of the colonies was necessary if the prosperity of the European economies were to be maintained. This was recognized implicitly by the German social democrat David, who called for a resolution at the congress stating that 'the socialist congress accepts the principle that the occupation and exploitation of the entire world are indispensable for the well-being of humanity.'[8] Presumably, an important tactical factor underlying the efforts of some social democrats to justify colonialism was the electoral popularity of colonial expansion at the time. To have rejected the very notion of colonial rule would have jeopardized the prospects of German and Dutch socialists.

Such views did not go unchallenged at the congress and in the socialist literature of the period. Kautsky in particular argued that the very idea of a socialist colonial policy was based on a logical contradiction. While accepting that the European proletariat had a civilizing mission, he maintained that a colonial policy which was of necessity one of domination and conquest could never be civilizing in its impact, as it degraded rather than uplifted the colonized. To exercise a civilizing influence required the confidence of 'primitive peoples', and this could only be gained 'when we give them their freedom'.[9] Elsewhere, he parried the argument concerning the civilizing influence of colonialism with the assertion that in many instances revolution necessitated the victory of a lower culture over a high one, where the latter had been created 'through the exploitation of labour'.[10]

While Marx viewed the non-European world as backward and of secondary importance, nevertheless he recognized the potentially constructive impact of colonial revolutions on proletarian revolution in the metropoles.[11] Anticipating later developments in the theory of imperialism, he noted, for instance, the importance of Asia as a market for manufactured goods and source of raw materials, drawing the conclusion that revolutions and disorders in Asia could accelerate the proletarian revolution in Europe by disrupting the metropolitan economies.[12]

Elsewhere, he wrote that the agrarian revolution in Ireland was an indispensable prerequisite for the workers' revolution in England, as a social revolution in this English dependency would seriously erode the position of the English ruling class. The overthrow of the aristocracy in England, according to Marx, was a necessary consequence of its demise in Ireland. On this basis, he criticized the English working class for its antagonism towards the Irish, warning that any nation that oppressed another forged its own chains in so doing.[13]

The mention of Ireland turns the analysis from the consideration of Marx's conception of the role of the colonies in world revolution to an examination of his ideas on nationalism and nationality. It is a commonplace that Marx had no significant theory of nationality.[14] Nationalism — here taken to mean the view that an individual's primary loyalties should be to the nation — was to him a form of reification and a manifestation of alienation. As an ideological construct of the bourgeoisie, it was designed to distract the workers from the social struggle between exploiting and exploited classes. The struggle against national oppression was in Marx's eyes clearly secondary to that against class oppression. Moreover, where national struggle resulted in the disintegration of large states into smaller and less economically viable units, it constituted an impediment to the capitalist economic progress which was a necessary objective precondition for the transition to socialism. Such a view also coloured his attitude to economic nationalism, which, given his commitment to global economic integration, could only be perversely anachronistic. Beyond this, Marx had little use for national particularism in its cultural form. He displayed little appreciation for cultural specificity, implicitly considered it an impediment to international proletarian solidarity, and predicted its gradual submergence into a universal proletarian culture of the future.[15] These perspectives are fundamentally at odds with the view of radical Third World writers considered in Chapter 4.

But, for Marx, nationalism, like other political phenomena was to be judged not so much in the abstract, but in relation to concrete political circumstances, and its impact in these circumstances on the struggle of the international proletariat against capitalism. Thus, despite his general hostility to nationalism , there were instances — like the Irish one — where Marx and Engels supported national struggles. Their reasons were tactical. They supported those national struggles which furthered the international proletarian revolution and opposed those which they judged to be inconsistent with the interests of the international working class. Given their assessment, for example, of the threat that tsarism posed to the working-class movement in Germany, Marx and Engels lauded any national movement which weakened Russia (cf.. their attitude towards Polish nationalism[16]). They condemned any national movement which might prove advantageous to that power (cf. their opposition to Panslavic and pro-Russian Czech and Balkan nationalism[17]).

Moreover, Marx's reservations about nationalism pertained most specifically to the capitalist epoch in which the conditions for proletarian revolution matured. It followed from Marx's materialist conception of history that at earlier stages, and in areas in which capitalist development was retarded, national struggle could be progressive, in that it assisted in establishing the politico-economic prerequisites for capitalist development. More explicitly, in situations such as that of Poland in the mid-nineteenth century, where the bourgeoisie, in conflict with the landed aristocracy, was struggling to consolidate the national economy as a basis for industrial development and participation in the world market, the national movement was socially progressive and, consequently, deserving of proletarian support.[18]

However, in situations where these two criteria (the interests of the international working class on the one hand and the desirability of replacing precapitalist with capitalist relations of production on the other) conflicted, it was the former that carried the day. The case of the Balkans is illustrative. Marx's concern about the pro-Russian character of national agitation against the Ottoman empire overrode whatever attraction he might have had to the anti-feudal nature of these movement's objectives. The priority of the interests of the international proletariat in the assessment of national demands anticipates much of what Lenin and Stalin had to say on the question of national self-determination.

Just as Marx and Engels subordinated the particular to the universal in discussing class versus national objectives and in defining their attitude to specific national struggles, so they were hostile to particularism in the development of theories of revolution. For Marx, socialist society was the outcome of conflict between forces and relations of production under capitalism, the agent of this transformation being the class-conscious proletariat. Capitalism produced the material and subjective prerequisites for the transition to socialism. For this reason, the notion that there might be paths to socialism other than through the stage of capitalism contradicts the essence of Marx's materialist conception of history. He welcomed the creation of a global capitalist economy because bringing precapitalist societies into the capitalist mainstream hastened the arrival of socialism.

But what of Marx's statement that his 'historical sketch of the genesis of capitalism in Western Europe' was not to be transposed into 'an historico-philosophic theory of the general path every people is fated to tread',[19] his view cited above that Russia might in certain circumstances skip the capitalist stage, or his assertion that the Asiatic mode of production lay outside of history? These suggest that the development (or lack of it) of non-European societies could diverge from his model. However, in the case of societies characterized by the Asiatic mode, it was necessary for an external agent, the European bourgeoisie, to set in train the movement towards socialism. In the case of Russia, the European proletariat rendered possible the transition to socialism. There is no indication in his writings that he believed that a non-European pre-capitalist society could autonomously define and successfuly pursue its own distinctive path to socialism . In Avineri's words:

> Since Marx's socialism is a dialectical outcome of the Aufhebung, transcendence, of European bourgeois civilization, he sees little reason to look for autochthonous roots for socialism in non-European society. 'Chinese communism' or 'African socialism' have no place in the universalistic scheme of Marx's socialist theory and make little sense within his philosophy of history.[20]

In situations where a society lacked the prerequisites for this transcendence, Europe provided them. This too prefigures some aspects of the Soviet discussion of national liberation.

Two further subjects should be addressed here. First, given that the question of alliances between classes greatly exercised later writers on national liberation, it is germane to recall Marx's views on the subject. The clearest treatment by Marx of alliance between the proletariat and other urban groups is in the 'Address of the Central Authority to the Communist League' (1850), in which he attempted to define the attitude of the socialist movement to the various liberal democratic revolutions of the late 1840s. Once again, concrete class interest dominates the analysis:

> The relation of the revolutionary workers' party to the petty bourgeois democrats is this: it marches together with them against the faction which it aims at overthrowing, it opposes them in everything whereby they seek to consolidate their position in their own interests . . . While the democratic petty bourgeois wish to bring the revolution to a conclusion as quickly as possible and with strictly limited demands, it is our interest to make the revolution permanent, until all the more or less possessing classes have been forced out of their positions of dominance.

Although the petty bourgeoisie strives to entangle the proletariat in their democratic party, such a union must be 'most decisively rejected' and an 'independent, secret, and public organization of the workers' party' established alongside the democratic party, putting forward proletarian demands in addition to those of the bourgeoisie.[21] Upon the victory of the petty bourgeoisie, Marx and Engels recommended the immediate organization, alongside the new official government, of revolutionary proletarian governments and the maintenance of armed workers' units, stressing that from the 'first moment of victory, mistrust must be directed no longer against the conquered reactionary party, but against the workers' previous allies'.[22] For our purposes, there are three important aspects to this analysis, all of which emerge strikingly in later Soviet, Chinese, and other *national communist* writing on national liberation: the acceptance of the principle of the united front (the alliance in this instance between the proletariat and the bourgeoisie in carrying through the 'bourgeois democratic revolution'); the stress on the temporary and partial character of the alliance; and the emphasis on the need for an independent working class organization.

With respect to alliances with rural groups, perhaps most instructive are Marx's comments on the peasantry in the '18th Brumaire of Louis Bonaparte'. Here, he put forward the opinion that the peasantry was too weak to enforce its own class interests. For it to engage in revolutionary action, it needed the support and the leadership of another class. This class, in the conditions prevailing in France in the 1850s, was the proletariat.[23] The worker-peasant alliance later became one of the fundamental strategic motifs of marxist-leninist doctrine on revolution and national liberation in underdeveloped societies, as did the view that the peasantry was incapable of *independent* revolutionary action.

Lastly, with respect to the use of force as an aspect of revolutionary struggle, it is clear from the bulk of their work that Marx and Engels perceived violent struggle as a necessary means of unseating dominant classes from their positions of power. The use of violence brought the bourgeoisie to power and maintained the bourgeois position. Violence would, in normal circumstances, sweep that position away. As Marx put it: 'Force is the midwife of every old society which is pregnant with a new one.'[24]

In conclusion, several aspects of early marxist thinking on the colonies and on revolution should be recalled. Some clearly coincide with, and in all likelihood considerably influenced, subsequent Third World views on national and social revolution. For instance, the emphasis on social and economic exploitation and the view that revolution ultimately brought not merely a change of rulers, but an end to all oppression. Others contrast markedly with the main body of national revolutionary thought in the Third World while informing to a certain extent Soviet attitudes on social and political change in Asia, Africa, and Latin America. Principal among these are his emphasis on the universal class rather than particular national character of revolution and revolutionary theory, his hostility to nationalism as such, and his stress on proletarian and European leadership of this world revolution.

## Lenin on National Liberation

### Introduction

Marx's commentary on revolution among oppressed nationalities in the less developed world was coloured by his attempt to square his theory of historical and social development with a support for revolutionary activity which weakened European capitalism, no matter in what historical circumstances it occurred. Thus, for example, despite his recognition of the progressive impact of capitalism in Asia, he enthused about the Taiping rebellion, which was in many ways reactionary from a marxist perspective, because this convulsion disrupted metropolitan capitalism and so could hasten the coming of the proletarian revolution in Europe.[25]

Similar dilemmas have affected Soviet marxist thinking about national liberation since Lenin. Here, the problem has been to render Marx's thought concerning the prospects for and nature of revolution in precapitalist societies consistent with the interests, first, of a movement devoted to the destruction of the 'imperialist world system' and, later, of a state facing a hostile world. These interests dictated the encouragement of anti-Western activity *per se* in the colonial and semi-colonial[26] countries, while the legacy of Marx favoured suspicion of particularist movements and ideologies and of the non-proletarian social groups they represented, and a profoundly Eurocentric focus in thinking about revolution. This tension between theory and political interest affected discussion by Lenin and his successors of the whole gamut of issues relating to Third World revolution: the objectives of national liberation, the place of the national liberation movement in the 'world revolutionary process', nationalism, the adjustment of theory to local conditions (national forms of socialism), leadership, membership, and class relations within the national liberation movement (the united front), and the use of force in struggles for liberation.

Lenin, in contrast to Marx and Engels, spent much time and energy grappling with the significance of colonialism and colonial revolution, and with the content and implications of the nationalist agitation of 'oppressed peoples' in Europe and elsewhere. Historical circumstance largely dictated this contrast, for the last decades of the nineteenth century and the first years of the twentieth witnessed a resurgence of colonial expansion to the point where practically the whole world outside Europe was divided by the European powers (and to a lesser extent the United States) into colonial and semi-colonial dependencies or spheres of influence. During the same period, the nationalism of subject peoples in the Balkans and in Central and Eastern Europe mounted a challenge of growing effectiveness to the multinational Ottoman, Austro-Hungarian, and Russian empires, while Western liberals displayed an increasing acceptance of the principle of self-determination for these peoples. In this context, a growing preoccupation with the national and colonial questions on the part of marxist writers was natural. The attempt by Russian marxists to deal with the national problem was particularly appropriate, given the large numbers of subject nationalities aspiring to self-determination within the tsarist empire.

Lenin went further in this direction than did most of his fellow Russian marxists and colleagues in the European socialist movement, not only in the amount of attention he devoted to these questions, but in the flexibility which characterized his attitudes to colonial revolution and national self-determination. His work, however, displayed little sympathy for the aspirations of subject peoples. Instead, his interest in their cause stemmed from an appreciation of the impact of their struggles on the balance of forces between the proletariat and its main adversary – European capitalism.

As such, it is not surprising that he devoted little attention to the objectives of national liberation movements. It was consequences in Europe and not motives in the colonies which held his interest. However, his discussions of revolution in general and his treatment of the nature of imperialism have some bearing on this issue.

With regard to revolution, and drawing from works such as *What Is To Be Done?* and *State and Revolution*, it is evident that he viewed the liberation of man to involve an end to exploitation through the expropriation of the means of production by the 'oppressed masses' led by the proletariat, and the creation of a classless society through the suppression by force of the exploiting classes. In other words, and as with Marx and Engels, liberation, for Lenin, had a profound social and economic, as well as political content. Perhaps the clearest example of the application of this line of reasoning to the struggle of subject nationalities against foreign rule is in a brief discussion of Balkan affairs.[27] Here Lenin noted that social progress in an anti-feudal and anti-capitalist direction was a necessary aspect of the overall liberation of the Balkan peoples. This went well beyond his definition of 'self-determination' which, in polemics with Polish and Austrian marxists, he defined simply as a right to secession (see below).[28]

Regarding imperialism, it was Lenin's view that the sources of colonial expansion were predominantly economic: the growing necessity in the period of 'monopoly capitalism' for secure sources of raw materials, markets for manufactured goods which could not be absorbed into the metropolitan market, and, perhaps more importantly, outlets for surplus capital. There is little of Marx's stress on the constructive impact of colonialism in Lenin's analysis. Instead, he underlines its character as a 'world system' of oppression. In discussing the building of railways, for instance, he rejected as bourgeois and philistine the idea that this was a civilizing enterprise. Instead he maintained that this was 'an instrument for oppressing a thousand million people [in the colonial and semi-colonial countries], that is, the more than half the population of the globe that inhabits the dependent countries'.[29] So much for Marx.

From this it may be inferred that the severance not only of the political bond of colonialism, but also of the economic links to the imperialist world system which underlie that bond, is a necessary condition of the liberation of subject peoples in the colonial and semi-colonial countries.

However, this is quite distinct from the advocacy of economic independence which, as shall be seen in Chapter 4, is such a prominent aspect of Third world doctrines of national liberation. Despite the efforts of later Soviet writers to establish that Lenin accepted the idea of economic independence, there is little if any mention of it in his work. Where he referred to the economic liberation of subject nationalities, he was speaking not of the creation of independent and autonomous economic units, but to the freeing of peasant masses from feudal oppression.[30] His attachment, as a follower of Marx, to large economic units carried with it an opposition to their dissolution into dysfunctional mini-states.[31] The termination of imperialist economic oppression in the colonies would, it was hoped, take the form not of a plethora of new and unviable nation states, but of the free association of formerly subject peoples in a world socialist economy.

## The World Revolutionary Process

The Eurocentrism of Lenin's approach to revolution in the Third World is particularly striking in his discussion of the significance of anti-colonial struggle in the context of global revolution. There is, however, more than a grain of truth in Stalin's remark that Lenin was the first among European socialists to grasp the importance of the anti-colonial movement in the struggle of the proletariat against capitalism. For Lenin, its importance derived from the contribution it made to the victory of the proletariat in the developed capitalist countries.

In 1912, Lenin underlined the world historical signifcance of China's revolution not only because it brought emancipation to Asia, but because it undermined the class rule of the bourgeoisie in Europe.[32] In 1913 he spoke of Asia, in terms later employed frequently by Chinese communists, as a 'new source of world storms' having serious repercussions in Europe and inspiring the international proletariat in their own struggle.[33] On this basis, he spoke of a new revolutionary alliance between 'Asian democracy' and the proletariat in the 'advanced countries'.[34]

In a later article, he went beyond arguing that revolution in the Third World was important and asserted that it was a necessary condition of the success of the proletarian revolution:

> The social revolution can come only in the form of an epoch in which are combined civil war by the proletariat against the bourgeoisie in the advanced countries and a whole series of democratic and revolutionary movements, including the national liberation movement, in the undeveloped backward, and oppressed nations.[35]

He kept to this line consistently in the aftermath of the revolution.[36] The view that the national liberation revolution was an essential condition of victory for the international proletariat is a substantial departure from Marx's conception of world revolution. While, as was seen above, Marx on rare occasions maintained that social conflict outside Europe might accelerate the proletarian revolution, nowhere did he state that national revolution outside Europe was a necessary condition for the consummation of the European socialist revolution. There is no reason to believe that he ever held such a view.

Lenin's departure from Marx in this respect follows from his treatment of imperialism. In Lenin's view, excess profits from exploitation of the colonies allowed the metropolitan bourgeoisie to stave off revolution at home by buying off the upper strata of the working class, giving them a stake in the *status quo* and thereby splitting the proletariat. The elimination of these superprofits as a result of colonial revolution would end this process of bribery and division, opening the door to socialist revolution in the metropole. As shall be seen below, this argument was later to become popular among Third World activists who sought to establish the primacy of their struggle in the overall process of world revolution.

Beyond this theoretical rationale, there was a practical one. Lenin was attempting the overthrow of the imperialist world system. With this in mind, it made sense to attract the broadest possible array of potentially anti-imperialist forces, including non-proletarian national revolutionaries. Such statements may be seen as justifications for overtures to such forces, or as appeals to them. In the latter context, it is not surprising that the clearest statements by Lenin and his colleagues of the link between revolution in Europe and that in the Third World came at gatherings at which national revolutionaries were included (the Second All-Russian Congress of Communist Organizations of the Peoples of the East, the Second Congress of the Communist International, and the 1920 Baku Congress).[37]

Despite his emphasis on the importance of national liberation to the proletarian revolution, Lenin was not willing to concede equality or primacy to the former in the world revolutionary process. This is evident in the 1919 speech quoted above, where he averred that 'the final victory can only be won by the proletariat'.[38] He came and comes out even more strongly in his polemic with M.N. Roy at the Second Congress of the Comintern in 1920. He refuted Roy's assertions (see Chapter 4) concerning the primacy of Third World revolution, asserting diplomatically that it was incorrect to belittle either proletarian or national revolutions as each was necessary to the other. Furthermore, the international proletariat was to be the avant-garde of the world revolutionary process.[39] This was not just the reflex of a committed marxist. He believed the Russian working class and its vanguard, the Russian Communist Party, to be in turn the vanguard of the international proletariat. His statements were, in effect, a claim to Soviet leadership of the 'world revolutionary movement'. His position on the role of the national liberation movement in the world revolutionary process balances the attempt, through doctrinal innovation, to attract the broadest possible array of allies with a concern to establish the primacy of the Russian Communist Party within the alliance of 'progressive forces', and to ensure the subordination of national demands to the interests of his party. This concern applied not only in the international context to anti-colonial movements, but, perhaps more importantly, to the demands of allies of the Bolsheviks among national minorities in the Russian Empire.

## National Particularism

The difficulty of walking the line between soliciting the support of national movements and maintaining the primacy of proletarian and, later, Soviet interests is also evident in Lenin's treatment of nationalism. Like Marx and Engels, he opposed nationalism in principle, considering it to be an ideological instrument of the bourgeoisie intended to dupe the working class into abandoning its transnational class interests.[40] Moreover, he opposed nationalism on economic grounds, holding the dissolution of the large multinational empires in central and Eastern Europe to be retrograde. The large markets which they encompassed stimulated the capitalist development which was a prerequisite for the transition to socialism:

> We social democrats are opposed to *all* nationalism and advocate democratic *centralism*. We are opposed to particularism and are convinced that, *other things being equal*, big states can solve the problems of economic progress and of the struggle between the bourgeoisie and the proletariat far more effectively than small ones can.[41]

Lenin extended his critique to broader forms of particularism, such as the Panislamic and Panturkic movements. These too, in Lenin's opinion, obstructed the development of proletarian internationalism by erecting artificial barriers between the various components of the working class. In 1920, he dismissed these two forms of particularist ideology as attempts by traditional elites to legitimize their leadership and privileges within the context of a struggle against imperialism.[42]

Lenin's rejection of particularism informed to a considerable degree his attitude to national self-determination. He quite consistently recognized the right of minority nationalities to determine their own future, if necessary by seceding from the larger states under whose jurisdiction they fell. He squared this with his preference for large economic units by maintaining that large units under proletarian rule could be based only on 'free voluntary association' rather than 'forcible association'.[43] The proletariat would win this voluntary association on the part of previously oppressed nationalities through the recognition of the right to self-determination. This, in his view, would wipe out the resentment and bitterness of minorities exploited by other national groups. As such, this recognition was a prerequisite for solidarity between oppressor and oppressed nations:

> In the same way as mankind can arrive at the abolition of classes only through a transition period of the dictatorship of the oppressed classes, it can arrive at the inevitable integration of nations only through a transition period of the complete emancipation of all oppressed nations and their freedom to secede.[44]

While this analogy is rather ill-conceived — a more logical conclusion based upon it would be that national integration could be achieved only through the dictatorship of oppressed nations (see the discussion of Sultan-Galiev in Chapter 4) — Lenin's position on the right to self-determination is clear.

The great significance of the right to self-determination in Bolshevik calculations is evident in its endorsement in one of the first documents of the Soviet regime, the Declaration of the Rights of the Peoples of Russia.[45] This endorsement was presumably intended to ensure the neutrality, if not the support, of subject nationalities in the Bolshevik struggle against 'white reaction', but it was not entirely empty. It was respected when the new government accepted the secession of the Finns, the Latvians, Lithuanians, Estonians, and Georgians in the years that followed. Of course there was little that the Soviets could do in the early days to prevent such departures, particularly on the periphery of what had been the Russian Empire, and when they were sufficiently strong to retake Georgia, they did so, though not without some misgivings on the part of Lenin himself.

In general, Lenin's view of the right to self-determination should not be confused with his, or the party's, attitude to the exercise of that right. Lenin stressed repeatedly that the acceptance of the right by no means implied the universal adovcacy of secession by subject peoples.[46] In the first place, he maintained that it was the self-determination of the proletariat of a given nation and not that of the nation as such which was the issue.[47] Secondly, and with regard to the national aspirations of the bourgeoisie of oppressed nations, Lenin qualified his position of self-determination by emphasizing that the party should support their objectives only in so far as they were directed against imperialism, and oppose those aspects of this nationalism which infringed upon the interests of the international proletariat.[48] The later history of the international communist movement displays the naiveté of his assumption that nationalism was divisible in this fashion. His position is significant none the less in that it displays his lack of sympathy for national aspirations *per se* and his concern above all to further the interests of the international communist movement led by the Russian Communist Party. This meant, as it did with Marx and Engels, the support of nationalist aspirations where and to the extent that these weakened the imperialist enemy and fostered the extension of Bolshevik influence and, later, the consolidation of Soviet rule, coupled with the rejection of any notion that these aspirations should be paramount.

## National Forms of Socialism

The balance between universal and particular in doctrines of revolution has always been a troublesome issue for marxist-leninists. To deny the relevance of specific circumstances in the formulation of strategy and tactics impedes progress towards desired ends. Moreover, it may alienate groups with theoretical pretensions of their own and whose support may be valuable. Accepting their relevance, on the other hand, may corrode ideological unity and the commitment to internationalism. In the extreme, such an acceptance draws into question the universality of marxist-leninism itself, as will be seen in Chapter 4. More practically, in a backhanded way, and like nationalism, such ideological diversity may constitute a challenge to the hegemony of the proletariat in the world revolution, or, to put it another way, to the vanguard role of the Soviet Union and its leading force, the CPSU.

Lenin's early writings on this subject are conditioned not only by his recent conversion to marxism, but also by the desire to undercut the social revolutionaries with whom his Russian Social Democratic Labour Party was competing for support within Russia. The social revolutionaries contended that it was possible, relying on the communal character of village life, to avoid the vicissitudes of capitalism in a transition to socialism peculiar to Russian conditions. This constituted, in effect, a denial of Marx's materialist concept of history.

For a marxist party to succeed in Russia at the expense of the social revolutionaries, it was necessary to refute this assertion. In his first major work,[49] Lenin set out to accomplish this by showing that capitalism had, in fact, arrived in Russia and hence could not be avoided. Later, he took a more direct tack, denying the possibility of a direct transition to socialism from precapitalist relations of production:

Marxism teaches us that at a certain stage of development a society

which is based on commodity production and has commercial intercourse with civilized capitalist nations must inevitably take the road
of capitalism. Marxism has inevitably broken with the narodnik
[social revolutionary] gibberish that Russia, for instance, can bypass
capitalist development.[50]

This appears to be a categorical rejection, with respect to Russia at
least, of national forms of transition to socialism.

He held comparable views in the pre-revolutionary period with
respect to similar ideological trends in colonial and semi-colonial countries. He referred to Sun Yat-sen's version of socialism as 'narodism'
and labelled it petty bourgeois and reactionary, rejecting specifically
an idea of Sun's later to achieve broad currency among Third World
nationalists and national communists — that a country's backwardness
facilitates rather than retards social revolution.[51] One may also infer
Lenin's rejection of specific Third World transitions to socialism by com-
bining his theory of imperialism, which stresses the integration of
colonies and semi-colonies into the international capitalist system with
his argument cited above from the *Two Tactics of Social Democracy*
that countries having commercial intercourse with advanced capitalist
nations can not avoid capitalist development.

On the other hand, one might argue that the stress on the worker-
peasant alliance in the *Two Tactics* and elsewhere displayed a willingness on his part to accept that the road to power varied according to
conditions prevailing in the society in question.[52] Allowing flexibility in
the tactics chosen in the quest for power, however, does not contra-
dict the assertion that a certain sequence of stages of development is
unavoidable. While form might vary, content remained constant.

As Lenin's thinking developed, he displayed growing flexibility with
respect to variety in 'the path mankind will follow from the imperialism of today to the socialist revolution of tomorrow'. In 1916, he
asserted that while all nations would arrive at socialism — which he
believed to be unique and universal — the course they took in the trans-
tion from capitalist imperialism would vary according to national conditions.[53]

He retained this acceptance of variety in the paths to socialism in the
aftermath of the revolution, urging communist workers among Eastern
peoples to adapt themselves to specific conditions which did not apply
to Europe and, in particular, to the fact that the bulk of the population
of their countries were peasants, and consequently, that the main revolutionary tasks were anti-feudal and not anti-capitalist.[54] That is to say,

the problem they faced was how to establish the preconditions for the transition to socialism rather than to effect that transition. For revolution to succeed in conditions of uneven development,[55] flexibility was necessary in the translation of general principles into tactics. As before, however, his writings betrayed no willingness to accept that Marx's laws of history — and in particular that a direct transition from precapitalist relations of production to socialist ones was impossible — were invalid outside of Europe. Any such acceptance would severely weaken the claim of the international proletariat and its vanguard to a hegemonic role in the world revolutionary process.

## The United Front

As will be seen in Chapter 5, the Soviet discussion of leadership and membership in Third World revolutionary movements revolves around the alliance of the proletariat with the national bourgeosie and the peasantry. Again, Lenin's and later Soviet comments on the subject reflect an attempt to deal with a number of uncomfortable tradeoffs. First, a united front with broad participation and popular support creates greater problems for the colonial powers than would a narrowly based one, and has a greater chance of success in the struggle against foreign rule. But it is far more difficult to guarantee the socalist orientation of, or proletarian control in, such a broad front. Second, accepting the revolutionary credentials of non-proletarian movements in the Third World expanded considerably the number of potential effective allies of the proletariat in the struggle against capitalism and after 1917, of the Soviet state in its struggle against the Western powers. But the endorsement of such claims could also mean curtailing the nascent proletarian movements in many of these countries, and co-operating or acquiescing in the suppression of 'fraternal parties' (for example, Turkey in 1920-2). Moreover, support for non-proletarian movements implied, in certain circumstances, aiding in the consolidation of the rule of 'reactionary elements' who might then make their peace with imperialism, collaborating with the latter against the Soviet state and the international communist movement and failing to complete even the 'bourgeois democratic revolution' (for example, China under the Kuomintang).

Lenin's pre-revolutionary writing on revolution in Russia displays a degree of sensitivity to these problems. He depicted the Russian bourgeoisie as incapable of fulfilling the tasks of its own 'anti-feudal' revolution because of its fear that democratic progress might strengthen the proletariat, the one 'consistently democratic' class in Russia.[56] This presumably reflects his unwillingness to relinquish the control of the movement against tsarist autocracy to the various Russian liberal parties. This consideration also informed his attitude towards the peasantry, which he viewed as an essential ally in the struggle, but as a force incapable of effective independent action and, hence, as subordinate to the proletariat.[57]

By contrast, he displays a somewhat more sanguine view of the 'bourgeoisie' in the colonial and semi-colonial countries. He maintained that 'in Asia, there is still a bourgeoisie capable of championing sincere, militant, and consistent democracy'.[58] He apparently perceived the bourgeoisie to be the natural leader of the various national struggles against imperialism outside Europe.[59] This reflected a degree of realism about the comparative strengths of social forces in non-European societies which was lacking in much later Soviet discussion of revolution in the Third World. Proletarian leadership of revolution might be preferable, but in conditions where the proletariat was numerically and organizationally weak, while the impact of the political activity of non-proletarian (in Lenin's terms predominantly bourgeois) groups was anti-imperialist, their efforts were to be endorsed and supported.

Early Soviet pronouncements on revolution in the Third World[60] reflect this perspective. Lenin put it most clearly in his exchanges with M.N. Roy at the Second Comintern Congress: 'There is not the slightest doubt that every national movement can only be a bourgeois-democratic movement, for the overwhelming mass of the population in backward countries consists of peasants who represent bourgeois-capitalist relations.'[61] The extent to which this position conforms to orthodox marxism may be questioned, and in particular the statement that peasants in pre-capitalist societies represent bourgeois capitalist relations. But the basic point that the conditions for proletarian revolution did not obtain is sound. It was also politically expedient, for it justified forcing local communists to co-operate with movements which were potentially useful to the Soviet Union from the perspective of foreign policy. It permitted, for example, co-operation with, rather than struggle against, regimes such as those of Reza Khan in Iran, Emir Aminullah in Afghanistan, and Kemal Ataturk in Turkey. All three governed areas contiguous to the Soviet republics and from which challenges to shaky Soviet control of peripheral areas in Central Asia and the Caucasus could be mounted.

Lenin's acceptance of bourgeois-democratic leadership was paralleled by support for broadly based class alliances. This is perhaps most evident in his use of the concept of the 'oppressed nation'.[62] In the

imperialist epoch, in his view, whole nations were victims of exploitation and, therefore, whole nations had an interest in liberation. A
number of Third World communists, departing from this analysis, went
on to assert that the world was divided into capitalist and proletarian
nations. Lenin, however, never went so far as to equate oppression by
imperialism with proletarian status.

It is worth stressing that Lenin's flexibility towards leadership and
breadth of participation in revolutionary movements in the Third World
did not involve any attachment to national unity as such. These multi-
class fronts, in which the proletariat of the non-European countries was
to participate and which received the approval and support of European
communist parties, were in his view temporary, lasting only so long as
the main direction and impact were anti-imperialist.[63] The alliance with
indigenous bourgeois groups was then to be replaced with struggle
against them. This suggests a conception of stages of revolution in
which social tasks were to be postponed until national (anti-imperialist)
ones had been completed, a position much contested in theory and
practice by a number of national revolutionaries from M.N. Roy, Li
Li-san, and Mao Tse-tung through to Amilcar Cabral and Samora
Machel, for reasons which will be discussed in the next chapter. On the
other hand, his insistence that social struggle was inevitable is at odds
with another main theme in Third World nationalist thought – that
national unity was an intrinsic value, not to be jeopardized by efforts to
achieve social change within the national group.

One other aspect of Lenin's thinking concerning class structure bears
mention here: his concept of the vanguard party.[64] In calling for proletarian leadership of the revolution in Russia, he envisaged not so
much a spontaneous uprising of a class conscious of its socio-historical
role, but a revolution engineered by a relatively small group of professional revolutionaries, largely drawn from the intelligentsia and subordinate to a tight decision-making centre which would orchestrate and
supervise mass proletarian action with a view to establishing a dictatorship of the party. The party would rule in a manner consistent with the
'objective interest' of the proletariat. The advantages of the organization of a revolutionary movement around a small centre of committed
intellectuals subject to the principles of democratic centralism are
obvious in the historical circumstances of pre-revolutionary Russia. The
masses were, with little exception, politically inexperienced, apathetic,
and resigned. The tsarist state possessed an extensive and reasonably
effective police power and was largely unconstrained by constitutional
niceties. The similarity of these to conditions prevailing in much of the

Third World during the colonial era, and the conspicuous success of the leninist recipe of political organization in 1917 assured that these ideas would gain considerable influence among disaffected colonial intellectuals. As Elie Kedourie put it:

> When Lenin imposed on the Social Democrats his idea of a party composed of an elite of professional revolutionaries who would lead the inarticulate masses willy-nilly toward the vision by which they themselves had been seized, he was, whether he knew it or not, summing up and codifying the rules of successful political action in all these societies which had been violently wrenched from their age-old moorings by European action or example.[65]

## The Use of Force

Lenin commented on revolutionary violence in two contexts which are relevant here: the revolution in Russia, and that in the colonies and semi-colonies. With respect to the Russian revolution, he stressed that the victory over tsarism would result in a dictatorship based on force, 'the arming of the masses, on an insurrection, and not in institutions of one kind or another established in a "lawful" or "peaceful" way'.[66] His analysis in *State and Revolution* rests on the assumption that the oppressing classes will not surrender their power voluntarily and, therefore, that it must be taken from them by force.[67]

With specific reference to anti-colonial revolution, he affirmed, paraphrasing Clausewitz, that 'The continuation of national liberation politics in the colonies will inevitably take the form of wars against imperialism.'[68] While to argue that wars of national liberation are inevitable is not equivalent to asserting that war is inevitably the form that every national liberation struggle must take, it is clear that Lenin saw violent struggle as the most likely form for the national liberation struggle, both in its anti-imperialist and social revolutionary aspects.

## Summary

As in the cases of Marx and Engels, a number of aspects of Lenin's treatment of the national and colonial questions stand out for their impact on later Third World thinking about revolution. Others contrast markedly with the main lines of this body of thought. In the first category are:

(1) his focus on the economic sources and character of imperialism, and, by implication, the socio-economic essence of liberation;

(2) his recognition of the great significance of anti-colonial revolution for the world revolutionary process as a whole; and
(3) his view that whole nations were oppressed by imperialism and, consequently, that all groups within the nation could participate in the struggle for national liberation.

In the second category fall:

(1) his silence with regard to economic independence;
(2) his reluctance to envisage the disintegration of large multi-national politico-economic units;
(3) his principled opposition to nationalism; and
(4) his subordination of the Third World revolution and of the right to self-determination to the interests of the international proletariat. Lenin shared Marx's and Engels' hierarchy of priorities. It was revolution in the industrial societies of the West which was important. National revolution in the Third World was judged in terms of its instrumental value in the struggle between the international proletariat and world capitalism.

## Notes.

1. Paradoxically, the division of labour was also the means by which human society accumulated the material prerequisites for this realization.
2. K. Marx and F. Engels, *A Manifesto of the Communist Party*, in K. Marx and F. Engels, *Selected Works in One Volume*, London, Lawrence and Wishart, 1968, p. 39.
3. K. Marx, 'The British Rule in India' (1853) in K. Marx and F. Engels, *On Colonialism*, Moscow, Progress, 1976, pp. 35-41.
4. Ibid., p. 41. This should be qualified, however, by noting that just as at one stage in history capitalism was constructive and to be encouraged, but at a later became an obstacle to further progress and therefore had to be destroyed, colonialism, while initially progressive, later held back colonial societies, for their economies were developed as dependent appendages of the metropole and only to the extent that such development was consistent with the interests of the metropolitan bourgeoisie. On this point see K. Kautsky, *Socialism and Colonial Policy: An Analysis*, Belfast, Athol Press, 1975, pp. 21, 30, 32.
5. S. Avineri, *Karl Marx on Colonialism and Modernization*, Garden City, Doubleday, 1968, pp. 3, 112, 19.
6. Cf. K. Marx, 'Preface to the 1882 Edition of the *Communist Manifesto*, in K. Marx and F. Engels, *Selected Works in Three Volumes*, Moscow, Progress, 1969, Vol. I, pp. 100-1. It is not the purpose here to judge the consistency of Marx's thought on the non-European world, but it bears mention that this line of argument verges on contradiction with that mentioned earlier concerning the necessity, prior to the proletarian revolution in the capitalist workd, of the universalization of capitalism.

7. F. Engels, 'Letter to Kautsky' (1882) in K. Marx and F. Engels, *Selected Correspondence*, Moscow, Foreign Languages Publishing House, 1953, p. 423

8. Extracts from the debate at the Stuttgart Congress, as reprinted in H. Carrere-d'Encausse and S. Schram, *Marxism and Asia*, London, Allen Lane, 1969, pp. 127-9.

9. Ibid., p. 132.

10. Kautsky, *Socialism and Colonial Policy*, p. 22.

11. It has been argued in fact that as the years passed, Marx's emphasis on colonial matters shifted from the positive aspects of colonialism to the role of anti-colonial revolutions as potential accelerators of the revolutionary process in the metropoles. Cf. M. Meisner, 'The Despotism of Concepts; Wittfogel and Marx on China', *China Quarterly* (henceforward *CQ*) (1963), no. 16, pp. 107, 110.

12. K. Marx, 'Revolution in China and in Europe' (1853), in Marx and Engels *On Colonialism*, pp. 19-26.

13. K. Marx, 'Confidential Communication to the General Council of the First International' (1870) in Marx and Engels, *On Colonialism*, p. 258. See also Marx's letter to A. Vogt (1870) in ibid., p. 335.

14. L. Kolakowski, *Main Currents of Marxism*, Vol. II, London, Oxford University Press, p. 88.

15. In Marx's view, the universalization of culture was an intellectual manifestation of global integration in material terms during the capitalist epoch. Marx, *Communist Manifesto*, pp. 39, 59.

16. Cf. P. Frolich, *Rosa Luxemburg: Ideas in Action*, London, Pluto, 1972, p. 22; and F. Engels, 'The Polish Debate in Frankfurt' (1848) in Carrere d'Encausse and Schram, *Marxism and Asia*, p. 122.

17. Cf. Kolakowski, *Main Currents*, II, p.89; and J. Nettl, *Rosa Luxemburg*, London, Oxford University Press, 1966, pp. 842-3.

18. Cf. Engels, 'The Polish Debate', pp. 121-2.

19. Marx, 'Letter to the Editors of Otechestvennye Zapiski', (1877) in K. Marx and F. Engels, *Selected Correspondence, 1846-1895*, London, Lawrence and Wishart, 1936, pp. 353-4.

20. Avineri, *Marx on Colonialism and Modernization*, p. 26.

21. K. Marx and F. Engels, 'Address of the Central Authority to the Communist League' (1850) in K. Marx and F. Engels, *Works* X, London, Lawrence and Wishart, 1975, pp. 280-4.

22. Ibid., pp. 280-3.

23. K. Marx, 'The 18th Brumaire of Louis Bonaparte' (1852) in Marx and Engels, *Selected Works in Three Volumes*, I, pp. 487, 482.

24. K. Marx, *Capital*, Vol. I, Harmondsworth, Penguin, 1976, p. 916. See also F. Engels, *The Anti-Duhring*, Chicago, Kerr, 1936, p. 187. It is true, however, that Marx recognised that in certain exceptional circumstances (namely, parliamentary democracy in Great Britain, Holland and the United States), a peaceful transition to proletarian rule could not be ruled out. It is none the less difficult to believe, given the thoroughgoing social revolution which necessairly would follow the assumption of power by the working class, that the entire process, even in these countries, could remain non-violent. See R. Tucker, *The Marxian Revolutionary Idea*, Princeton, Princeton University Press, 1970, p. 144.

25. Marx, 'Revolution in China and in Europe', p. 22.

26. The term semi-colonial is used in marxist-leninist commentary to denote countries in the Third World, which, while retaining nominal political independence, are subject to substantial economic penetration by the 'imperialist' powers, and whose leaders, therefore, have little flexibility, acting in effect as puppets of foreign economic interests.

27. V. Lenin, 'The Significance of the Serbo-Bulgarian Victories' (1912),

*Collected Works* (henceforward *CW*) XVIII, p. 398. See also V. Lenin, 'To the Indian Revolutionary Association' (1920), *CW* XXXI, p. 138.

28. V. Lenin, 'The Right of Nations to Self Determination' (1914), *CW*, XX, p. 400.

29. V. Lenin, 'Preface to the French and German Editions of *Imperialism, The Highest Stage of Capitalism* (1920), *CW* XXXII, p. 190.

30. Lenin, 'Significance of Serbo-Bulgarian Victories', p. 398. For an example of recent misuse of this reference, see D. Kunaev, 'V. Lenin i Natsional'no-osvoboditel' naya Revolyutsia', *Kommunist* (1969), 17, p. 54.

31. Cf. V. Lenin, 'On the Question of National Policy' (1914), in *CW* XX, pp. 223; and V. Lenin, 'The National Question in Our Programme' (1903), *CW* VI, p. 463.

32. V. Lenin, Resolutions of the 6th All-Russian Conference of the RSDLP' (1912), *CW* XVII, p. 485.

33. V. Lenin, 'The Historical Destiny of the Doctrine of Karl Marx' (1913), *CW* XVIII, p. 584.

34. V. Lenin, 'The Awakening of Asia' (1913), *CW* XIX, p. 86; and V. Lenin, 'Backward Europe and Advanced Asia' (1913), *CW* XIX, p. 100.

35. V. Lenin, 'A Caricature of Marxism' (1916), *CW* XXIII, p. 60.

36. Cf., for example, V. Lenin, 'Address to the 2nd All-Russian Congress of Communist Organizations of Peoples of the East' (1919), *CW* XXX, p. 159, in which he stated that victory for the European proletariat was impossible without the assistance of colonial peoples. See also V. Lenin, 'Preliminary Draft Theses on the National and Colonial Question' (1920), *CW* XXXI, p. 146, where he insisted that a close alliance with the national and colonial liberation movements 'must be pursued'.

37. Relevant documents from the first two meetings are cited in the previous note.

38. Lenin, 'Address to the 2nd All-Russian Congress', pp. 161-2.

39. V. Lenin, 'Report of the Commission on the National and Colonial Questions' (1920), *CW* XXXI, pp. 243, 44; and A. Reznikov, 'Lenin o Natsional'-no-osvoboditel'nom Dvizhenii', *Kommunist* (1967), 7, p. 94.

40. Cf. V. Lenin, 'Critical Remarks on the National Question' (1913), *Collected Works* XX, pp. 25-8; V. Lenin, 'Theses on the National Question' (1913), *Collected Works* XIX, p. 245; Lenin, 'The Right of Nations to Self Determination', pp. 411, 424. See also J. Stalin, *Marxism and the National Question* (1913) in J. Stalin, *Marxism and the National and Colonial Question*, London, Lawrence and Wishart, 1942.

41. Lenin, 'On the Question of National Policy', p. 223.

42. Lenin, 'Draft Theses on the National and Colonial Question', p. 149.

43. Lenin, 'A Caricature of Marxism', pp. 67-8.

44. V. Lenin, 'The Socialist Revolution and the Right of Nations to Self Determination' (1916), *CW* XXII, p. 147.

45. 'Declaration of the Rights of the Peoples of Russia' (1917), as cited in I. Deutscher, *Stalin*, Harmondsworth, Penguin, 1977, p. 188.

46. Cf. Lenin, 'Theses on the National Question' (1913), p. 244; Lenin, 'A Caricature of Marxism', p. 66.

47. Lenin, 'The Right of Nations to Self Determination', p. 428; Lenin, 'The National Question in Our Programme', pp. 454-6. At the risk of over-systematizing his views, this may explain in part his misgivings about the Red Army's 1921 conquest of Georgia, which was ruled by a socialist (Menshevik) regime with strong trade union support. Stalin followed Lenin in the emphasis on the right of self-determination of the masses, and not of the bourgeoisie. Cf. J. Stalin, 'Speech at the 3rd All-Russian Congress of Soviets', cited in Deutscher,

*Stalin*, p. 190; and J. Stalin, 'The October Revolution and the National Question' (1918) in Stalin, *Marxism and the National and Colonial Question*, p. 74.

48. Lenin, 'The Right of Nations to Self Determination', pp. 411-12.

49. V. Lenin, *The Development of Capitalism in Russia* (1899), *Collected Works*, III, pp. 21-607.

50. V. Lenin, *Two Tactics of Social Democracy in the Democratic Revolution* (1907), Moscow, Progress, 1977, p. 43.

51. V. Lenin, 'Democracy and Narodism in China' (1912), *CW*, XVIII, pp. 163-4.

52. Lenin, *Two Tactics*, pp. 38, 80-1. In this vein, Meyer argued that 'despite his argument about the rise of capitalism in Russia, Lenin did take into account the fact that the predominance of the peasantry in Russia's economy would necessitate changes in the marxist sociology'. A Meyer, *Leninism*, Cambridge, Harvard University Press, 1957, p 114.

53. Lenin, 'A Caricature of Marxism', pp.69-70.

54. Lenin, 'Address to the 2nd All-Russian Congress of Communist Organizations of the Peoples of the East', p. 116.

55. I.e., where some societies were behind others in the creation of the 'material and subjective conditions for the transition to socialism'.

56. Lenin, *Two Tactics*, pp. 46, 55, 96.

57. Ibid., p. 41.

58. Lenin, 'Democracy and Narodism in China', pp. 163-9.

59. For a similar view on the part of Stalin in a work closely supervised by Lenin, see Stalin, *Marxism and the National Question*, p. 14.

60. Cf., for example, the breadth of the appeal in Council of People's Commissars, 'Appeal to the Muslims of Russia and the East' (1917), in J. Degras, ed., *Soviet Documents on Foreign Policy*, New York, Octagon, 1978, I, pp. 15-17.

61. V. Lenin, 'Report of the Commission on the National and Colonial Questions', p. 241.

62. Ibid., p. 240.

63. Ibid., p. 242.

64. Cf .V. Lenin, *What Is To Be Done?* (1902), *CW* V, pp. 375, 385, 396-7, 400, 422-3, 428, 438, 446, 462, 464, 466.

65. E. Kedourie, ed., *Nationalism in Asia and Africa*, New York, Meridian, 1970, pp. 27-8.

66. Lenin, *Two Tactics*, p. 58.

67. V. Lenin, *State and Revolution* (1917), *CW* XXV, pp. 396, 400, 460, 461-2.

68. V. Lenin, 'The Junius Pamphlet' (1916), *CW* XXII, p. 310.

# 4 THE THIRD WORLD AND NATIONAL LIBERATION

## Introduction

This chapter discusses the development by Third World nationalists of ideas of national liberation and of strategies and tactics designed to translate these ideas into reality. It covers those movements in the colonial and semi-colonial countries of the Third World which have been most prominent in armed struggle against foreign rule or against indigenous conservative regimes closely linked with outside interests. The analysis focuses on the doctrines of the kemalist movement in Turkey, the Kuomintang, the Chinese Communist Party (CCP), the Viet Minh and the Vietnamese Workers Party, the Algerian Front de Liberation Nationale (FLN), the African Independence Party of Guine and Cabo Verde (PAIGC), the Popular Movement for the Liberation of Angola (MPLA), the Mozambique Liberation Front (FRELIMO), the South West Africa People's Organization (SWAPO) and the African National Congress (ANC). It pays particular attention to the writings of Sun Yat-sen, Mao Tse-tung, Ahmed Sukarno, Ho Chi Minh, Frantz Fanon, Che Guevara and Amilcar Cabral. It also includes a number of early national revolutionaries who, while they were not involved in armed struggles of the type mentioned above, none the less influenced later thinking on anti-Western revolution or whose ideas prefigured later trends in Third World revolutionary thought. The most important of these are the Tartar national communist Mir Said Sultan-Galiev and the Indian marxist M.N. Roy.

The struggle against Western domination in the Third World is a very broad one geographically, chronologically, culturally and ideologically. Some justification for concentrating on this slice of it is, therefore, necessary. Chronologically, it is possible to argue that the history of the phenomenon of national liberation goes back at least as far as the exodus of the Jews from Egypt and takes in such salient episodes as the revolt of the Macabees, of the Hussites uprising in Bohemia, the American Revolution, the independence of the Spanish and Portuguese colonies in Latin America, the unification of Italy, and the collapse of the Ottoman Empire in Europe. But this work focuses on national liberation as an aspect of the struggle of non-European peoples against European colonial and semi-colonial domination in the aftermath of the industrial revolution and the expansion of Western power throughout the globe. It is since the First World War and, with greater force, since the Second World War, that indigenous forces in the Third World have mounted a challenge of increasing strength to Western hegemony.

As was noted in Chapter 1, the study concentrates on movements which have chosen violence as a form of struggle, because the term 'national liberation', particularly in the last two decades, has come to be associated, in international law, at the United Nations, and in Western commentary on Third World politics with movements engaged in armed struggle. This volume gives special attention within this group to movements and figures prominent in the struggles in China, Indonesia, Vietnam, Algeria, Cuba, Portuguese Africa, and the rest of southern Africa, because these are the principal instances of violent national revolution in the Third World.

For purposes of comparison and completeness, this examination of national revolutionary thought in the Third World is supplemented by some consideration of the thought of prominent Third World nationalists who have been involved in conflicts in which violence was *not* the dominant form of struggle in order to determine whether and how the objectives and strategies of national liberation movements resemble or differ from those of figures such as Nehru ,Nasser, Toure, Nkrumah and Nyerere. From such a comparison, it should be possible to deduce whether there has occurred a transition, in ideological terms, from a 'moderate' period of decolonization and national self-determination to a more radical phase of national liberation, or whether in important respects Third World thinking *as a whole* is distinct from Soviet and Western views of political and social change in non-European societies. In addition, though the focus of this study is on secular movements and the doctrines they espouse, where useful, reference is made to Catholic liberation theology and to 'Islamic liberation', again for purposes of comparison.

Three further points concerning the sample should be made. First, the geographical focus of the study is the Third World. As such, whatever the merits of the concept of 'internal colonialism', the efforts of contemporary separatist movements in the West (the Bretons, the Basques, the Welsh, the Northern Irish, the Quebecois) do not fall within its purview. Nor do the struggles of national minorities in the European USSR (the Lithuanians, the Latvians, the Estonians, and the Ukrainians) or in Eastern Europe (for example, the Croats and

Albanians in Yugoslavia).

Second, although the category of national revolutionary movements described above may appear rather narrow, in ideological terms it is quite broad. Those included range from national communists (Sultan-Galiev and much of the leadership of the CCP, for example) through those who eschewed the communist label while claiming to be marxists (cf. the MPLA in Angola), those who rejected the label of marxist while acknowledging the influence of Marx (for example, Amilcar Cabral), to those who claimed to have developed autochthonous doctrines of revolution, rejecting marxism *per se* for religious reasons (for example, the FLN).

Thirdly, there is a temptation in an analysis of this sort to quote more or less randomly from various writers in attempting to establish common ground between them, without attending to the fact that thinking evolves over time in response to changing historical circumstances and as militants develop a more sophisticated understanding of the problems they face and of the options available to them. Where the doctrines of these movements do show significant change over time, it is noted in the analysis. However, in most of the cases considered below, there are sets of objectives and strategies which remain relatively constant over time, despite changing circumstances, once they have been defined in basic statements of doctrine.

The analysis below follows a pattern similar to that in the previous chapter. From a discussion of the essential idea of national liberation, it passes on to discuss the role of the struggle for national liberation in world history and then various aspects of the process by which the objectives contained in this idea are to be achieved.

### The Definition of National Liberation

Among those movements which have been involved in armed struggle against foreign domination, from Ataturk onward there has been a near universal recognition that political independence from foreign rule, while an essential precondition of national liberation, is insufficient. This perspective has also been shared by those nationalist figures considered here who did not mount armed challenges to external domination.

At least three other objectives have been generally recognized as integral components of the idea of national liberation. The first of these is economic independence, control of the nation's resources and of economic activity within the state's boundaries. This emphasis is shared by both non-marxists and marxists, from Sun Yat-sen onward. Sun maintained that China was not free to develop because of foreign economic domination. By implication, freedom from external economic control was necessary for improvement in China's economic situation.[1] The Turkish National Pact of January, 1920, which is, in some respects, the first more or less coherent statement of 'kemalist' ideology, declared that it was a fundamental condition of national survival that Turkey should enjoy control over the means of economic development. For this reason, the nascent republican government rejected any perpetuation of trade and financial capitulations which the Ottoman Empire had accepted in its relations with the European powers.[2] In internal policy, this principle translated itself into a very broad role for the state and for state-controlled enterprise in the industrial, raw materials, and financial sectors of the Turkish economy. In Indonesia, Sukarno defined his nation's struggle as one against the economic as well as the political 'chains of imperialism'.[3]

In the case of the CCP, as early as 1928, Mao Tse-tung, in arguing that the completion of the 'democratic revolution' in China implied the overthrow of imperialist privleges,[4] was in effect calling for economic as well as political independence. The privileges he decried were largely economic in content (foreign control of Chinese trade, customs, and finance, foreign ownership of Chinese industry and infrastructure, etc.). When the CCP took power in 1949, this concern over the foreign economic presence expressed itself in widespread nationalization of foreign property, and again, in more and more widespread state control of economic activity.

As Chinese involvement in Afro-Asian politics grew in the 1950s and 1960s, party commentators extended the discussion of economic independence as an aspect of national liberation to the newly independent states. An article in *People's Daily* in 1960 argued, for example, that:

> To the imperialists, economic control and political enslavement have always been like the two indivisible edges of a sword used against the oppressed peoples. In order to obtain genuine independence all oppressed peoples must therefore free themselves from the economic control of imperialism[5]

The Chinese communist emphasis on economic independence from the world capitalist system, coupled with their radical rejection (from the Great Leap Forward onwards) of integration into the Soviet block, led logically to the advocacy of self-reliance – the creation of self-sufficient national economic units. This also followed from their experience during the struggle against the Kuomintang (KMT) of insufficient aid from the Soviet Union and the consequent necessity in remote base areas of relying on internally generated resources.

The commitment to self-reliance was perhaps most evident during the Great Leap Forward of 1957 to 1958. The abandonment of this line in 1958 was not a renunciation of the principle. Chinese writers continued to recommend it as an economic course for the newly independent states. Instead, it reflected a recognition of impending economic disaster . Again, the economic opening to the West in the aftermath of Mao's death may not indicate an abandonment of the eminently nationalist objective of economic independence and self-sufficiency. Instead, it can be argued that the recourse to Western know-how and capital in the four modernizations constitutes an attempt to construct the material prerequisites for an economically strong and self-sufficient China, reliant on no one and consequently capable of free choice in foreign and domestic policy.

Later liberation movements have displayed a similar concern to achieve not only political but economic independence. Truong Chinh succinctly expressed the Vietnamese communist view in 1946, when he asserted that the 'complete independence' sought by Vietnam required that the 'Vietnamese economy must be independent, not tied to the French economy or to that of any other country'.[6]

A contributor to the FLN's theoretical journal *El-Moudjahid* captured the Algerian movement's perspective in noting that: '[Le peuple algerien] n'entend pas se debarasser de l'oppression politique pour se resigner a une oppression economique qui interdit tout progres social et confere a l'independance novellement acquise un caractere illusoire.'[7] In the Algerian case as elsewhere, this principle was operationalized in widespread seizures of foreign property after independence and in a dominant role for the state in industrial development.[8]

Elsewhere, Che Guevara in one of his better known statements of revolutionary theory, stressed that there could be no true independence or, for that matter, sound development unless the 'economically dependent peoples' freed themselves from economic domination by foreign capital.[9] In the Cuban case, the attempt to put this kind of thinking into practice through selective nationalization of American industrial and agricultural property, and to assert far more active control over foreign investment in general, was a key factor in the deterioration of Cuban-American relations in 1959-60.[10]

The theme of economic liberation is also conspicuously present in the statements and policies of revolutionary movements in Lusophone Africa. The first programme of the PAIGC mentioned economic independence as an aspect of national liberation.[11] Amilcar Cabral, its founder, called for economic independence through his writings.[12] Marcelino Dos Santos, an early leader of FRELIMO who later became prime minister of Mozambique, in 1962 cited economic independence as a principal objective of his movement.[13] A series of FRELIMO articles in the mid-1960s stressed that the movement was fighting not only colonialism, but neocolonialism (that is, economic exploitation by the foreign power).[14] Eduardo Mondlane, FRELIMO's first president, mentioned 'economic exploitation' along with colonialism as a principal target of the revolution.[15]

In the case of Angola's MPLA, the movement's 1962 programme called for economic independence as an integral aspect of national liberation.[16] In 1974, Agostinho Neto, the movement's president, declared that no country in Africa was yet free from economic domination and, consequently, that the struggle for national liberation necessarily extended well beyond the attainment of political sovereignty.[17] There is no difficuly in finding similar formulae in the programmatic documents of SWAPO, the ANC, and ZANU.[18]

Where these movements have succeeded in establishing themselves as governments, there has been considerable variation in the degree to which they have attempted to put into practice the principle of economic independence. This may be the result of factional struggle in the new leaderships betwen 'pragmatists' and 'ideologues' (as is arguably the case in Angola), and/or, more basically, of the constraints imposed by lack of skills, undercapitalization, and insufficient aid from the socialist camp. In all three Portuguese African cases, the seriousness of the commitment to national control of the economy was evident in extensive nationalization of foreign property — much of it abandoned during the exodus of the Portuguese, in close scrutiny over and regulation of remaining foreign economic involvement, and in the frequent insistence upon state participation in foreign direct investment. In the years since independence, however, all three, in the face of persistent low growth, poor performance in the state sector, and shortfalls in foreign public assistance, have sought broader foreign private participation, and have accordingly softened the terms governing that participation.

In the case of Zimbabwe, any elan in the direction of economic independence has been inhibited by the regime's concern to prevent any flight of capital and skills and to ensure continued access to foreign public and private sources of capital.

One might conclude from this that in instances where economic independence is seen to conflict with economic well-being, even these 'Afro-marxist' regimes will sacrifice the former to the latter. However, as Crawford Young has noted with reference to Africa:

> Overriding political or economic imperatives may force upon a regime choices that appear to be inconsistent with ideological preference. Such dissonance may be rationalized as either not truly inconsistent with ideology correctly understood or as a conscious and temporary departure from rectitude; it does not annul the world view with which it is in tension.[19]

To summarize from the above, there would appear to be among movements which have embarked on armed struggle for liberation in colonial and semi-colonial countries a near universal recognition that national liberation does not stop with political independence, but includes economic liberation as well.

The third element of the idea of national liberation is a commitment to profound social change. It was generally recognized that this involved not only changes in longstanding indigenous socio-political structures (the displacement of traditional elites) and in relations of production in the agrarian sector (such as land redistribution), but also the avoidance or elimination of capitalism. The outcome of this social change was to be one form or another of socialism.

The focus on social revolution as an element of national liberation again goes back to the early period of anti-Western struggle. As with the emphasis on economic independence, it is common to both marxists and non-marxists. Among the former, the Tartar Bolshevik Mir Said Sultan-Galiev, a major theorist of what has been termed 'Muslim national communism' in the Soviet Union, maintained that the process of national liberation involved both national (the overthrow of Great Russian domination) and social (the elimination of indigenous feudal and nascent capitalist oppression) tasks. The process of liberation in his view culminated in socialism.[20]

Similar attempts at a synthesis between nationalism and socialism were common in the 1920s and early 1930s in the Arab communist movement. Taking advantage of a period of what might be called 'left sectarianism' (the rejection of broad united front tactics — see Chapter 5) in Comintern doctrine, these groups sought to combine the quest for national independence with the preparation of the masses for class struggle and social revolution. Maxime Rodinson has referred to this trend as 'marxist or proletarian nationalism'.[21]

In the case of Turkey, prominent kemalist ideologues such as Tekin Alp called for a social revolution directed against 'religious and socio-economic aristocracies' which oppressed the people and which impeded the development of Turkey into an economically strong modern state. This revolution, in Tekin Alp's view, was to be directed not only against traditional indigenous power structures, but against capitalism as well. He quoted Ataturk as affirming that: 'Nous sommes de ceux qui tiennent a lutter en tant que collectivite nationale contre le capitalisme qui veut nous engloutir.' Alp justified this anti-capitalist and, incidentally, anti-democratic thrust by arguing that liberal economic policies not only were the source of the misery of Turkey's masses, but also facilitated foreign domination by opening the door to foreign economic penetration.[22] His and Turkey's spearhead in this resistance to foreign economic penetration was, as noted above, state involvement in the economy, a phenomenon he referred to as 'veritable state socialism'.[23]

In China, Sun Yat-sen characterized the revolutionary movement as one directed not only against foreign domination, but also against the entire elite of 'avaricious officials, evil gentry, and corrupt scholars' which had allowed the country to be humiliated.[24] He went beyond targeting the traditional elite, however, to reject capitalism as a path of development for China and to advocate a radical redistribution of national resources in favour of the poor.[25]

Sukarno went beyond this on a number of occasions to identify capitalism as the economic| expression of colonialism. This led him to call for revolution directed not only against foreign rule, but against capitalism as a socio-economic system, and for its replacement with a just and prosperous socialist society.[26] Sukarno too, therefore, in his discussion of social objectives, presents a dual justification for social change – the uprooting of imperialism and the creation of a 'just' society.

Similar concerns are evident in the Chinese communist discussion of their own and other Third World revolutions. The principle that the liberation revolution was directed against both internally and externally originating exploitation is a persistent theme. As early as 1928, Mao was arguing that the external aspect of China's revolution was paralleled by an internal one, namely the liquidation of compradors, the overthrow of warlords, and the completion of the agrarian revolution (that is, land reform).[27]

This social struggle was justified not only in terms of the socialist orientation of the movement (it was repeatedly asserted that the eventual outcome of the revolution was the creation of a socialist society through the elimination of both feudal and capitalist relations of production),[28] but also as a consequence of the co-option of indigenous elites by foreign interests. The latter made social revolution a necesssary condition for success in the struggle against foreign domination.[29] Along these lines, the party leadership argued in 1927 that since the national bourgeoisie had abandoned its own revolution and thrown in its lot with imperialism and 'reaction' the fight by the proletariat for the fulfilment of its own (that is, anti-capitalist) class interests was a 'necessary prerequisite for success in the revolution for national liberation'.[30]

While the radicalism of this particular statement may be explained largely in terms of its historical context (it was issued at a time of severe repression of the CCP by Chiang Kai-shek and by the left KMT regime in Wuhan), there is ample evidence from later years (both in doctrine and policy) to suggest that this particular identification of domestic with foreign exploiters was not exceptional. In 1961, for example, in a retrospective article on the role of the peasantry in the Chinese revolution, a writer in *Red Flag* stated

> Feudalism was the ally of imperialism and bureaucratic capitalism and the foundation of their rule. Therefore, to bury imperialism and its lackeys in China, we had to eliminate feudalism; only when we firmly led the peasants in waging an anti-feudal struggle could a powerful anti-imperialist force be organized.[31]

There is a hint of a third reason for including social revolution as an element of the struggle for national liberation. Meeting the concrete needs of an impoverished peasantry for land and for debt relief was a potent mobilizing device.

This line of reasoning has important implications for the delineation of stages in the revolutionary process. In effect it denies the separability of the national liberation revolution into distinct phases. Through much of the history of the Chinese revolution, the anti-imperialist and social revolutionary phases were to some extent combined. Part of this was the result of necessity. Through the late 1920s and the early and mid-1930s, and much of the 1940s, the KMT was attempting physically to eliminate the CCP. In these circumstances, struggle against the KMT would have been difficult to avoid. But it was also in some respects deliberate policy, as, for example, when the CCP combined military struggle against the KMT encirclement of the Kiangsi soviet with social struggle (rent reduction, land confiscation, etc.) within the base area in the early 1930s. Another example is the period after 1939, when during the struggle against the Japanese, the party encouraged similar social struggle within the areas under their control.

The theme of social revolution and its justification in terms of ethical commitment, the links between indigenous elites and foreign exploiters, and its utility in mobilizing mass support are common in the literature of later movements as well. The Vietnamese communist discussion of social revolution is illustrative. Ho Chi Minh, Vo Nguyen Giap and Truong Chinh repeatedly stressed that the process of liberation involved anti-feudal agrarian revolution (confiscation and redistribution of land, reduction of rent and debt, destruction of traditional political structures), as well as anti-imperialist struggle.[32] The point of the Vietnamese revolution was, in Truong Chinh's view, the socialization of the means of production, the abolition of the 'regime of exploitation of man by man'.[33]

Algeria's FLN maintained in its first platform that the struggle for liberation included several revolutions, one of which was a profound social transformation in Algerian Muslim society. This involved the liquidation of indigenous 'medieval and feudal structures' upon which colonialism rested.[34] Ferhat Abbas extended the attack to capitalism, maintaining in terms that recall Sukarno that since capitalism was indissolubly linked to colonialism, it was not possible to fight the one without assailing the other.[35] Ahmed Ben Bella, Algeria's first president, took this line to its logical conclusion, stating in 1963 that the ultimate goal of the FLN was the establishment of a 'revolutionary Arab socialism'.[36]

In policy, this Algerian commitment to social change and socialism reinforces the implications of the quest for economic independence. Both have favoured the expropriation of private (particularly foreign) enterprise and the growth of a substantial state sector in the Algerian economy. In the rural sector, the consequence of this commitment was a degree of land reform immediately following independence. The expropriation of some five million acres of quality farm land for redistribution was facilitated by the exodus of thousands of French settlers. The process was continued under the 'Charter of the Agrarian Revolution' in 1971 with attempts to establish model collective villages and, by 1978, with the further acquisition of some 4.6 million acres by a

National Land Fund, 3.1 million of which the government subsequently redistributed to poor peasants.[37]

Turning to Latin America, one sees again, in the writings, for
example, of Che Guevara, Regis Debray and Carlos Marighela, all three
arguments for social revolution noted above: the point of the process of
liberation being the elimination of all exploitation; the ties between
indigenous bourgeois and landowning elites and foreign interests
making anti-imperialist and social struggle inseparable; and the utility
of social revolutionary slogans in mobilizing the masses.[38] In the case
of Cuba, Castro and his colleagues translated this commitment to social
change into practice in the aftermath of Batista's fall in take-overs of
foreign agricultural and industrial property, the progressive socialization
of agriculture, industry, retail and wholesale trade, and finance,[39] that
is to say, in a massive expansion of the state role in the economy and a
considerable degree of centralization of economic decision-making.
Similar trends have appeared in the post-revolutionary economic and
agrarian policies of Nicaragua's FSLN.

Turning to sub-Saharan Africa, the movements in the Portuguese
colonies again all emphasized the significance of social revolution as an
aspect of national liberation. Cabral maintained that the struggle
targeted both indigenous and foreign oppression, the aim being the
termination of all forms of exploitation (feudal, as in the case of hier-
archical relationships among the Fulah, and capitalist, as with price
manipulation by Portuguese traders) of man by man. In Cabral's view,
the essence of the process of national liberation was the regaining of
control by the people over the nation's productive forces. This necessitated a socialist solution through the destruction of capitalist and pre-
capitalist relations of production. Cabral also shared the other two
rationales for social change as an integral aspect of national liberation.
He cited the links between indigenous elites (or example, the Fulah
chiefs) and the colonial power. Beyond this, he asserted that, particularly in Fulah areas where exploitative social relations characterized
indigenous society and where persisting loyalty to tribal elites impeded
the activities of the PAIGC, the embrace of social objectives (that is,
the attempt to destroy the power of traditional elites) was necessary
in order to attract mass support.[40] More generally, he noted:

> Always remember that the people do not struggle for ideas, for
> things in the heads of individuals. The people struggle and accept
> the sacrifices demanded by the struggle, but in order to gain material
> advantages, to be able to live a better life in peace, to see their lives

progress and to ensure their children's future.[41]

In the case of the MPLA, social reform was implicit in early documents, which spoke of 'agrarian reform', the 'social promotion of the masses', and the need to fulfil the claims of 'oppressed peasants and workers'. Agostinho Neto later echoed Fanon in arguing that if there were not significant social progress as part of the process of national liberation, Angola would fall into a new kind of discrimination 'as negative as the first'. For this reason, the national liberation struggle was one directed against both internal and external exploitation and the MPLA embraced a 'firm' anti-capitalist as well as anti-imperialist socialist option.[42]

Similar assertions may be found in FRELIMO,[43] ANC,[44] ZANU[45] and SWAPO[46] programmatic and theoretical writings. In the cases of the MPLA, FRELIMO, the ANC and SWAPO attitudes towards social revolution have increasingly come to be couched in marxist-leninist vocabulary, whether because of the radicalizing effect of prolonged armed struggle, because of growing dependence on Cuban and Eastern bloc technical, economic, and military assistance, and/or because of a perceived need to identify with a powerful external potential ally.[47]

The practical implications of this concern with social transformation among these movements are again evident to varying degrees in their pre-victory policies in zones which they controlled and in the post-independence economic and social measures taken by the governments which they formed. In Guine-Bissau, before victory the PAIGC made major efforts to encourage co-operative agricultural production, socialized retail trade through the 'people's shops' system, and organized a rudimentary political structure centred around village committees where youth and women were encouraged to play a prominent role. FRELIMO followed a similar course, though it is unclear to what degree village committees replaced rather than merely co-opted, and thereby perpetuated the social position of, traditional elites.

In the aftermath of independence, all three Lusophone movements have moved to socialize economic activity through nationalization of key sectors. Angola and Mozambique have attempted ambitious transformation of the agricultural sector through the establishment of large state farms on former plantations and, particularly in Mozambique, through the sponsorship of production co-operatives. Agrarian reform has not been a critical issue in Guine-Bissau, as there was no serious problem of concentration of ownership, exploitation of rural labour, and, for that matter, no shortage of arable land.

It is therefore legitimate to conclude that, in general, revolutionary social transformation (substantial land reform and the attempt to impede the development of or to replace as far as practically possible capitalist relations of production) constitutes an integral aspect of the concept of national liberation for the bulk of the groups considered here. This commitment has generally been justified in three ways.

(1) as a tactic to broaden a movement's mass support;[48]
(2) as a necessity given the profound links between indigenous elites and foreign oppressors; and
(3) as part of a basic ethical commitment to end all exploitation, indigenous and foreign.

These movements have generally accepted that the outcome of this process of social transformation is one form or another of socialism. To judge from the practice of these movements both before and after victory, 'socialism' implies the expropriation and redistribution of the property of those considered to be exploiters, co-operative or public ownership of key sectors of the economy, and a highly visible role for the state in the management and control of economic activity. In the latter sense, the policy implications of the commitment to social revolution closely approximate those of the objective of economic independence.

In addition to these political, economic, and social aspects of the idea of national liberation, there is a generally accepted cultural or subjective dimension. The Muslim national communism of Sultan-Galiev and other Tartar members of the Bolshevik Party was in part a defence of and attempt to reform Islamic Turkic culture in the face of the challenge of Great Russian chauvinism. Many of the more salient aspects of Kemal Ataturk's programme were cultural in content and aimed at fostering the subjective prerequisites for modernization and national unity through an assault on traditions impeding them. One could cite here the abolition of Koranic schools and the reorganization of education on a secular state-controlled basis, the literacy and orthography campaigns, the outlawing of polygamy and the granting of equal status in divorce proceedings to women, and the rewriting of Turkish history along national Turkish rather than Islamic Ottoman lines.[49]

Sukarno stressed the importance of a colonized people's sense of inferiority, declaring in terms which prefigure Fanon's analysis considered below, that: 'Colonial people are a faceless people, a people without an identity they can call their own, a people who to their very core bear the brand of imperialism, the sears of its pervasive-ness'.[50] He pointed out that the success of colonialism depended on convincing brown-skinned peoples of their inferiority and backward-ness, and maintained that one purpose of his party was to eradicate this sense of inferiority.[51]

The notion of cultural revolution or cultural liberation has a long history in Chinese communist writing. In the first place, there is in much CCP commentary on revolution, from Li Ta-chao to Mao Tse-tung, a pronounced voluntarism, a belief in the potency of will in over-coming objective obstacles in the struggle for liberation.[52] The emphasis on subjective rather than objective prerequisites for revolu-tionary activity implies a concern to create cultural conditions which foster or release the power of the will of the masses. In this sense, cultural regeneration is a precondition of national liberation as well as an aspect of it.

Mao displayed his awareness of the importance of cultural liberation among other places in 'On New Democracy': 'For many years we com-munists have called for a cultural revolution as well as a political and economic revolution.' He appealed for the destruction of the 'old culture' which served colonial and feudal interests.[53] This suggests the elimination not only of those aspects of Western culture which demoralized and denied self-respect to the Chinese people, but also of those elements of the Chinese cultural heritage which impeded a vigorous and effective Chinese response to Western penetration. Mao's emphasis here on cultural renovation paralleled and perhaps to a degree drew upon a broader trend in cultural life in the 1920s and 1930s — the New Culture Movement. Those involved in it conducted a revolution in Chinese literature, replacing classical literary Chinese with prose accessible to the common people and satirizing the stultifying effects of traditional social relations, the point being to create the cultural prere-quisites for a rebirth of China.

During the Cultural Revolution, Chinese writers suggested that such efforts were an integral aspect of national liberation elsewhere in the Third World.[54] Liu Ta-nien (deputy director of the Academy of Sciences Institute of Modern History) identified the content of cultural liberation in at least one sphere when he called for a complete rewriting of Asian history which would emphasize anti-Western revolution and remove all 'Eurocentric, Western, chauvinist falsifications'. In his view, this would 'help the people free themselves from the mental enslave-ment of imperialism'.[55]

The cultural regeneration envisaged in Chinese communist writing and practice during the 'cheng feng' or rectification movement in the late 1930s and early 1940s and in the Cultural Revolution was nationally specific rather than universal in content. In the first of these periods, Mao called for the development of a sinified marxist consciousness, one 'that in all of its manifestations [would be] imbued with Chinese peculiarities'.[56] The Cultural Revolution of the mid-1960s combined a like emphasis on Chinese specificity with a pronounced xenophobia expressing itself, for example, in the banning of classical music and Western dance.

Vietnamese communist writers, like their Chinese counterparts, emphasized the importance of cultural renovation in the process of national liberation. Ho Chi Minh called in 1951 for more intense cultural work with a view to creating a 'new man' through the systematic elimination of 'all vestiges of colonialism and the servile influence of imperialist culture'.[57] Again, the new culture envisaged by Vietnamese writers was specifically national in character. Ho called for the development of 'the fine traditions of national culture', along with the assimilation of 'what is new in the progressive culture of the world with a view to building a *Vietnamese* culture'.[58] Truong Chinh likewise stressed that, as the Vietnamese people had to be masters of their country in every respect, 'Vietnam must develop its national culture'.[59]

Fanon, drawing upon his experience as a psychiatrist in Blida, devoted much attention to the cultural impact of colonialism and its psychological consequences. In his view, the destruction of indigenous culture, coupled with the racial barriers preventing or strongly inhibiting assimilation of the colonized into the culture of the colonizer, resulted in the atomization of colonial society and the dehumanization of individuals within it.[60] Whether or not leading figures in the FLN shared this diagnosis, they clearly agreed with Fanon that the restoration of the dignity of the oppressed individual, of his respect both for himself and for his culture, was an aspect of the struggle for liberation.[61]

For Fanon, cultural liberation was an integral part of the armed struggle against colonial rule rather than something to be begun once political independence had been achieved. The armed struggle itself — the decision to reject submission and to assert oneself as a subject in history and the action which followed from this decision — liberated those involved in it.[62] The individual decision to revolt was the key to self-liberation, and the sum of these decisions the essence of national liberation.[63] Freedom which was granted and not won by force was not freedom, for it did not involve individual self-assertion in struggle, the deliberate and conscious rejection of the cultural and psychological structure of colonial domination.[64]

Later discussions of national liberation by Black African revolutionary nationalists reflect Fanon's emphasis on the cultural aspect of colonialism and anti-colonialism. It was widely maintained that the intrusion of a dominant foreign cultural presence resulted in a sense of humiliation, inferiority, and self-contempt among indigenous peoples. This demoralization redounded to the advantage of the colonial power.[65] As such, the restoration of the dignity of the oppressed individual and of his respect for himself and for his culture were essential aspects of the overall process of liberation. Liberation was itself a 'struggle for culture'[66] or, as a representative of SWAPO put it:

> . . . the liberation process itself, the armed struggle, is a cultural act. By this I mean that we are trying to liberate ourselves not only politically but culturally. Economic and political liberation is not possible if people are not culturally linked, in that they must have a belief in their own identity, their own dignity.[67]

For these groups, too, cultural liberation meant not only the elimination of 'all traces of colonialism',[68] but also an attack on those elements of surviving traditional culture which facilitated external domination (for example, deference to traditional rulers who were collaborating with the colonial administration) and/or which obstructed the creation of an egalitarian socialist society. In the latter vein, the PAIGC, the MPLA, FRELIMO, and ZANU all have challenged the subordination of women in African society. In the case of the Lusophone African movements, this was put into practice in the reservation of leadership positions for women, in the banning of forced marriages, and in the involvement of women in military activities in both auxiliary and combat roles. In certain instances, these movements also struggled against the hold of traditional superstition, attempting to convince the rural population that they were responsible for their own destiny rather than being helpless in the face of unseen irresistible forces.[69]

Again, the particularistic character of the cultural liberation sought by these African movements should be underlined. Their conception of the 'new man', the product of this revolution in consciousness, is not so much a universal humanist idea as it is a nationally specific one. These movements seek to create or to recreate a culture of their own rather than to transcend national or religious differences in a homogeneous

world culture. Cabral, for instance, spoke of the 'reafricanization' of
the people of Guine-Bissau, and of the need to conserve and strengthen
popular culture within a *national* framework.[70] FRELIMO, in a post-
independence statement on education policy, stated that the party's
efforts in education were 'aimed at forming a new Mozambican African
personality', while Machel earlier stressed the salience of national consciousness in the 'new mentality' which his movement sought to
foster.[71]

To summarize, those included in this sample share a common perception of the prerequisites for and basic constituents of national liberation. National liberation for these groups involves the acquisition not
only of political but also of economic independence. Their practice
suggests that the latter means national control over the most important
sectors of economic life. Beyond this they embrace radical social
change, which they characterize as socialist in character or as movement in the direction of socialism. This includes dispossession of
dominant economic groups or classes, be they foreign or indigenous, and
the redistribution and/or public ownership of national economic
resources. Both economic and social objectives favour what has been a
common policy outcome in instances where these movements have
taken power, the nationalization of privately owned financial, agricultural, industrial and natural resource enterprises. Beyond this social
dimension, these movements and their writers include a cultural dimension in their definition of national liberation, calling for the creation of
a new liberated mentality.[72] It has come to be commonly, though by
no means universally, accepted that the political and social aspects of
national liberation should be pursued contemporaneously, given the co-
option of indigenous elites by foreign interests and given that social
revolutionary programmes are deemed to motivate the masses to take
up the cause of national liberation. Cultural liberation also accom-
panies the struggle for political independence, as the elimination of
the subjective consequences of foreign domination is considered to be a
precondition for effective struggle against foreign rule.

A number of these elements are particularistic in content: freedom
from foreign political control and economic dependence, and the
resurrection or creation of national culture. The social aspect of national
liberation has a more universal character. It pertains to the situation of
all men in presocialist society and involves an end to the exploitation
of man by man, an end to poverty and deprivation, and the creation of
the preconditions for each individual human being to realize his full
creative potential. These universalist social objectives were, as was seen

above, shared to some extent by earlier national movements in Europe and elsewhere (see Chapter 2). But the role which they play in the ideologies of Third World national revolutionary movements is different. For the latter group, a social revolutionary programme is not only a means of obtaining mass support. It is also a necessary condition for successful national revolution, because of the ties which exist between indigenous elites in colonial and semi-colonial countries and the 'foreign oppressor'. Beyond this, social revolution is, for these groups, an essential element of liberation because the latter is held to involve an end to all oppression, indigenous and foreign.[73] This recalls the discussion of the marxist theory of revolution in Chapter 3 and would suggest that in this respect, the idea of national liberation is an attempt to synthesize basic attributes of both nationalist particularism and marxist universalism.

Before identifying the sources of this common conception of national liberation, its relation to the nationalism of Third World figures not involved in wars of national liberation and not subject to the radicalizing effect of such wars should be examined. A perusal of the writings of such figures as Jawaharlal Nehru, Gamal Abdel Nasser and other Arab nationalists, Marcus Garvey, George Padmore, Kwame Nkrumah, Sekou Toure and Julius Nyerere suggests that these perspectives on the problem of liberation fit into the broader context of nationalist thought in the Third World in this century.

It was widely accepted, for instance, that political independence was not so much an end in itself as a prerequisite to or means for the attainment of other more important objectives. With respect to economic independence, we see Nehru asserting that British economic domination was a brake on Indian progress, suggesting that this domination had to be thrown off if India were going to realize the aspirations of her leaders.[74] Nkrumah, particularly in his later years, repeatedly averred that neocolonialism (economic control) was the essence of external domination. A similar preoccupation with the economic dimensions of liberation may be found in the writings of the likes of Sekou Toure, Tom Mboya, Julius Nyerere, and in various documents of the Pan-African movement in the late 1950s and early 1960s.[75]

The growing concern throughout the Third World to restrict and to regulate foreign economic activity and, more particularly, the wave of nationalizations of foreign enterprises in the late 1960s and 1970s and the growing insistence on joint ownership where new investment occurs, suggest that the notion of 'dependencia' and its obverse, the desire for economic independence, have come to play an important role in the policy-making of most states in the Thid World. That they have also informed these states' international diplomacy may be seen in the efforts, not just of radical states, but of the Third World as a whole, to secure recognition by the international community of national sovereignty over resources and over economic activity within national frontiers.[76]

With regard to social change, Nehru held that traditional elites, like foreign economic interests, were an impediment to progress, and called for their removal. He also supported agrarian reform and embraced socialism as the necessary path for India.[77] In earlier writings, his radicalism was more pronounced. In the 1930s, for instance, he sought not merely national independence but the ending of all exploitation through 'vast revolutionary changes' in the political, economic, and social regime.[78]

In the Arab world, the tendency to link national tasks (pan-Arabism, economic independence, national consolidation) with social ones, to combine nationalism with socialism, is perhaps clearest in the theoretical writings of Nasser, who called for a social revolution to secure economic justice for all, to accompany political revolution against imperialist occupation or indigenous tyranny.[79] The Ba'athists, and Iraq's General Kassem shared this dual commitment to anti-imperialism and social change.[80]

In Africa, the literature of nationalist movements and political parties abounds with references to the necessity of social change and of an end to exploitation if real freedom is to be achieved, to the need for displacement or emasculation of traditional elites, to the rejection of capitalism as a mode of development, and to socialism as the culmination of the struggle for freedom.[81]

One should not perhaps overestimate the doctrinal accomplishment of many of these writers. Often the 'socialist 'aspect of these programmes was only vaguely conceived. Nor, however, should this socialist dimension be undervalued. The commitment it embodies has had significant policy consequences in Egypt, India, Syria, Iraq, Guinea, Tanzania, Mali, Ghana, Cuba and Nicaragua, among others. All of these states have undertaken programmes of land reform, and/or have emphasized public ownership of key sectors of the national economy.

Finally, the theme of profound social change to eliminate indigenous oppression is also clearly present in the writings of liberation theologians such as Gustavo Gutierrez and in various products of the progressive Catholic movement in Latin America in the 1960s and 1970s. One could cite here, for example, the Medellin Bishops' Conference 'Document on Justice'.[82]

Turning to the cultural aspect of national thought, an examination of these sources shows that the association of cultural regeneration with national liberation is accepted not only by the liberation movements considered above, but by a much wider array of Third World nationalists. Nehru, for example, echoed Sukarno in speaking of the 'shameful subservience and timid submission to an arrogant alien authority' among Indians, and, consequently, of the need to raise his people's psychological and spiritual level as part of the struggle for freedom.[83] In the Arab world, Rodinson notes among many intellectuals and political figures a general desire for cultural as well as political independence.[84] A conscious rejection of Western culture also appears to be a significant aspect of the recent Islamic revival, particularly in its recent Iranian manifestation. However, although there are many different currents in this revival as a whole, the cultural aspect at least of its more conservative wing would appear to be conspicuously more atavistic and reactionary than most of the movements considered here. This is perhaps clearest in attitudes towards the place of women in Islamic society.

Early black nationalists voiced similar concerns. Marcus Garvey anticipated much later commentary in his argument that it was the inferiority complex of blacks which allowed others to take advantage of them.[85] Leopold Senghor's response to the problems of inferiority complexes, lack of self-respect, and sense of 'culturelessness' among black elites was to launch the concept of 'negritude'. This amounted to the assertion of a consciousness and cultural essence shared by all black people, both in Africa and in the diaspora, which united them and distinguished them from other races, and in which they could take pride.[86]

Sekou Toure, while rejecting Senghor's solution, shared his view of colonialism as a system of cultural as well as economic and political domination and his recognition of the need for a psychological emancipation if 'total liberation' were to be achieved.[87] One encounters similar themes much later in the writing of Steve Biko, a founder of South Africa's Black Consciousness Movement. Biko followed Fanon and numerous others in stressing that the cultural alienation of and self-negation by blacks in white dominated societies was one of the principal bases of white ascendancy. 'Mental emancipation' was, therefore, a precondition for political freedom.[88]

It appears, therefore, that the idea of national liberation entertained not only by those engaged in armed struggle against foreign and/

or indigenous oppression, but also by a broader spectrum of nationalist opinion in the Third World goes well beyond political independence to embrace economic, social and cultural dimensions. Indeed, the idea of national liberation as it is defined by the movements considered earlier seems to fall into the mainstream of Third World nationalist thought.

That such a geographically, culturally and ideologically diverse group should reach this broad agreement on the meaning and objectives of the process of national liberation is surprising. Two categories of explanation seem promising in accounting for this concurrence. First, the extent to which these ideas reflect developments in Western thought is striking.[89] The various dimensions of the idea of national liberation may be explained partly in terms of the global dominance of European thought and the diffusion of European ideas concerning society, the nation, and the international system throughout the non-European periphery.

With regard to political independence, the growing acceptance by the great powers of the right of national minorities in Europe to self-determination brought in its wake a growing assertion of that right by the colonial subjects of these powers, for they were being denied the same right. The example of successful struggles for national unification and self-determination in southern, eastern, and central Europe in the nineteenth and early twentieth centuries also favoured such an assertion.

The cultural aspect of demands for national liberation drew upon the growing emphasis in European nationalist thought on cultural specificity and authenticity evident most clearly in the work of Gustav Herder and, subsequently, in that of Balkan nationalists.[90] One might also trace the focus on economic independence to the work of economic nationalist such as Friedrich List and, through him, to the concerns of early Americans such as Hamilton with the need to insulate the national economy from more powerful external economic influences in order to establish the preconditions for national economic development.

It was noted in Chapter 2 that the programmes of European nationalists also contained ample reference to social objectives. In this sense too, Third World thinking on national liberation follows earlier nationalist thought. Beyond this, in inter-war Europe and North America, there was evident a growing preoccupation of governments with social welfare and the management of the economy. Western electorates and those they elected increasingly accepted that the state had a legitimate role to play in the redistribution of income, and that it was the responsibility of the state to prevent, in so far as was possible, excessive variation in the business cycle, and to sustain economic growth through fiscal and monetary policy.[91] This considerable broadening of the role of the state in Western society resulted from the evolution in economic thought associated with the work of Keynes, from the growing political power of the organized working class, and from the hardship of the Great Depression. The focus of anti-colonial movements not only on political independence, but also on social change and the acquisition of sufficient economic autonomy to allow the state to manipulate domestic economic activity in order to maximize both development and and gains from development, reflects a prior evolution in European theory and state practice.

The educational experiences of many leaders of anti-colonial movements in leading European and American universities, and the close connections which many of these figures developed with the socialist and trade union movements in Britain, France, and the Netherlands, favoured not only the transmission of the principle of national self-determination, but also of Western social reformism to nationalist movements in the colonies. In this sense, it could be argued that the colonial regimes (with the exception, perhaps, of Belgium, Portugal, and Spain), by permitting the emergence of such elites, indeed by fostering this emergence through granting access to advanced education, sowed the seeds of the destruction of colonialism.

These developments in the Third World conception of national liberation also derived from exposure to marxist-leninist thought, primarily in two areas. The first was marxist-leninist thinking on the nature of oppression and revolution in pre-capitalist and capitalist societies. As was noted in Chapter 3, marxist-leninist theory favoured a preoccupation in political action with the interests of the poor and a concern to improve their lot through the expropriation of the property of comparatively wealthy indigenous and foreign elites. In its leninist manifestation, it also favoured an emphasis on the role of the revolutionary state in the implementation of social and economic policy. Moreover, it called for a radical rejection of capitalism as a necessarily exploitative economic system.

The second — marxist-leninist theories of imperialism — also favoured a rejection of private sector capitalism in a manner that was particularly potent in the colonial and semi-colonial world. Lenin in particular isolated capitalism as the principal cause of colonialism and hence of the colonial subjugation of non-Western peoples which was so noxious to Third World nationalists. A natural conclusion to draw from this contention was that capitalism was inextricably linked to colonialism. It followed (particularly if one accepted, as many Third World nationalists did, that, where an indigenous commercial and manufacturing bourgeoisie emerged, it was dependent on foreign capital) that anticolonialism carried with it anti-capitalism. Hence, the social tasks taken on by anti-colonial movements included not only those which were commonly referred to as 'anti-feudal' (land reform and the unseating of indigenous hereditary elites), but also those directed against private capital, autochthonous and foreign.

The anti-capitalist implications of the leninist theory of imperialism spill over from the discussion of the social objectives of national liberation movements into the definition of economic goals. For Lenin and his disciples, colonialism was for all intents and purposes merely a political expression of European capitalist expansion. Though Lenin himself did not do so, it was natural to take this argument further to the position that real freedom could be obtained only by decoupling colonial from metropolitan economies. Moreover, if one accepted the view, implicit in Lenin's work, that such development as did occur within the confines of capitalist colonialism was designed to render more efficient the exploitation of indigenous peoples, then it followed that dissociation from, or a radical redefinition of peripheral participation in, the world capitalist economy was a necessary prerequiste for development in a manner consistent with the interests of the 'oppressed nations'. In this sense, as was suggested in the previous chapter, the leninist theory of imperialism, to the extent that it had an impact on radical Third World thought, favoured the adoption of economic independence and of self-reliance as basic objectives in the process of national liberation.

The avenues by which elements of marxism-leninism were transmitted to the colonial and semi-colonial countries were manifold. It is clear that many nationalist figures were exposed to these ideas during periods of education, employ, or military service in North America and Europe. One could cite here Chou En-lai, Nguyen Ai Quoc (Ho Chi Minh), George Padmore, Sutan Sjahrir, Kwame Nkrumah, and Frantz Fanon, among many others. Marxism held particular interest for the colonial intellectual sojourning in the West, since it was above all groups on the left in metropolitan societies which were consistently and radically questioning colonial policy.[92] Moreover, its radical critique of capitalism made its adoption a natural means of separating or differentiating themselves ideologically from the colonial power.[93]

The Bolshevik Revolution of October 1917 also stimulated interest in marxism-leninism. This event was particularly encouraging from the

Third World perspective as it was in an overwhelmingly rural, peasant, non-industrial society, rather than in one of the advanced capitalist states, that a revolutionary party dealt this severe blow to the European imperialist system. Moreover, the revolution created a state that, in word at least, rejected the colonial idea and unequivocally asserted the right of colonial and subject peoples to self-determination. Accounts of the May 1919 movement of unrest in China, for example, as well as the reminiscences of Chinese communists and nationalists, emphasize the inspirational role of the October Revolution for Chinese nationalism. It was in large part the revolutionary example and the anti-colonial rhetoric and policy of the nascent Soviet state which drew many gifted Chinese intellectuals, among them Li Ta-chao and Ch'en Tu-hsiu into the communist movement.[94] The Soviet example gained new significance in the late 1920s and 1930s as the USSR embarked on an essentially autarkic, and for this reason all the more impressive, period of rapid economic development based on the marshalling and allocation of all available resources of the nation according to a pre-determined development plan.[95] This came to be perceived in the Third World as a viable economic alternative and one which was preferable to continued participation on unequal terms in the Western-dominated international capitalist economy.

Yet the diffusion of marxist-leninist ideas was not purely passive. The Soviet government has, since its inception, attempted to influence nationalist and anti-colonial movements in the Third World in the direction of socialism. The conscious efforts of the international communist movement had an important active role in the transmission of socialist ideas to national liberation movements. There is some truth in Ulam's remark that:

> The injection of communism into the anti-colonial and nationalist movement and elsewhere, while it did not pay any immediate dividends, helped to swerve that movement away from the liberal, parliamentary, and essentially Western direction it had followed prior to 1914.[96]

In the first place, a number of the figures whose thought was discussed above participated in the early Comintern (among them Ho Chi Minh, M.N. Roy and George Padmore) or in the Russian Communist Party (as in the case of Sultan-Galiev and his Tartar colleagues). Secondly, the Comintern, through agents such as Voitinsky, Dalin, and Maring (Sneevliet) was instrumental in the establishment of a number of Asian communist parties and in the definition of their early doctrines.

Thirdly, the Soviet Union, in the 1920s in the case of China and, since the death of Stalin in both Asia and Africa, has seconded political and economic advisers to friendly governments and movements. In a number of cases (for example, the Kuomintang, and later, in the Middle East, Southern Africa, and Ethiopia) these advisers have used their positions to influence the policies of these governments and movements towards what has come to be called in Soviet terminology a 'socialist orientation', and, in a number of cases, to enhance the position of left-wing groups at the expense of more moderate ones.

Fourthly, the Soviet Union, again with a hiatus in the stalinist period, has sponsored, participated in, and/or supported numerous international congresses and conferences with a view not only to stimulating anti-Western activity in the Third World, but also to inculcating the participants in these meetings with marxist-leninist concepts. The earlier congresses of the Comintern were important in this context, not only because they brought together Asian communists who were playing prominent roles in specific anti-colonial movements, but also because of the Soviet success in associating non-communist movements such as the Kuomintang to the Comintern.

But of greater significance were meetings such as the Baku Congress of Near Eastern nationalists (1920) and the 1927 Brussels Congress of the Anti-Imperialist League. The latter attracted a broad range of leading nationalist figures, most notably Nehru and Mohammed Hatta, who later became prime minister of Indonesia. The sponsorship of such meetings has been accompanied by the creation of what might uncharitably be called 'front organizations', designed again not only to further anti-Western sentiment, but also to spread marxist ideas. These date back to the early days of the Soviet state. It was intended that both the Baku and the Brussels Congresses should result in the formation of permanent anti-colonial organizations, but in both cases these rapidly came apart, falling afoul of Soviet foreign policy or of sudden shifts in Soviet doctrine. The Baku Committee disappeared as the Soviets sought to improve relations with Great Britain in the early 1920s. The Anti-Imperialist League never really got off the ground, given the nearly contemporaneous Soviet leftward turn away from co-operation with non-proletarians (see Chapter 5).

One of the spinoffs of the Anti-Imperialist League and of the trade union international, the International Trade Union Committee of Negro Workers (the Negro International) serves as a useful illustration of active Soviet attempts to influence Third World opinion in the direction of socialism. The avowed purpose of the organization, formed in the late 1920s and extant until the mid-1930s, was to spread anti-imperialist and socialist propaganda through Africa and the West Indies. Its principal vehicle, a journal called *The Negro Worker* and edited by George Padmore (later a prominent participant in the Pan-African movement and an adviser to Kwame Nkrumah) was published in Hamburg and disseminated clandestinely by black sailors on ships calling at that port.[97]

Perhaps the best later example of an organization which the Soviets have used to disseminate marxism-leninism is the Afro-Asian People's Solidarity Organization (AAPSO), formed in the late 1950s in cooperation with groups in friendly Third World countries such as India and Egypt and based in Cairo. In the mid-1960s, the organization grew beyond Africa and Asia to include Latin American movements, representatives from throughout the Third World meeting in 1966 at the Tricontinental in Havana. The AAPSO has served as a conduit for Soviet ideas more than it has been an instrument of Soviet foreign policy. Soviet control over AAPSO has never been complete, and has on a number of occasions been challenged by contenders for influence such as Cuba and the People's Republic of China.

Three other aspects of conscious Soviet attempts to spread its interpretation of marxism in the Third World should be mentioned. The first was the 'on-again off-again' attempt to use metropolitan communist parties to influence colonial nationalists, an example of which would be the sponsorship by French communist militants of marxist study circles in francophone Africa during and immediately after the Second World War. Another was the organization of study groups by the Portuguese Communist Party in the late 1940s and early 1950s. Among prominent Lusophone African nationalists, Agostinho Neto and Amilcar Cabral first came into contact with marxism in this setting. This means of transmission was in a number of instances constrained severely by the need of these metropolitan parties to respond to the internal political realities of the metropole. The volatility of the issue of Algerian nationalism in French domestic politics and the prominence of white settlers in the Algerian Communist Party, for example, prevented the development of significant ties between the French Communist Party (PCF) and the FLN.

Beyond this, the Soviets have attempted to ensure that the Soviet example does not go unnoticed by inviting prominent Third World nationalists and leaders of new states to the USSR in order that they should have direct exposure to the achievements of socialism. That they

have had some success in this regard is evident from the memoirs of
Nehru among others, who professed after such a visit that the broad
features of communism as well as the tremendous post-revolutionary
changes in Russia greatly attracted him (see note 95). They have supplemented this effort over the years, and once again with lapses during
Stalin's rule, with special education programmes for Third World
students, two examples of which are the Communist University of
Toilers of the East (KUTV), intended for the training of left-wing Asian
cadres in the 1920s, and its more recent descendant, Patrice Lumumba
University.

The relatively general agreement on objectives of the process of
national liberation may be traced not only to direct exposure to European ideas, but to a cross-fertilization among Third World nationalist
and national revolutionary movements themselves. The ideas of successful movements frequently provided models for later ones.[98] As Amilcar
Cabral once noted, the doctrinal independence of the PAIGC was only
relative, because:

> We are also influenced by the thought of others ....We are not the
> first to wage an armed struggle for national liberation, or a revolu-
> tion. Others have done this. There are other experiences ... We did
> not invent guerrilla war.[99]

This transmission too was facilitated by interaction between groups, as,
for example, when African nationalists were trained in China and
Algeria, or by contacts at international conferences, such as the Tricontinental, the 1967 Organization of Latin American Solidarity (OLAS)
meeting in Cuba, and the 1969 Khartoum Conference of 'progressive'
liberation movements in the Portuguese colonies and southern Africa.
Moreover, smaller groups of liberation movements sometimes established co-ordinating bodies of their own, such as the Conferencia de
Organizacoes Nacionalistas das Colonias Portuguesas (CONCP), which
brought together Angolan, Mozambican and Guinean cadres.

However, it would be insufficient to explain the wide acceptance of
a combination of political, economic, social and cultural goals as the
definition of national liberation solely in terms of external ideological
influence. Some attention to the historical circumstances faced by
movements in revolt against Western domination in the Thirld World is
also necessary. Third World nationalists adopted these ideas because
they appeared relevant to the problems they faced. What was it in the
concrete conditions faced by Asian, African and Latin American move-

ments which made these objectives, rather than some others, germane? The answer lies in the nature of imperialism itself, in both its colonial and neocolonial forms.

One should not underestimate the diversity of the manifestations of colonialism in different empires (for example, that of the United Kingdom versus that of Portugal), in different territories within a single empire (for example, Southern Rhodesia versus Nigeria), and in the administration of different populations within a single artificially defined colony (as with Nigeria or Chad). Nevertheless, its essence was common to all those territories and peoples which experienced it. In the first place, it constituted a denial of self-determination to the indigenous peoples on whom it was imposed.[100] Whatever the form it takes, colonialism involves a withdrawal of some measure of political power from these people and vesting it in the hands of an imposed foreign administration. This circumstance rendered European thought concerning the self-determination of nations relevant to Third World elites.

Moreover, while economic exploitation historically has not been the monopoly of the colonial powers; and while the economic impact of colonialism on the colonies was not *necessarily* negative; the imposition of external control has frequently been accompanied by the use of power to restructure colonial economies in a manner consistent with metropolitan interests. One could cite as examples French cotton production in Southern Chad, British, French, and Dutch plantation agriculture in South East Asia, Portuguese forced labour practices in agriculture in Angola and manipulation of pricing on indigenously produced cotton in Mozambique, Belgian concentration of the Congolese population in the mining areas and the extremely oppressive labour practices of the early years of Belgian rule in the Congo. There is no guarantee that the interests of metropolitan investors — cheap labour, uninhibited access to stable colonial markets, the suppression of local competitition, the structuring of colonial production and infrastructure around primary goods export and, where such goods were purchased from indigenous producers, low prices on for such commodities — coincided with what new indigenous elites considered to be the national interest of the territory and population they sought to represent.[101] Nor was there any guarantee that metropolitan interests would not use their access to political power — an access far greater than that enjoyed by indigenous peoples — to override the preferences or interests of the local population. The inclusion of economic independence derived to a substantial degree from the nature of the external imposition.

With respect to social change, three elements of the historical situation should be noted. First, in many instances, and in particular in areas which were ruled indirectly, colonial nationalists were right in maintaining that colonial administrations co-opted traditional elites (cf., for example, the Portuguese use of Fulah chiefs in Guine-Bissau or British co-operation with the traditional rulers of Northern Nigeria). As such, these groups constituted an obstacle to national independence.Beyond this, the power of these groups was rooted in traditional communal structures and patterns of authority. They could be expected to oppose processes of modernization — with attendant urbanization and greater vertical and horizontal mobility  — which disrupted this power base. Modernization, and the economic development and improvement in standards of living which were perceived to be part of it, were basic goals of Westernized national elites struggling for independence. Traditional elites could be expected to, and often did, attempt to impede the development of competing foci of authority and power and for this reason too were potential adversaries of anti-colonial nationalists.

Second, the colonial administration and economic interests based in the metropole employed skilled and semi-skilled indigenous personnel, often giving them standards of living well above the norm for the colonial population. Moreover, to the extent that an entrepreneurial group emerged, the interests of a substantial portion of it (for instance, those licensed to distribute foreign goods) were closely linked to those of external economic actors, and to the system which perpetuated the conditions in which they profited. These groups too had a stake in colonialism. Many members of them were distinctly ambivalent towards, if not actively hostile to, the demands of nationalist movements.

Third, previous chapters have alluded to the problem of mobilizing mass support among apolitical rural populations isolated from the penetration of Western ideas, and for whom the concepts of the nation and national self-determination were often nebulous if not meaningless abstractions. The way to reach these people was to address their basic needs and the concrete problems they faced as a result of external challenges to traditional lifestyles. In many instances, addressing these concerns involved a challenge to existing distributions of property, modes of production, and social hierarchies. All of these factors favoured the inclusion of social revolutionary objectives in the programmes of Third World nationalist movements. The stronger ᵗʰe external resistance to national aspirations, the greater the need for mass participation, and hence the stronger the necessity to address systematically the social grievances of the masses. For this reason, it is natural that movements engaged in prolonged armed struggle and needing reasonably secure base areas and the support of a population facing dangers of reprisal were often those who most assiduously incorporated social revolution into their theory and practice (for example, the CCP, the Vietnamese communists, the Lusophone African movements, etc.). In a related vein, this focus may be partially explained by the fact that in a situation where modernizing elites were 'unestablished', the adoption of a social revolutionary ideology was a means of differentiating themselves from their established predecessors and a means of strengthening their group cohesion.[102]

Finally, the subjective impact of colonial rule constitutes the concrete basis for the inclusion of cultural and psychological liberation among the fundamental goals of liberation movements. The cultural impact and psychological consequences of the external penetration of Third World societies again varied considerably, depending, among other things, on whether white settlement followed the imposition of colonial rule and on whether that rule was exercised directly or indirectly. Yet as a general phenomenon colonialism was justified in terms of the superiority of Western culture and of the white man. It was accompanied by an intrusion of the conqueror's customs and *mores*. In intent and/or consequences, it challenged, destroyed, or rendered irrelevant for large sections of the colonial population indigenous cultural patterns which defined each man's place and role. In addition, colonial regimes often demanded a conscious rejection of indigenous cultural heritage on the part of those 'natives' who sought advancement within the colonial system. Having demanded this, they seldom gave substantial returns.[103]

Colonial rule was usually accompanied by severe and highly visible discrimination in access to amenities, government services and education, and in guarantees of basic civil and political rights. The discrepancy between discriminatory practice and liberal theories of universal rights was blatant. The result (in urban areas at least) was frequently a loss of identity and self-respect, a sense of powerlessness, inferiority and bitterness. This cultural oppression and its results not only go a good distance towards explaining why Western-educated elites adopted nationalism in the first place. They also render intelligible two aspects of the cultural preoccupation of national movements: the creation through consciousness-raising of the subjective prerequisites for victory in anti-colonial struggle, and the elimination, both during and after the struggle for power, of those aspects of colonial culture and ideology which devalued colonial man.

A third aspect of 'cultural liberation', the challenge mounted by modernizing nationalists to traditional values, may also be ascribed largely to the colonial experience. It has already been noted that the colonial powers often co-opted colonial elites. This favoured struggle by national movements against these elites. Yet the power which these elites drew upon derived in large part from traditional value systems which prescribed obedience to religious leaders and hereditary chiefs, sheikhs, sultans, kings, etc. The attempt to supplant these figures or to subordinate them to the nationalist movement involved not only struggle against specific personalities, but a challenge to the ideological structure which legitimized their rule. Beyond this, national movements were on the whole committed to modernization and development of one form or another and to national integration. It followed that they should attack those aspects of traditional culture which on balance impeded these processes. One could cite in this context traditional medical practice (with some reservations), popular superstition and the widespread use of magic, the subjection and isolation of women, tribalism, and, in the economic sphere, customary agricultural and husbandry practices which limited productivity and damaged the land.

The analysis thus far has referred principally to colonial situations. However, many areas of the Third World not subjected in a formal sense to colonial rule shared to some degree these circumstances. Many were subject to varying degrees of intervention and political domination (for example, the protectorate status of a number of states in the Arab Middle East, the division of Persia into spheres of influence, the capitulations forced upon Persia, Turkey and China, and American interference in the Caribbean and Central America), economic dependence (for example, the European and American penetration of Latin America and China, and the American role in Liberia), external manipulation of social structure in order to perpetuate elites who served foreign interests (for example, China and Central America), and Western cultural penetration calling into question indigenous cultural patterns. The conditions conducive to the development of the conception of national liberation outlined above, therefore, obtained beyond the colonies themselves.

To summarize, the widespread acceptance of a definition of national liberation comprising political, economic, social and cultural objectives responds to historical realities in the Third World at the time national movements were formed and articulated their objectives. It was these historical conditions which rendered attractive to emerging Third World elites the ideas of political, economic, social and cultural change which they borrowed from Western sources.

## Other Aspects of Doctrines of National Liberation

Beyond this general concurrence on the meaning of national liberation, the groups covered in this analysis display ample disagreement on matters of doctrine. With respect to the 'world revolutionary process', there are wide variations in opinion on what forces outside the Third World were allies of the national liberation movement. While some writers accepted, indeed urged, alliance with the international proletariat or the international communist movement, others rejected it, asserting that the Western proletariat had lost its revolutionary character and had become a collaborator with imperialism. Some saw the Soviet bloc as a critical ally. Others saw it as a new imperialist. With regard to nationalism, some writers rejected it as bourgeois ideology. Others embraced it as the essence of their commitment. With reference to the origins and nature of revolutionary theory, some asserted the critical role and universal character of marxism-leninism. Others denied the applicability of marxist analysis and prescription to their own situations. On the questions of breadth and leadership of the national liberation movement, some asserted the vanguard role of the domestic proletariat, while others ridiculed such assertions. With regard to the use of force in the struggle for liberation, some glorified violence, others viewed it as a regrettable necessity, while still others rejected it out of hand. In such circumstances, to look for a widely shared, coherent ideology of national liberation — a system of ideas setting down not only basic objectives, but also defining the place in world history of Third World revolution, a methodology for analysing socio-political reality, and strategies and tactics for realizing goals — is unrealistic.

Careful examination of the writings and practice of national liberation movements suggests that there are a number of widely shared themes beyond the adherence to a common basic idea of national liberation, themes which distinguish Third World from both Soviet and Western thinking and which have significant implications in both the domestic and international political contexts. Three aspects of Third World theory and practice stand out: the balance between universal and particular (that is, internationalist and nationalist) commitments; the balance between universal and particular in theories of revolution; and the breadth and structure of the national liberation movements and the nature of interactions within it.

## Nationalism and Internationalism

With regard to the place in history of national liberation, it was generally accepted that the struggle against imperialism was international, in that it involved the joint effort of all non-Western peoples against Western domination. This consciousness was perhaps strongest among marxists, who saw the efforts of their peoples to free themselves from foreign domination as part of a world socialist or world proletarian revolution.

M.N. Roy's first supplementary thesis at the Second Comintern Congress,[104] Sultan-Galiev's series of articles on 'Social Revolution in the East',[105] Li Ta-chao's equation of the Western nations with the exploiting classes and of non-European peoples with the proletariat,[106] Mao Tse-tung's situating the Chinese Revolution within the context of the world struggle against imperialism and for socialism,[107] Ho Chi Minh's characterization of the world revolutionary movement as an alliance of oppressed colonial peoples with the international working class,[108] and Che Guevara's assertion that the national liberation struggle was necessarily an international one because imperialism was a world system and had to be defeated in a world confrontation[109] are all typical of the internationalist focus of marxist-leninists involved in national revolutionary struggles.

Similar views were entertained by movements which were not avowedly marxist-leninist during their struggle for independence. Sun Yat-sen, for example, held that China would be vulnerable to the threat of foreign domination as long as imperialism survived anywhere and, therefore, that China shared an interest with other oppressed peoples in the destruction of the imperialist world system.[110] Sukarno maintained that the Indonesian struggle was part of a broader Asian and African revolution, the objective of which was 'to uproot imperialism, to uproot colonialism, to uproot capitalism, in order to build socialism, to consolidate a new world'.[111]

An FLN writer wrote in *El-Moudjahid* that the Algerian war was but 'un épisode de la lutte universelle qui souleve les peuples africains et asiatiques contre le colonialisme europeen'.[112] Fanon held that the Algerian war was one part of the liberation of man, both in the colonies and in the metropolitan countries.[113] Cabral averred that the ultimate objective was the 'total liquidation of imperialism', and that Guine-Bissau's war 'was only one aspect of the general struggle of oppressed peoples against imperialism, of man's struggle for dignity, freedom, and progress'.[114]

Again, this recognition goes well beyond movements engulfed in wars of national liberation. It can be traced through most of the development of anti-Western thought in the Third World. Nehru, for example, viewed the Indian struggle as part of a broader struggle against imperialism.[115] To cite another example, Sekou Toure emphasized the common objective in the colonies and the metropole of overturning the rule of imperialism.[116]

The reasons for this internationalist focus are not difficult to discern. Among marxist-leninists and those such as Nehru, Sukarno, Toure, Nkrumah, Fanon, Cabral, etc., who were influenced more or less strongly by marxist ideas, it is not surprising, given the ostensibily internationalist character of that ideology. Not only is the revolutionary objective of marxism — the ending of man's exploitation by man — universal. The enemy (capitalism and, later, imperialism) too, while perhaps national in form, is perceived to be a global transnational phenomenon. The very nature of this body of ideas encourages thinking which transcends national boundaries.

The influence of circumstance again reinforces that of ideas. It is natural for men in difficult circumstances to have a sense of solidarity with those facing similar difficulties elsewhere. The ubiquity of Western domination favoured the spread of a sense of common cause against the West.

Internationalism on the part of anti-colonial movements in the Third World was also dictated by considerations of political interest. In the first place, it was recognized by people as diverse as Sun Yat-sen, Che Guevara, and Frantz Fanon, that the prospects for success in a specific struggle for liberation depended to a great extent on the degree of pressure placed on the colonial power in other venues. This assessment is reasonably accurate. It is probable that the Algerian war, for example, accelerated the process by which French colonies elsewhere in Africa gained their independence. In the Portuguese African case, colonialism was defeated not in any single struggle, but as a result of the pressure that movements in all three countries (and particularly in Guine-Bissau and Mozambique) jointly brought to bear on the Portuguese.

A second interest in emphasizing the international character of the struggle for liberation lay in the utility of such statements in soliciting external assistance. In the first place, it may have been assumed that an emphasis on the universal significance of particular struggles for national liberation would encourage outsiders to proffer the assistance necessary to win and to stay in power once victory had been achieved.[117] Specifically, for many of the movements considered here, the Soviet bloc has been a crucial source of military and other forms of assistance. Soviet writers, as shall be seen below, have stressed the significance of national liberation as part of a broader world revolutionary process. A willingness to conform to Soviet doctrinal pronouncements concerning the character and role of the process of national liberation presumably facilitates access to such assistance.

The internationalist focus and commitment of Third World liberation movements was not, however, rhetorical. It was frequently institutionalized in inter-regional organizations such as the Anti-Imperialist League, AAPSO, and the Tricontinental, and in regional and sub-regional groupings, such as the Organization of Latin American Solidarity (OLAS) and the CONCP. Among the purposes of such groupings were the exchange of information and the co-ordination of strategies (for example, the CONCP), and the channeling of material support from within the group and from external sources. Although some of these organizations were on occasion manipulated by external agents, there is little reason to doubt that they constituted an institutional manifestation of a desire to co-operate transnationally in the pursuit of what were perceived to be universal objectives.

Organizations or proto-organizations such as the Group of 77, the nonaligned movement, and, at the regional level, the liberation committee of the Organization of African Unity (OAU) display an analogous institutional expression of the commitment of new states to the international struggle against the remnants of colonialism and against Western economic hegemony. The UN voting patterns of Afro-Asian states on issues such as apartheid, the decolonization of Portuguese Africa, the liberation of Namibia, and the new international economic order also reflect a commitment of sorts to these concerns.

There are also numerous instance of liberation movements and the states formed by them translating theory into practice in rendering concrete support to like groups struggling for freedom elsewhere. One might cite here Tunisian and Moroccan provision of bases to the FLN, Algerian and Cuban training of PAIGC, MPLA, FRELIMO and SWAPO militants, and their financial support of and weapons transfers to these movements, Tanzanian provision of sanctuary and base facilities to

FRELIMO, ZANU and the ANC, Zambian provision of like facilities to the Zimbabwe African Peoples' Union (ZAPU) and SWAPO, Guine-Bissau's assistance to the MPLA, Mozambican assistance to ZANU and the ANC, and Angolan support of SWAPO. It would be difficult credibly to maintain that this behaviour reflected not a sense of solidarity, but mere self-interest. In a number of cases (for example, Zambia, Mozambique and Angola, or in Central America, Nicaragua) states acting in this fashion have incurred substantial economic and military penalties. It might plausibly be argued that such policies were undertaken to gain prestige in the Third World community. Yet the very fact that these states might gain prestige in this fashion underlines the importance in Third World politics of this sense of common cause.

The assertion of the transnational character of struggle against the West was frequently accompanied by a recognition that there was a potential contradiction between the universalist commitment to the 'liberation of man' and national particularism. The uncritical embrace of nationalism is rare in the writings of those in the Third World involved in the anti-colonial and broader anti-Western struggle. Of the various figures considered here, Sun Yat-sen was perhaps the strongest in defending nationalism. He maintained that China's principal problem was the country's fragmentation of loyalties, and the focus of the Chinese on clan and family rather than national concerns. The lack of a national spirit meant that China was 'but a sheet of loose sand', weak and incapable of resistance and self-assertion.[118] It was nationalism which would make it possible to reverse China's decline. As such, Sun condemned 'cosmopolitanism', which he viewed as an imperialist device inimical to the survival of China. Internationalism was a matter for the distant future when China had been unified and strengthened to the point where she could hold her own.[119]

Far more common, however, among the writers considered here was the condemnation of 'narrow nationalism' as part of the intellectual baggage of Western domination. Sukarno displayed his misgivings about national particularism when he distinguished between 'Western nationalism', which he considered to be petty and chauvinistic, and 'Eastern nationalism', which was for all intents and purposes indistinguishable from a universalist humanism.[120]

Chinese communists condemned nationalism in strict marxist-leninist terms,[121] as did Ho Chi Minh, who attributed it to 'imperialist reactionaries'.[122] Fanon described what he termed excessive nationalism as a perverse imitation by colonial populations of the ideology of colonialism.[123] Debray warned that national chauvinism facilitated the 'imperialist penetration' of Latin America by balkanizing the continental revolution.[124] Marcelino Dos Santos of FRELIMO characterized 'primitive nationalism' as a manipulation of national symbols in order to replace colonial with indigenous oppression.[125]

Similar concerns are evident in the writings of those who did not take the path of armed struggle. Nehru argued early in his career that the Indian anti-colonial movement should 'discard a narrow nationalism in favour of world cooperation and real internationalism'.[126] Among African figures, George Padmore, Sekou Toure, Kwame Nkrumah and Julius Nyerere all denounced national particularism.[127]

However, this internationalist commitment and condemnation of national particularism were greatly tempered in theory and, perhaps more importantly, in practice in a number of ways. In the first place, there was little if any willingness on the part of Third World national revolutionaries to recognize the leadership of the international proletariat or the 'socialist camp' in the common struggle against imperialism or for that matter the leading role of any force other than their own. Only in a very limited number of cases where a clear dependency exists between a national movement and an external force such as the Soviet Union or China, has a movement recognized such a claim to primacy.[128] It is reasonable to surmise that, in such a context, this recognition reflects a concern to avoid problems in the patron-client relationship. Beyond this, there is little attempt in the Third World literature to define just who, if anyone, does lead, other than numerous assertions by CCP, FLN, Vietnamese, and other figures that they themselves are a principal or central force in the world struggle.

Moreover, Third World writers have commonly asserted that it is the contradiction between the peoples of the non-Western world and Western imperialism, rather than (as Soviet writers would have it) that between socialism and capitalism or between the proletariat and the bourgeoisie, which is the fundamental contradiction in world politics.

Analogously, it has been widely maintained that the Third World revolution is the principal force in the world revolutionary process, and that revolution in the Third World is a necessary condition of successful socialist revolution in the West. This view was common even among marxist-leninists involved in armed struggle for liberation, despite its glaring inconsistency with Marx's materialist conception of history and for that matter, with the Soviet conception of national liberation (see Chapter 5). The movement to such a position was, among these groups, seemingly based on Lenin's argument in *Imperialism* that metropolitan capitalists used the profits stemming from exploitation of the colonies and semi-colonies to buy off sections of the metropolitan proletariat, thereby postponing revolution. Lenin worked his way around the obvious question of how proletarian revolution could succeed in such circumstances by maintaining that once colonial expansion had reached its limit, inter-imperialist war over the allocation of colonial possessions was inevitable. This in turn would create the conditions for socialist revolution.

Third World nationalists, however, over time and in the absence of revolution in Europe, arrived at different conclusions from his analysis — that revolution in Europe had been stymied and would remain so until the colonies had detached themselves from the 'imperialist world system'. M.N. Roy, for example, held that until the European bourgeoisie was deprived of colonial profits, 'the European working class [would] not succeed in overthrowing the capitalist order'.[129] In the debates at the Second Comintern Congress, he argued that it was essential for the Comintern to accept that the fate of world communism depended on revolution in the East.[130] Sultan-Galiev maintained similarly that:

> So long as international imperialism, incarnated by the entente, can retain the East as a colony of the natural wealth of which it may dispose as an absolute master, so long will it remain confident of a favorable outcome to an isolated economic conflict with the labouring classes of the metropolis, since it has the possibility of 'shutting their mouths' by satisfying their economic demands.[131]

In the case of the CCP, this sentiment was muted at times when the party was particularly solocitous of the CPSU, such as 1923-36 and 1950-6, but it is none the less a persistent characteristic of party writing throughout its history. Li Ta-chao shared the view that it was revolutionary activity in the colonial and semi-colonial countries which would stimulate the general crisis of capitalism in the metropoles. Moreover, in a formulation prefiguring developments in Mao Tse-tung's thought in the late 1950s, Li consciously inverted Marx's belief that the most industrially advanced countries were those with the greatest revolutionary potential by arguing that backwardness stimulated revolution, and that it was in the hands of backward non-European peoples that the future of the world socialist revolution lay.[132]

In the late 1940s there developed in Chinese communist doctrine the concept of an intermediate zone composed primarily of colonial and semi-colonial countries between the USSR and the USA. It was the contradiction between revolution in the intermediate zone and imperialism which was imminent and dominant in the conditions of the day, rather than that between the USA and the USSR, for in order to attack the USSR, American imperialism first had to subdue the intervening ground.[133] Later assertions of the primacy of the national liberation movement in the struggle against imperialism may be found in Liu Shao-ch'i's famous speech to the Pacific conference of the World Federation of Trade Unions (WFTU) in 1949,[134] and in the 1960s when the Sino-Soviet dispute removed the incentive for restraint on this subject, while in the mid-1950s, as was noted above, Mao revived Li Ta-Chao's argument concerning the advantages of backwardness.

The 1960 editorial 'Long Live Leninism' pointed to the relative stagnation of the revolution in Europe and cited Asia and Africa as a 'new source of world storms'.[135] Yu Chao-li (a pseudonym for the expression of views reputedly close to those of Mao), in a series of articles in the same year, asserted that it was against the national liberation movement that the main forces of imperialism were concentrated, and that 'the real immediate contradictions' of the period were those between the United States and the colonial and semi-colonial countries, rather than those between the US and the USSR.[136]

Even greater frankness was evident in the open polemic between the CCP and the CPSU in 1963-4, when Chinese commentators argued that national liberation revolutions were 'decisive for the cause of the international proletariat as a whole',[137] and in the period leading up to the Cultural Revolution when Peng Ch'en was heard to argue that the principal contradiction of the period was that between imperialism and 'the oppressed nations of Asia, Africa, and Latin America'.[138] Lin Piao meanwhile characterized the world revolution as 'a picture of the encirclement of the cities [the developed West and the Soviet Union] by the rural areas [the Third World]'.[139] This amounted to a challenge to the the centrality of the Soviet role in world revolution and, by extension, to Soviet leadership of the world revolutionary process, and ultimately, to Soviet status as a revolutionary force in international politics.

In the aftermath of the Cultural Revolution, as China embarked on a more active diplomacy, the terms employed to describe the character of international politics shifted (there was a greater emphasis on states rather than peoples, and a shift in usage from the phrase 'the national liberation movement' to the 'Third World'), but the essence of their commentary on this subject changed little. The Third World remained the focal point of world contradictions and the centre of revolutionary struggle. The main contradiction was that between rich and poor nations, between North and South.[140]

As China drew closer to the United States and its allies, comment on the Third World and its struggle against the developed world decreased. This reflected a narrower definition of Chinese diplomatic priorities — a focus above all on the conflict with the Soviet Union and the need for rapid development and a quest for partners who might be useful in these tasks — and perhaps a concern not to alienate unnecessarily possible allies in the West.[141] While it is clear that the Chinese position on the role of the national liberation revolution in the world revolutionary process varies with the character of Chinese relations with the Soviet Union, the fact that the argument that the national liberation movement is the principal force in world revolution emerges during periods when the Chinese are asserting independence from the USSR (and for that matter from the United States) suggests that it is the more deeply felt position and that its muting during periods of close Sino-Soviet relations and Chinese wooing of the West was a matter of tactics.

Among other marxist-leninist groups the Vietnamese have avoided taking a clear position on the matter. This reflects perhaps their concern during the war against South Vietnam and the United States to avoid alienating either side in the Sino-Soviet dispute. By contrast, Che Guevara, for example, argued on more than one occasion that the focus of the world's contradictions had shifted to the Third World and to the struggle for national liberation.[142]

Such views were, not surprisingly, even more widely held by movements and writers who were not avowedly marxist-leninist. To cite a few examples, Sukarno at the Belgrade Conference (1961) betrayed his conviction that the contradiction between imperialism and the Third World was paramount in arguing that while peaceful coexistence was possible between the socialist and capitalist systems, 'there [could] be no coexistence between independence and justice on the one hand and imperialism-colonialism on the other'.[143] Fanon maintained that it was the fate of the Third World rather than socialism's competition with capitalism which was the fundamental problem in world politics, again using the argument that the withdrawal of the colonies from the capitalist system would cause the latter's collapse.[144] A similar stress on the primacy of struggle in the Third World is evident in Amilcar Cabral's writing.[145] Elsewhere, Herbert Chitepo, a ZANU functionary, also shared the view that revolution in the Third World created the preconditions for revolution in the metropole by cutting into 'imperialist superprofits'. As such, it was the most pressing task of the world revolution.[146]

Not surprisingly, this leads to a common and important qualification of indiscriminate internationalism — the advocacy specifically of Third world solidarity in the struggle against external domination. The call for Third World solidarity has over the years taken many forms and has had many justifications. Some writers (for example, Ahmed Sukarno and Marcus Garvey) have cast it in racial terms, arguing for a unity of all non-white peoples against white oppression.[147] Others have called for a unity of all colonial peoples based upon the common experience of oppression and exploitation within the Western, imperialist-dominated world system, but without reference to race (for example, Tai Chi-t'ao's proposal for an international of oppressed peoples to struggle against imperialism and Sultan-Galiev's call for a colonial international independent of the Communist International).[148]

In the 1950s, similar ideas were embodied in the Bandung Movement of Afro-Asian solidarity, the product of a perception of a common experience of domination and oppression by the West and a concern to put forward more effectively the specific concerns of new states in the international system. Associated with the growth of 'Afro-Asianism' was the spread of neutralism and nonalignment in the Third World, culminating in the 1961 Belgrade Conference which established the nonaligned movement. Nonalignment, at least as originally conceived, was based on the premise the the smaller, poorer, states in the international system shared an agenda quite distinct from those of the two superpowers. For this reason, they should remain aloof from the Soviet-American competition and attempt as a group to promote issues of particular concern to them (the completion of the process of decolonization, the problem of development, the restructuring of economic relations between the developed and less developed worlds, etc.). As Julius Nyerere put it in 1962:

It would be both utopian and dangerous to blindly entrust our destiny to the sole experience of Europeans from either East or West. Every great power develops a colonial vocation of annexing the weak countries to serve its tactics and to further its most important objectives in the world.[149]

The concepts of Afro-Asianism subscribed to by the likes of Nehru, Sukarno, Nasser, Toure, and Nkrumah, as well as Nyerere, though fluid in content, all contained an implicit, if not explicit, common denominator — the vision of a Third World distinct from and united (prescriptively if not descriptively) in the face of 'the others'. While the salience of particular issues on the agenda of the nonaligned movement has varied over time, and while the importance attached to 'anti-imperialist' causes has at times fostered the impression that the nonaligned movement has been 'captured' by the Soviet bloc, it has never lost its original concern to remain aloof from both East and West and to promote its own specific agenda. Where this agenda has conflicted with the Soviet one (for example, on Afghanistan), the movement has not hesitated to take positions which, while they may seem equivocal from a Western perspective, are none the less wrongheaded and uncomfortable from a Soviet one. Such a conclusion is reinforced by the voting patterns of nonaligned states in the United Nations, and in the Islamic Conference on issues such as the Afghan and Kampuchean ones.

A further outgrowth of this Third World sense of solidarity in the face of outsiders has been the movement for a new international economic order and its institutional manifestation, the Group of 77. The efforts for a reallocation of global resources by this group of Third World states are not directed solely against the West, but against 'rich' states as such, including the USSR again to the discomfort of the Soviets, who argue that as they did not participate in the colonial plunder of the Third World, they have no responsibility of restitution (see Chapter 5).

Universalism in the Third World has been diluted further by regionalist ideologies and commitments. Here one can cite Sun Yatsen's, Nehru's, and Sukarno's Pan-Asianism, Sultan-Galiev's and Kemal Ataturk's Pan-Turanism, and the PanAfrican commitment of every major African or black nationalist figure from Marcus Garvey to Robert Mugabe. Several aspects of regionalist, pan-ethnic, or pan-religious ideologies — the view that the inhabitants of a particular region (for example, Africa), those who share a particular linguistic heritage (for example, the Arabs), or those who adhere to a particular faith (for example, Islam) share an identity which sets them apart from (and often above) other groups and which they should value, preserve, and strengthen — conflict potentially if not actually with the universalist embrace of human liberation discussed above. This is particularly true when it is held that this identity implies a duty to emphasize the group's interests and objectives at the expense of both narrower and broader commitments.

Yet the most substantial qualification or dilution of internationalism is at the national level, in the discussion of nationalism, and, more clearly, in the pursuit of nationalist policies. In the first case, one fre-

quently finds in Third World writing a tendency to supplement the condemnation of 'narrow Western nationalism' with an attempt to render
their own forms of nationalism respectable through redefinition.
Sukarno, for instance, after rejecting Western nationalism, contrasted it
with what he termed Eastern nationalism, a 'feeling of love for [one's]
country' which was 'immune to petty and narrow views'.[150]

Marxists have tended to approach the issue by distinguishing
between 'bourgeois nationalism' on the one hand and patriotism or
'revolutionary nationalism' on the other. Ho Chi Minh, for example,
distinguished between chauvinism, an attribute of 'reactionaries', and
patriotism, which, while remaining undefined, far from being inconsistent with internationalism, was 'part and parcel' of it and hence desirable.[151] Later, one finds Debray positing the existence within the
castroite movement of a 'revolutionary nationalism' which was an *'a
posteriori* synthesis of two currents, nationalist and internationalist,
nationalist and communist'.[152] Unfortunately, he neither elaborates on
the dimensions of this purported synthesis of bourgeois and proletarian
ideology nor explains it with reference to objective social and historical
forces. This suggests that he is attempting through a spurious dialectic
to render the nationalism of the Cuban elite respectable in marxist-
leninist terms.

Elsewhere, Marcelino Dos Santos spoke similarly of a distinction
between primitive nationalism and revolutionary nationalism, which
synthesized nationalism and socialism in a commitment to the
'objective' interests of the whole people. This took the form of a
struggle both against imperialism and for internal social change.[153]
Whatever the merit of these attempts at redefinition, they provided a
justification for diluting the commitment to human liberation with a
particularistic focus on the needs of specific peoples.

Another common theme in Third World writing about nationalism
which dilutes the internationalist commitment of these movements is
the recognition that appeals to national sentiment have significant
tactical utility in mobilizing popular support and in integrating diverse
and often hostile segments of ethnically diverse populations. One sees
elements of this in Mao Tse-tung's and the CCP's appeals to the
Chinese people in the late 1930s to join in a 'national salvation movement' to defend the motherland, and in Mao's calls for the upholding
of 'the dignity and independence of the Chinese nation'.[154] During the
initial phases of the war against Japan, communist cadres stressed the
inculcation of a national consciousness which provided an impetus for a
mass upsurge in support of the war effort in base areas.[155] Sun Yat-sen

also stressed the importance of nationalism in inspiring popular participation in the struggle for social change and against foreign rule.[156]

Debray, in later writing, took this line of argument even further, maintaining that the mass identification with the nation was stronger than were internationalist class loyalties, and, consequently, that the embrace of nationalism by proletarian revolutionary movements (for example, the CCP, the Vietnamese Workers Party, and Castro's 26th of July Movement) was a necessary precondition of their success.[157] This stands Marx and Lenin — who argued that nationalism, being an aspect of bourgeois ideology designed to impede the development of the internationalist class consciousness which was a prerequisite for the international socialist revolution, was a severe impediment to success in the socialist revolution — on their heads.

Elsewhere, one finds in the writings of the Lusophone African movements a similar appreciation of the mobilizational and integrative value of national symbols.[158]

It was only a short step from this kind of argument to the assertion that a nationalist phase of Third World revolution was both unavoidable and necessary for the transition to a future internationalist universalism. In this vein, one can cite Nehru, Sukarno, Fanon and Debray.[159]

Although there may be a certain theoretical validity, even in a marxist-leninist framework, for this notion, and while the assessment of the tactical utility of nationalism discussed above may be eminently sensible, both constitute attempts to legitimize nationalist appeals and sentiments, and both may be used to rationalize a failure to subordinate particular national objectives to universal ones. To summarize then, although recognition of the universal character of the struggle for liberation and of the commitments which movements took upon themselves was widespread, this internationalism was qualified in doctrine by the refusal to accept external leadership, by the assertion of Third World primacy in world revolution, by calls for the unity of and common action by the Third World exclusively and by various regional, religious, and pan-ethnic subgroups within it, and by a distinct equivocation about national particularism.

But the relative weights of revolutionary universalism as opposed to more or less exclusive forms of particularism is perhaps best indicated in the behaviour of these movements once they take power. Although the internationalist character of the foreign policies of many new states is by no means inconsequential, it is dwarfed in significance by the preoccupations of their governments with the establishment and defence of national sovereignty and autonomy and the pursuit of national interests in the conduct of policy. Moreover, the 'internationalist' activities in which these regimes involve themselves frequently coincide with their perceptions of national interest. In such circumstances, the depth of their internationalism may be questioned.

The case of the People's Republic of China is an eloquent demonstration. The foreign policy of China since 1949 suggests that the CCP, despite its internationalist rhetoric, was and is profoundly nationalist in its concern to remove all manifestations of China's inferior status in world politics, to establish China as a great power, and to guarantee the security of Chinese territory from foreign attack.

Superficially, Chinese intervention in the Korean War might appear to reflect a commitment to proletarian internationalism, and perhaps to some extent it did. Yet a close examination of Chinese behaviour suggests that the dominant factors underlying Chinese actions were the sense of an American threat to China associated with the UN involvement in Korea, a desire to deter that threat by showing that China meant business and was capable of backing up its warnings with the effective use of military force, and to establish China's right to a say in matters of regional security in North East Asia. Other aspects of Chinese internationalism – such as the support for Thai and Vietnamese communist challenges to colonial or 'neocolonial' regimes friendly to the United States – may be ascribed to a Chinese desire to prevent the establishment by the United States of a South East Asian cordon sanitaire from which to threaten the security of the Chinese communist regime. Likewise, much of the assistance rendered to new states and liberation movements in the 1960s and early 1970s reflect not so much disinterested revolutionary solidarity as they do a concern to reduce or replace Soviet influence among such groups.

The Chinese concern to reestablish the full territorial extent of previous Chinese sovereignty and/or to undo territorial settlements imposed on China by foreign powers is evident in the annexation of Tibet, in the Sino-Indian conflicts of the late 1950s and early 1960s, in the persistent claim to sovereignty over Taiwan, and in the willingness to take great risks in the pursuit of this claim in the crises over the offshore islands in the mid and late 1950s. In the case of the conflict with India, it is evident that national concerns were given greater weight in Chinese policy than were those of Third World solidarity. In the Tibetan and Taiwanese cases, it is clear that national Chinese imperatives weigh more heavily than do the desires of the people occupying the territories in question.

With respect to the Soviet Union, Chinese sensitivity over the question of sovereignty and the legacy of unequal treaties has been evident in the Chinese reluctance to accept concessions to the USSR in Manchuria and at Port Arthur during negotiations over the Sino-Soviet friendship treaty in 1950, in their refusal to accede to Soviet requests in the late 1950s for military facilities on Chinese territory,[160] and in the various Sino-Soviet border clashes of the 1960s. To summarize, there is much in the conduct of China's foreign policy since 1949 to support the contention of leading sinologists such as Stuart Schram and John Gittings that nationalism has been a consistent and prominent dimension in the thinking of Mao and his associates.[161]

Western specialists on the Vietnamese communist movement have similarly assessed Ho Chi Minh.[162] The Vietnamese preoccupation since the departure of the French to reunify Vietnam and to establish Vietnamese hegemony in Indochina at the expense of Kampuchea and Laos underline the importance of 'narrow nationalism' as a basic determinant of Vietnamese policy. Likewise there is little doubt that despite Algeria's financial and material assistance to liberation movements, Algerian foreign policy has been dominated by an emphasis on specifically Algerian objectives.

The internationalism of Lusophone African governments is also severely limited in policy by an unwillingness to compromise their sovereignty and a primary concern for national welfare rather than global revolution. Hence, the Angolans and Mozambicans, despite close ties with the USSR have resisted Soviet pressure for military base rights. Both Angola and Mozambique have cultivated ties with Western multinationals. As one commentator put it, with reference to Angola:

> Notwithstanding their official support of Neto, the Soviets had reason to be displeased with him because of his uncompromisingly nationalist stance which has led him to persist in dealing with 'imperialist' firms such as Gulf Oil and Boeing and to refuse permission for Soviet military bases on Angolan soil.[163]

Mozambique, and to a lesser extent Angola, have also retained cooperative economic relations with South Africa despite their support of SWAPO and the ANC. The Mozambican government has severely constrained ANC activity on its territory so as not to jeopardize these ties. More recently, both the Angolans and Mozambicans have responded to South African military pressure and South African-sponsored disruption of their economies by even more strictly controlling anti-South African activity on their territory. In short, when international solidarity involves significant national costs, it is sacrificed.

It would be superfluous to multiply examples of this type, both from governments formed by liberation movements and from the wider Third World community. Suffice it to say that the practice of Third World states suggests that particular national interests come well ahead of regionalist loyalties or revolutionary internationalism in the policy-making of their governments, moderate and radical, right wing, centrist, or left wing.

Several factors having to do with the structure of the international system, with the historical situation of the societies from which movements for liberation emerged, with the character of the struggles they waged, and with the nature of the agenda they faced upon assuming power account for this qualification of revolutionary internationalism. First, national particularism is favoured in a structural sense in a world of defined territorial entities organized into nation states. Those movements in areas of extinguished or reduced sovereignty striving for equal treatment and self-determination did so within a state-centric international structure for which nationalism (a theory concerning the natural division of humanity into culturally defined groups) was the justification. Morever, as in the most immediate sense the institutions against which these movements struggled were particular, it was natural that the form and content of their struggles should also be particular. Further, once they took power, the immediate problems they faced — consolidation of their control, organization of a governmental structure, legitimation, self-definition in relation to other state actors — were overwhelmingly particular rather than universal in content. Finally, it would be unrealistic to expect that groups having waged often arduous struggles to free their societies of external domination should forgo the enjoyment of the fruits of victory and accept subordination to other external actors and the possible dilution of their achievement in a broader quest for liberation.[164] For such movements, autonomy is itself a value, as well as a means to other ends.

## Universal and Particular in Theories of Liberation

The concern among national liberation movements to assert autonomy extends to the discussion of the sources of theory. The hostility of Marx to particularism in the theory of revolution was noted in Chapter 3. Lenin evinced a greater flexibility with respect to the adaptation of theory to concrete historical circumstance, but retained a strong emphasis on the universality of Marx's laws of history and on the uniqueness of socialism.

The movements considered here by and large accepted that certain principles of revolution were of universal application. Opinions varied widely with respect to the balance between universal and particular in the development of revolutionary theory and strategy. None the less, Third World writers have on the whole placed far greater weight on the relevance of cultural and historical specificity and on the need for originality in the elaboration of theory than did Marx and Lenin, or, for that matter, later Soviet writers. This difference in emphasis reflects not only pragmatism — the awareness that theory, if it is to be useful, must not depart radically from the specific conditions faced by particular liberation movements — but also a concern to assert national creativity and to reject external domination in the realm of ideas.

The acceptance of universal laws of revolution was strongest among self-avowed marxist-leninists. Even in these cases, however, the concern to assert the importance of situational specifics was strong, presumably because of the irrelevance of much of orthodox marxist thought in Third World precapitalist conditions. This concern has seriously impeded the development or maintenance of doctrinal unity within the international communist movement.

In the Chinese communist case, the disastrous experience of repression in 1927, when slavish adherence to the twists and turns of Comintern doctrine exposed the party to decimation by the Kuomintang, did much to encourage doctrinal autonomy. The displacement of substantial elements of the party to rural areas such as the Chingkangshan and, later, the Kiangsi Soviet, also favoured creativity in doctrine. Mao underlined the implications of Chinese specifics for revolutionary strategy in the initial elaboration of the rural base area concept. He argued that it was characteristics specific to China (that is, the disunity of the 'white camp') which 'provided the conditions under which one or more base areas [could] emerge'.[165]

Eight years later, Mao wrote that studying the Russian experience was insufficient for Chinese communists. The laws of the Russian Civil War embodied characteristics specific to Russia. It was of greater importance to draw upon 'the great number of conditions special to the Chinese Revolution' — uneven political and economic development, the disunity of outside powers striving for control, and the salience of the agrarian revolution, among others.[166] Leninism was developed in response to specific Russian conditions. It had to be modified by principles derived from local practice. This resulted in a new and *higher* form of theory.[167]

This trend in Mao's thought culminated in his report to the 6th

Plenum of the CCP Central Committee in 1938, where he stated:

> There is no such thing as abstract marxism, but only concrete
> marxism. What we call concrete marxism is marxism that has taken
> on a national form, that is, marxism applied to the concrete condi-
> tions prevailing in China, and not marxism abstractly used. If a
> Chinese communist talks . . . of marxism apart from Chinese pecul-
> iarities, this marxism is merely an empty abstraction. Consequently,
> the sinification of marxism, that is to say, making certain that in all
> of its manifestations it is imbued with Chinese peculiarities, using it
> according to these peculiarities, becomes a problem that must be
> understood by the whole party without delay.

It was the viewpoint and method of marxism and not the letter of it
which were important. Consequently, he called for an 'end to the
writing of eight-legged essays on foreign models'.[168] The latter presumably referred to Soviet attempts to impose theoretical discipline
on member parties of the Comintern and was aimed in particular at
Wang Ming, the Chinese party luminary sent out from Moscow to rein
in the errant local leadership of the CCP. That the 'sinification of
marxism' was a weapon in intra-party struggle does not suggest,
however, that Mao was insincere. The insistence on the importance of
national characteristics in the adaptation of revolutionary theory and
the rejection of foreign models remained constant themes in CCP
writing until the liberation.[169]

The years of close dependence on the Soviet Union in the early and
mid-1950s brought a muting of this line of argument, but by 1956 the
Chinese were once again taking pains to emphasize the distinctive character of China's path towards socialism.[170]

This is not to say that the universal character of marxism-leninism
was contested. Chinese leaders referred repeatedly to the general
applicability of marxist fundamentals and to the importance of the
Soviet experience of revolution and socialist construction.[171] They were
apparently unwilling at this time to risk the consequences of an open
ideological break with the Soviet Union. Beyond this, the CCP showed
no willingness to accept the idea that there could be non-marxist forms
of socialism.

Yet statements intended for internal consumption emphasized
specificity in the Chinese revolutionary experience, and the *superiority* of that experience to others (most notably the Soviet one), and
rejected servile adherence to foreign models.[172] In policy, the stress on

national creativity is most clearly demonstrated in the late 1950s in the Great Leap Forward.

As the Sino-Soviet dispute developed, and, subsequently, during the Cultural Revolution, the Chinese stress on the originality and universal significance of their own contributions to revolutionary theory grew all the more strident.[173] This was accompanied by a deliberate rejection of much of Soviet doctrine concerning political and social change in the Third World. Chinese commentators not only showed themselves willing to differ fundamentally with established Soviet positions (for example, peaceful coexistence and the non-inevitability of war), but consciously used theory as an instrument to discredit the Soviet Union which, it was maintained, had abandoned marxism-leninism. Comment on the subject in the aftermath of this upheaval shows some retreat on the applicability elsewhere of the Chinese experience, but little change in the stress on originality.[174]

Vietnamese communists, while to a considerable degree constrained in their discussion of the topic by their need to remain on good terms with both the CCP and the CPSU, echoed the Chinese emphasis on national specifics in the elaboration of strategy. Ho Chi Minh, for example, praised Mao's efforts to 'sinicize' marxism (compare this with Soviet attitudes towards the 'sinification of marxism', as outlined in Chapter 5), advocating in his turn what amounted to a Vietnamization of marxism and calling for the adaptation of marxist-leninist theory in accord 'with new conclusions drawn from our revolutionary practice'.[175] Both he and General Giap betrayed more than a hint of nationalism in stressing that lessons drawn from the Vietnamese experience constituted an important creative contribution to the universal science of marxism-leninism.

Among Latin American radicals, the stress on national originality in the development of theory is less evident, the protagonists viewing themselves more as participants in a regional struggle than in national ones. At the regional level, however, the concern to establish the importance of specific conditions in the development of revolutionary theory, remained. Guevara, for example, held that the states of the region shared a sufficient number of fundamental characteristics for it to be possible to develop a theory of revolution applicable to Latin America as a whole.[176]

Debray was more explicit and adamant in his stress on the specifics of revolutionary situations, rejecting categorically the import of foreign models. Theory in his view was inductive, developing out of tactical data and specific experience. It was, therefore, intrinsically particular rather than universal. To base practice on imported theory rather than to develop theory on the basis of indigenous practice was an inversion of the only feasible path to victory. Basing theory on indigenous roots was, in his view, not a rejection of marxism-leninism, but an affirmation of it.[177] Apparently, in order to affirm the essence of marxism, it was necessary to reject the substance of it.

Among African movements which ultimately proclaimed a marxist-leninist orientation (for example the MPLA and FRELIMO), there was also a stress on national specifics, particularly in the period prior to the development of strong dependence on Soviet material and diplomatic assistance. Samora Machel in writings in the early 1970s emphasized heavily the practical origins of theory.[178] Agostinho Neto underlined the importance of historical factors and specifically national objectives and individual perceptions on the character of the liberation struggle.[179] Even during the period of close relations with the Soviet Union and seemingly greater marxist-leninist orthodoxy since 1976, MPLA writers have been quick to stress the dynamic evolving character of marxism-leninism and the enrichment of the corpus of revolutionary theory with the particular experiences of national revolutionary struggles.[180] One student of recent Angolan politics characterizes the Angolan variant of 'scientific socialism' as 'eclectic, within a broad socialist framework, but the Angolan element is preponderant within it'.[181] The above suggests the difficulties likely to be faced by any external actor attempting to impose its own vision of Third World revolution even on self-avowed marxist-leninist national revolutionary movements.[182]

The stress on theoretical originality was even stronger among non-marxist-leninist movements. It often extended to an explicit rejection of orthodox marxism as a strategy of revolution or framework of analysis. Sun Yat-sen, in dissociating himself from marxism suggested that method should be based not on 'abstruse theory', but on concrete *Chinese* facts.[183] Sukarno too underlined the importance of local characteristics in the elaboration of what he referred to as 'Indonesian socialism', a form 'adjusted to conditions prevailing in Indonesia, adjusted to Indonesian nature, to the people of Indonesia, to the customs, the psychology, and culture of the Indonesian people'. He bluntly rejected foreign models, stating that Indonesia should not imitate others, but should seek institutions in accord with Indonesia's 'inner nature'.[184]

Although even the more radical elements in Algeria's FLN underlined the originality of their own revolutionary model,[185] the leadership apparently judged the movement's doctrinal independence to be insufficient. The party's first post-independence programme criticized the party's militants for having relied excessively on the revolutionary experience of other countries and for conforming 'blindly to established dogmas' with little appreciation of the 'uniqueness and spontaneity of the revolutionary dimension of the national struggle'.[186]

Fanon echoed this perspective and diverged dramatically from contemporaneous Soviet and Chinese doctrine by denying the necessity of choice between capitalism and socialism, which he saw as alternatives relevant to the past:

> The underdeveloped countries ought to do their utmost to find their particular values and methods and style which shall be particular to them. The concrete problem we find ourselves up against is not that of a choice, come what may, between socialism and capitalism as they have been defined by men of other continents and of other systems.[187]

Guine-Bissau's Amilcar Cabral, while willing to admit the utility of marxist methodology in analysing social reality, denied that the PAIGC was in any sense a 'communist or marxist-leninist party', and maintained that it was utopian to attempt to apply imported models in the African revolutionary context, an ironic inversion of the Soviet line that it was utopian not to apply general revolutionary principles (see Chapter 5). In Cabral's view, liberation and social revolution were a 'local national product . . . essentially determined by the historical reality of each people'.[188] The principal sources of theory were national specifics. This explains the fact that Cabral's own political writing is essentially a description and analysis of what was or had been going on in the local struggle, rather than a set of abstract universalizable principles.[189]

In the South African case, finally, the 1969 ANC programme stated flatly that revolutionary programmes not reflecting the specific South African situation were devoid of value and that the blind application of the revolutionary experience of other countries was 'extremely fatal' (*sic*).[190] The position of non-marxist movements serves to reinforce the conclusion that it would be extremely difficult for any outside force to exercise leadership in the elaboration of doctrine over revolutionary nationalist movements as a group.

The concern among these movements to preserve autonomy and to assert originality in the realm of theory falls into the mainstream of

Third World nationalist thought about paths to independence and socialism. To cite a few examples, while in early writings Nehru embraced what he referred to as a universal 'scientific socialism'.[191] in his mature work he argued that although he accepted the fundamentals of socialist theory, he rejected the notion of a fixed universal doctrine, life being too complicated to be confined within such a construct.[192] European (including Soviet) socialism was largely irrelevant to India, given its emphasis on the industrial proletariat. The dominant considerations in India were, in his view, nationalism and the rural economy.[193]

Among African writers, the assertion that the struggle for freedom and development should be distinctively African dates back well into the nineteenth century. The Liberian educator and diplomat Edward Blyden, for example, declared in 1881 that:

The road by which one man may attain to the highest efficiency is not that which would conduce to the success of another. The special road which has led to the success and elevation of the Anglo-Saxon is not that which would lead to the success and elevation of the Negro.[194]

Much later, Sekou Toure rejected communism as a path for Guinea, noting that it was absurd that African nations should act according to supposedly universal principles, ignoring historical conditions. In a manner reminiscent of Fanon, he denied the necessity of choice between capitalism and socialism as that choice was cast by marxist-leninists.[195] While in the mid-1960s he moved towards a position which he referred to as 'scientific socialism' and stressed the universality of socialism as an ideology, he continued to show considerable originality in the ways in which socialism was to be achieved in Guinea.[196] George Padmore advocated a combination of African nationalism and socialism as an alternative to the 'myopically pseudo-marxist doctrinaire policy' of the international communist movement.[197] In the same passage, he demonstrated that it was not only the practical desire to adapt theory to specific conditions which was the basis for the rejection of universal theory, but also the desire to assert autonomy: 'The European, communist or non-communist, fails to realize that one of the first reactions of politically awakened, self-respecting coloured leaders is the desire to be mentally free from the dictation of Europeans, regardless of their ideology.'[198]

Elsewhere, Nyerere contested the marxist and Soviet view that socialism was unique, rejected foreign models, and maintained that Tanzania was building a socialism which was hers alone and with methods which were also specific to that country.[199]

One might argue that it is inappropriate to situate the 'scientific socialism' of self-acclaimed marxist-leninist movements within the broader context of national or regional socialism. The MPLA, for example, adamantly asserts the difference between 'African socialism' and its own 'scientific socialism'.[200] But to judge from MPLA theory and practice, this difference is exaggerated. As one analyst has noted, 'what is most surprising is that for all [the MPLA ideology's] supposed radicalism, a careful examination reveals a programme not dissimilar to European social-democratic thinking'.[201] Indeed, in a broader context, there would seem to be little agreement on, or for that matter little attempt to define, just what the universal substance of 'scientific socialism' is among the movements which have embraced it.

But what of recognized communist parties leading national liberation revolutions, such as the CCP or the Vietnamese Workers Party? It is true that the socialist component of these parties' programme may be more extreme than that, say, of Sukarno or Sekou Toure. Yet the basic substance of their conceptions of what socialism is (an end to exploitation through public ownership or control of the basic means of production and redistribution of national resources such as land in such a way as to benefit the poorer classes) are quite similar. There would appear to be an elemental common ground to the concept of socialism, despite the wide variations in its policy manifestations.

At least four common themes characterize the contributions of Third World revolutionary movements to the corpus of theory concerning revolution in the non-European world. The first is the importance of subjective prerequisites in the process of revolution.

## Voluntarism and Leadership of the National Liberation Movement

Third World discussions of revolution are marked by a voluntaristic aspect which distinguishes them dramatically from orthodox and Soviet marxism. By voluntarism is meant the accentuation of such subjective factors as will, consciousness and ethics, as opposed to objective characteristics such as the level of economic development, as preconditions for successful revolution. This tendency is a logical consequence of the dilemma which orthodox marxism poses for the Third World revolutionary. In underdeveloped precapitalist conditions, one has either to abandon any hope of 'truly liberating' revolution and to accept the inevitability of prolonged suffering as capitalism develops and then declines, or to modify the theory in such a way as to get around the objective constraints on social development in such conditions. This voluntaristic element is difficult to square with Marx and Engels. Although these two did not deny the importance of subjective factors in revolution, these factors were themselves a superstructural product of developments in the economic base. They could not, therefore, compensate for deficiencies in that base. Although Lenin's thought displays a greater emphasis on subjective factors, notably in his concept of the vanguard party — an association of professional revolutionaries which would organize and lead the revolution — nowhere in it is there the suggestion that revolutionaries can skip stages of history by developing an appropriate degree of revolutionary consciousness, or that the existence of a numerous urban proletariat was not a prerequisite for socialist revolution.

A voluntaristic perspective is implicit in the widespread focus on cultural revolution as an aspect of national liberation. Beyond this, such a tendency is evident not only in the explicit treatment of the importance of consciousness as opposed to material preconditions, but also in the consideration of the nature of class and leadership and in the frequent disregard in doctrine and policy of objective limitations in the attempt to build socialism.

Both Sun Yat-sen and Sukarno betrayed a voluntaristic tendency, the former in his view that the revolution would be directed by a conscious and disciplined elite of 'selfless idealists' which would guide the masses towards a new China, and the latter in his argument that it was the individual human being and not the level of development which was 'the decisive factor in the struggle'.[202] In neither case do objective factors receive any substantial emphasis in their accounts of the conditions of revolution.

In the case of the CCP, voluntarism has been an aspect of theoretical development since the foundation of the party. Meisner notes that Li Ta-chao rejected Marx's account of the materialistic origins of socialist consciousness. Socialism was for him not a result of economic or basic determinants, but was a subjective product of human knowledge, emotion, and will.[203] Mao too stressed the importance of revolutionary will rather than material prerequisites in the making of social revolution. Indeed, in his argument that 'poor and blank' societies enjoyed the highest revolutionary potential, he verged on inverting Marx's materialist conception of history, in that it was pre-industrial societies rather than industrial ones which could make the most rapid advance to socialism.

The subjective character of much Chinese communist doctrine is also evident in their discussion of the nature of the proletariat. Except in periods of intense Soviet pressure to accept the leadership of the Kuomintang in China's struggle for liberation, Chinese writers, and most particularly Mao himself, have stressed the importance of proletarian leadership of that struggle (see below). This meant essentially the leadership of the CCP, an elite group of revolutionaries of diverse class origin. This reflected Lenin's thinking in *What Is To Be Done?* But in Lenin's view, this elite was to lead the working class in making the socialist revolution. As was noted above, at no time did he intimate that the proletarian revolution could be made without the participation of organized industrial workers. Soviet marxism has always stressed the role of the working class (that is, industrial labour), and the need to avoid a divorce between the party and what is, in the Soviet view, its main base of support.

But events in China favoured a different direction in CCP theory. As in the case of a number of movements to be considered below, the CCP first tried to focus its organizational activities on the urban working class. The defeats of 1927 and, subsequently, the reverses dealt to the party in its ill-advised pursuit of the Li Li-san line in 1930-1, dictated a retreat to rural areas and severed the links between the party and urban workers. This forced reliance on the peasantry. An accentuation of the peasant role in the revolution was also favoured by the populist inclinations of key figures in the party such as Li Ta-chao and Mao Tse-tung. Given that the party, for reasons of self-legitimation and in order to retain its legitimacy in the eyes of the international communist movement, was compelled to retain its verbal commitment to the vanguard role of the working class, this train of events favoured a redefinition of the concept of the proletariat which de-emphasized the individual's role in the production process and stressed instead the possession of 'correct proletarian consciousness' as the critical determinant of proletarian status.[204] Such a line of argument implies that socialism is a product not of a given level of socio-economic development, but of correct consciousness. As such, societies at any level of development can make revolutions which establish the conditions for socialist development.

The voluntaristic tendency in Third World marxist thinking on revolution was also evident in much Latin American writing on the preconditions of revolution. Guevara, for example, maintained that the individual and his 'heroic attitude' were of fundamental importance in the struggle for liberation.[205] There is ample stress in Castro's speeches on the importance of spirit in revolution.[206] Debray's voluntarism is best illustrated by his concept of the guerrilla foco. In his view, the revolution was to be led not by the urban working class, but by a military cell made up principally of intellectuals of bourgeois origin, possessed of a 'proletarian' consciousness which allowed them to transcend their objective class origins and to lead peasants and workers in the socialist revolution. It was the capacity of these intellectuals to overcome their objective limitations − to 'commit suicide as a class' (Debray was here quoting Amilcar Cabral) − which created the possibility of anti-imperialist and anti-capitalist revolution in Latin America.[207]

Similar views concerning the catalytic revolutionary role of conscious intellectuals may be detected in the work of Fanon. In *The Wretched of the Earth*, he argued that the revolutionary elite was to be found in a group of intellectuals dissatisfied with the gradualism of the mainstream nationalist movement and having realized the revolutionary potential of the peasantry. He explicitly denied what was, in the marxist-leninist view, the objectively determined vanguard role of the industrial working class.[208]

To cite a further example, Cabral's treatment of leadership in the struggle for liberation also displays a pronounced weighting in favour of subjective conditions of revolution. In the conditions of Guine-Bissau, leadership fell to what he termed the petty bourgeoisie, and more specifically, to a small group within that 'class' which was politically conscious and which consequently could surmount the objective interest which those in that social category had in collaborating with and reaping the benefits of colonialism. In the period after the winning of independence, it was again revolutionary consciousness which would permit this group to resist their natural proclivity to use power for their own narrow interests and instead to continue the revolution in Guinean economic and social structure.[209] The critical factor in this continuation was thus a *moral* commitment to the goals of the PAIGC.[210] Turning finally to the MPLA, although the movement in its later statements referred quite consistently to the need for working-class leadership of the Angolan revolution, a closer analysis shows that, as with, the CCP, its conception of the proletariat was sufficiently broad to take in almost the entire population.[211] In this sense, one might say that here the concepts of the 'proletariat' and the 'people' verge on being coterminous, the critical factor again being not so much an individual's place in the relations of production, but his degree of revolutionary consciousness (that is, his support for the MPLA and its programme).

The impatience and wilfulness which this voluntarism betrays reinforces the conclusion above concerning the ability of outsiders to maintain control over Third World revolutionary movements. And indeed, in practice it has created or exacerbated difficulties in relations between the USSR and radical Third World revolutionary movements. For example, Soviet doubts about the Chinese Great Leap Forward (see Chapter 5) were a major factor in the falling out between China and the USSR in the late 1950s, the Chinese apparently believing that Soviet resistance to this project reflected a desire to condemn China in perpetuity to second-class status as a world power. In the 1960s, the voluntarism of Guevara and his colleagues evident in their efforts to sow revolution throughout Latin America severely strained relations with Cuba at a time when the USSR was seeking to avoid additional problems in the Soviet-American relationship.[212]

## Class Participation and Struggle in the National Liberation Front

The discussion of leadership leads to the broader question of class participation and structure in the national liberation front. The second distinguishing characteristic concerns breadth of participation and the nature of class relations within the national liberation front. The struggle for national liberation is seen principally as a national one, rather than as a class struggle within nations. Accordingly, the vision of the united front tends to include virtually the entire population of the area concerned. Early Third World marxists attempted to cloak the appeal for national unity in appropriate terminology.

Sultan-Galiev, for example, denied the relevance of class distinctions to the situation of the Turkic peoples in Soviet Russia, emphasizing the primitive character of class differentiation in Muslim society. He took the view that, since this society was as a whole oppressed by outsiders, it was as a whole proletarian. As such, despite the low degree of social and economic development, the Tartar national revolution was socialist in character.[213] Sultan Galiev's concept of the 'proletarian nation' drew to some extent upon Lenin's argument that whole nations could be oppressed by imperialism and hence that nations as a whole could have an interest in anti-imperialist struggle. However, Lenin never equated oppression *per se* with proletarian class status. For Lenin, as for Marx, it was primarily position in the relations of production which determined class. Moreover, his view of national fronts was more clearly dialectical than was Sultan-Galiev's. He placed a greater emphasis on class differentiation within the oppressed nations, and perceived the common interest in anti-imperialist struggle to be balanced by competing interests among different classes within the emergent nation. By contrast, class struggle had little place in Sultan-Galiev's thought.

Both Li Ta-chao and Mao Tse-tung in his early works also envisaged very broad particiption in the liberation struggle and stressed strongly the need for the unity of the nation *as a whole* barring a numerically insignificant group of irredeemables). One of Mao's first programmatic works called for the participation of the vast majority of Chinese in the anti-imperialist cause.[214] Li Ta-chao, in a manner similar to Sultan-Galiev's, drew an analogy between the oppression of the proletariat within capitalist countries and that of the weak nations on the international level. He therefore argued that China was as a whole a proletarian nation.[215] This allowed the equation of nationalism and socialism.

While in the early 1930s, Mao and his colleagues displayed considerable reluctance to re-establish a 'united front from above' with the Kuomintang (and this despite considerable pressure from the Comintern to do so), they called upon individual members of the Kuomintang to join them in the struggle for national liberation.[216] Their appeals for support showed little concern about class contradictions and it was accepted at least from 1935 (the Maoerkhai appeal) that the bourgeoisie could participate in a government of national defence.[217] In 'On New Democracy', and despite the renewal of elements of class struggle in the base areas, Mao continued to entertain the vision of a broad united front led by the CCP and including the bourgeoisie, though he considered the latter an unreliable ally and envisaged a combination of alliance and struggle within the national front.[218]

This position on participation in the united front persisted until victory in 1949,[218] and is maintained in Mao's conception of the 'four class bloc' (workers, peasants, urban petty bourgeois, and national bourgeois) outlined in his 'On the People's Democratic Dictatorship' (1949).[220] In the aftermath of victory, CCP writers continued to stress that the national liberation struggle was one of the 'whole people'[221] including the national bourgeoisie, despite the tendency of Soviet writers at this time to write off this social group. The basic preference for broad national participation in the liberation struggle was not affected by the subsequent twists and turns of Chinese doctrine with respect to Third World regimes *led* by the national bourgeoisie from the 1950s to 1970s.[222] In summary, despite all the variation over time in response to historical circumstance (for example, the 'betrayal' by the Kuomintang in 1927) and to Comintern and Soviet pressure, there is evident in CCP doctrine a clear preference for the unity of all Chinese

in the struggle against imperialism. This presumably follows in part
from their realization of the fact that divisions in Chinese society facilitated imperialist penetration and exploitation of China. Even in
periods of open struggle against the Kuomintang, the CCP continued to
solicit the participation of the bourgeoisie as a class in their revolution.

A similar conclusion may be drawn from Vietnamese communist
doctrine and policy. The stress on uniting the whole people in the
struggle against the French and later the Americans was a persistent
theme. Ho was quite consistently open to bourgeois participation in a
liberation front structured around the 'worker-peasant alliance' and led
by the Vietnamese Workers Party.[223] It was the concern to maintain
unity that caused the party to postpone the agrarian revolution into the
early and mid-150s.

It is true that this emphasis on national unity may have been tactical
in both the Chinese communist and Vietnamese cases. In both
instances, class struggle followed the party's seizure of power. However,
the emphasis in these intra-national struggles was not so much on
liquidating indigenous exploiters but on winning them over. As Mao put
it in 'On the Ten Great Relationships' (1956):

> Can a negative element turn into a positive element? . . . Can a
> counter-revolutionary change? This depends on social conditions.
> Completely stubborn, dyed-in-the-wool counter-revolutionaries
> undoubtedly exist. But where the majority of them are concerned,
> given our social conditions, the day may come when they do change
> . . . Because of the people's strength, and because of our correct
> policy towards counter-revolutionary elements of allowing them to
> reform themselves through labour and become new men, there have
> been many counter-revolutionaries who have given up being counter-
> revolutionary.[224]

Class struggle was in a sense a device for strengthening national unity
rather than a devaluation of that unity.

Elsewhere, Sun Yat-sen maintained that all Chinese could participate in the nationalist revolution and played down internal class contradictions in Chinese society. He argued that such divisions were weak,
there being 'no especially rich class', but only varying degrees of
poverty.[225] Tai Chi-t'ao put forward the now familiar view that the
Chinese people constituted a single class exploited by imperialism.[226]
Sukarno asserted similarly that there were in Indonesia no significant

class divisions, the whole nation having been pauperized by imperialism.[227] This created the basis for participation by all groups in the
struggle against colonialism.[228]

Among other liberation movements, the FLN saw their project as
one involving all Algerians.[229] Debray, while excluding landowners
from his conception of the national liberation front, held that national
bourgeois membership, in addition to that of workers, peasants, and intellectuals, was both possible and desirable.[230] Cabral took an essentially non-class subjective view of participation, maintaining that any
group could participate, as long as their attitude was correct. The
people of Guine-Bissau were those who opposed Portuguese colonial
rule.[231] The MPLA, prior to independence, called for a 'liberation
coalition' of all parties, popular and religious organizations, ethnic or
national minorities, and social classes.[232] FRELIMO, too, invited all
Mozambicans of whatever class, ethnic, religious, racial and political
affiliation to join, the main criterion of eligibility being acceptance of
the FRELIMO programme.[233] While in the cases of both the MPLA and
FRELIMO, there appeared in the later stages of the struggle for independence and in the aftermath of victory a growing emphasis on class
differentiation and conflict within the nation, the emphasis remained
on the need to re-educate 'exploiting elements' in order to integrate
them more fully into the national front, to overcome internal contradictions in order to strengthen national unity.

On the whole, it is fair to say that among Third World national revolutionary movements there was a tendency to de-emphasize internal
contradictions and to seek to construct a national liberation front
encompassing all groups within the nation or nation to be. Where the
necessity or inevitability of class struggle was recognized, the numbers
of 'class enemies' were generally held to be very low (cf. Sultan-Galiev
and Mao Tse-tung). Such groups were to be won over rather than elimi-
nated. Class struggle was a means of consolidating national unity
through overcoming internal contradictions, through the integration of
isolated elements of the population into the national whole. Implicit in
this conception is the view that class contradictions are secondary, less
developed than in industrial societies, and eradicable in the process of
developing a revolutionary national identity. This too is in some sense
an inversion of Marx, who viewed class contradiction as essential and
national identity as superstructural fetishism, with no intrinsic value. It
also differs considerably from the Soviet perspective for the same
reason.

The emphasis on broad national unity among these movements again lies in the mainstream of Third World nationalist thought. One encounters frequently themes touched upon above elsewhere in the literature. Nehru, despite his recognition of divisions within the Indian population, stressed the possibility and the desirability of broad participation in the struggle for independence and in later national construction.[234] Sekou Toure, in early writings, held the view that internal social contradictions in African society were insignificant when compared to the contradiction between Africa and imperialism. He maintained that in Africa there was only one social class, 'that of the dispossessed'. As a result, the Parti Democratique Guineen (PDG) was not to be the representative of a single social group, but was instead the party of the entire nation, and indeed all adult Guineans became members of the party. As time passed, and in response to challenges to his position, Toure began to lay greater emphasis on class struggle within the Guinean nation, positing the emergence of an 'exploiting class' opposed to the 'people's class'. None the less, Toure apparently refused to contemplate the exclusion of the 'exploiting class' from the PDG, instead taking the view that this contradiction was secondary to national unity and could be contained within the context of this unity.[235]

Nkrumah maintained similarly in earlier writings that it was the 'people as a whole who revolt and struggle as a "nation-class" against colonial oppression', though he too in later years, and particularly following his ouster by the Ghanaian military, displayed a growing acceptance of the concept of class struggle.[236]

The policy implications of this general stress on the unity of the nation in the face of outsiders are evident in Africa, for example, in the prevalence of one party unitary states. As two Western commentators have put it: 'Recent African politics have been characterized by the opposition of most African governments to competitive party systems, their lack of sympathy for federalism, and their attack on political liberties.'[237] The obverse of the insistence on the unity of the entire nation in the face of an external enemy or in the tasks of social and economic transformation is a stress on the illegitimacy of opposition and the undesirability of competing centres of power within the nation. The prevailing conception of politics is centralist and unitary rather than pluralist.

The origins of this focus on unity are not hard to discern. Third World societies tend to lack cohesion at the national level. Instead, loyalties focus on family or kinship groupings or subnational ethnic or religious communities. The emphasis on national cohesion and the discouragement of subnational competition are attempts to contain or to defuse centifugal forces within national liberation movements or within the states which they form.

As will be seen below, both Soviet and American conceptions of political development place a certain degree of stress on divisions within the new states, both prescriptively and descriptively. The prescriptive aspect of Soviet doctrine concerning class struggle in the aftermath of independence, and in particular concerning the need to displace bourgeois elements within 'national democratic goverments' and to clear the way for the working class and its vanguard to occupy a leading place in the politics of new states have on occasion caused serious problems in Soviet relations with otherwise friendly states. This is so not only because of the non-proletarian, non-communist charcter of many of the leaders of these states, but also because of a reluctance to sanction doctrines or policies which undermined national unity (see Chapter 5). In this sense, while, as was noted in Chapter 3, Third World elites often saw much merit in leninist and Soviet theories of party *organization* and *function* (the stress on mobilization, the penetration of society through party-affiliated and controlled mass organizations, the decision-making principles of democratic centralism, and the importance of a vanguard elite), their acceptance does not on the whole extend to types of class struggle which would seriously erode national cohesion or their own leadership. A similar qualification attaches to their advocacy of social revolutionary change.

On the American side, the prescriptive stress on division takes the form of appeals for the construction of a pluralist democratic order in new states (see Chapter 6). This also conflicts with the tendency in Third World thinking to view the nation as a collective entity, all citizens participating as one in the struggle to win or to consolidate national independence and to develop the country. Pluralism, in the sense of competition within the nation for political and social goods, is pernicious. Attempts to encourage it are viewed as imperialist penetration. Where rights are discussed, it is the collective rights of the community as a whole rather than rights pertaining to individuals or groups within the community which receive the greater stress.

The third aspect of doctrines of national liberation which deserves comment here is the nearly universal stress on the critical role of the peasantry and on the primacy of rural struggle. Among Chinese communists, this theme again runs through party commentary from the party's very early days. Li Ta-chao's thought on revolution, for example, was strongly populist in character. He displayed a conspicuous distaste (curious for a marxist) for urban life and a belief in the purity and dynamism of the rural existence. Li called on China's youth to disperse to and learn from the villages and cast the peasantry as the basic force of Chinese regeneration.[238]

Mao from very early in his career displayed a similar appreciation of the peasantry. This apparently dated from 1925, when he withdrew temporarily from active politics and returned to his home province of Hunan.[239] A return to Hunan in 1926-7 further heightened his awareness of the revolutionary potential of the peasantry. His report on the visit emphasized the contribution of rural areas to the revolution, the role of the working class hardly bearing mention.[240]

Mao's retreat to the countryside in 1927 and his subsequent dependence on peasant support only reinforced this orientation in his thinking. By the late 1920s he was being indirectly criticized for his 'peasant mentality' and his insufficient appreciation of the party's need for solid working-class support.[241] In the face of this criticism, and during the protracted struggle for control of the party in the early and mid-1930s, Mao held his piece on this topic. However, after the consolidation of his control over the party in the mid-1930s, reference to the peasantry as the 'main strength of the revolution' re-emerged.[242] This position remained more or less constant in later discussions of 'anti-feudal' and 'anti-imperialist' revolution.[243] As the Sino-Soviet dispute heated up, Chinese emphasis on the importance of their own revolutionary model, on rural struggle, and on the encirclement of the cities from the countryside as the basic strategy of revolution, grew less restrained.[244]

In practice, the CCP emphasis on the essentially rural character of the national liberation revolution is even clearer. Driven from the cities in 1927, they took refuge in base areas in remote parts of the countryside, built an army out of the peasantry, and carried on the struggle from 1928 until victory in 1949 largely without substantial urban working-class participation.

The Vietnamese communist movement shared the CCP's emphasis on the role of peasants, referring to the liberation struggle as a peasant war and stressing that the support of the peasantry was the basis for success.[245] In practice, the war of liberation pitted communist forces rooted in the rural areas against towns held first by the French and then, in the south, by the Americans and their local allies. Victory was based on the construction and expansion of rural base areas, culminating in seizure of the cities.

In Algeria, the FLN too emphasized rural organization and the status of the peasant as the decisive force in the anti-colonial struggle.[246]

Fanon went further, viewing the peasantry as the only true revolutionary group in colonial society. All others were to varying degrees compromised by ties to imperialism. The peasantry alone had 'nothing to lose and everything to gain'.[247]

A similar focus on rural struggle may be found in the writings of Guevara and Debray, the latter justifying the shift from proletariat to peasantry by maintaining that the most explosive contradiction in Latin American society was that between peasants and landowners, the countryside being, therefore, the weakest link in the 'imperialist/ oligarchic' system.[248] He stressed elsewhere that the traditional marxist-leninist focus on working class rather than peasant struggle, along with such Soviet marxist concepts as 'national democracy' were 'outworn' and 'discredited'.[249] This presumably reflected his impatience with the official Latin American communist parties whose support for armed revolutionary struggle along castroite lines was lukewarm at best.

A number of the Lusophone African radical movements considered here came to a similar focus on peasant participation and rural struggle after originally attempting more orthodox tactics and finding them inappropriate, if not suicidal, in the conditions which they faced. The PAIGC, MPLA, and FRELIMO, all reflecting perhaps the urban backgrounds of their leaders and their exposure to marxism, originally tried urban struggle. In each case, after the failure of protest and strike activities in the towns, they shifted to the countryside, and to the creation of rural base areas. Cabral reflected the consensus of the three movements when he referred to the peasantry as the 'major physical force in a national liberation struggle'.[250]

This stress on the peasantry and on rural struggle differs rather sharply from orthodox marxist-leninist characterizations of socialist revolution, which focus on contradiction between labour and capital, on urban rather than rural social processes, and on the decisive role of the conscious working class. The focus of Third World revolutionary nationalists on rural struggle may be ascribed to a number of factors. First, as noted above, it was a logical consequence of prior failure in urban struggle. The power of 'counter-revolutionary forces' was usually concentrated in urban areas and, therefore, urban struggle held a high probability of defeat. Moreover, a concentration on the peasantry followed from a recognition of the demographic and socioeconomic realities of less developed countries. The working class was generally small. The vast majority of the population was rural and engaged in agriculture. It may also reflect the influence of a populist strand in revolutionary thought which dates back at least to the Russian narodniki, if not to earlier European romanticism, a strand which embodies the urban intellectual's disillusionment with the materialism and corruption of the urban environmentand industrial society, and his atavistic longing for traditional rural life. The belief in the essential goodness and purity of peasant life is reflected not only in much of the thinking of the liberation movements, but is also implicit in Gandhi's antimodernism, Nyerere's ujamaa, and Sekou Toure's notion of com-- munaucratie.

## Violence and National Liberation

The final distinguishing aspect of doctrines of national liberation is the treatment of violence. There are three relatively widely shared characteristics of the discussion of this subject among radical revolutionary movements in the Third World. First, it is accepted implicitly or explicitly that the objectives of the struggle for liberation are sufficiently important to justify the use of violence to achieve them. There is no need to document this in the case of movements which opted for armed struggle. Had their militants not believed this, they would not have made such a choice. But this view was also widely shared by nationalists who strove for and obtained power by non-violent means.[251] Even Nehru, while embracing the Gandhian perspective on violence, once wrote that while violence was bad, slavery was worse, and that violence could be preferable to non-violence in circumstances where the latter promised no results.[252] Indeed, Gandhi's own position that violence could be justified only when the perpetrators of it were not aware of the non-violent approach to the struggle for independence suggests that the end of freedom was sufficiently important to justify violence.[253] Certain radical Latin American Catholics have gone further in suggesting that where oppression is particularly severe, the concerned Christian is left with no alternative to violence. As the Peruvian priest Camilo Torres put it in announcing his decision to join the guerrillas in 1965: 'I believe that revolutionary combat is a Christian and priestly combat . . . It is the only way in the circumstances of our country for us to love our neighbour as we should.'[254]

Second, national revolutionaries generally maintained that armed struggle was a necessary aspect of revolution in the Third World, not just in their own country, but everywhere. Sun Yat-sen maintained that revolution was inevitably violent.[255] In the case of Mao, a belief in the necessity of violence dates back to very early in his political life when he criticized Bertrand Russell for having maintained in a series of lectures in China that revolutionary objectives could be achieved without violence.[256] The view that violence is an unavoidable aspect of the revolutionary struggle dominates CCP literature until the victory in 1949,[257] a reflection of the fact that for much of the period the party was fighting for its survival against a varied array of warlord, Kuomintang, and Japanese forces. The occasional inferences that a peaceful transition to socialism was possible[258] are suspect as they occurred in the context of appeals to other classes for unity and as such were tactically motivated. Moreover, the statement cited referred specifically to the resolution of class contradictions *within* the Chinese nation.It did not bear upon the struggle against imperialism.

Emphasis on the necessity of violence persisted in the aftermath of victory and was applied across the board to anti-imperialist struggle everywhere.[259] While this strain of CCP thought was muted in certain periods (for example, the mid-1950s), this may again be explained in contextual terms, rather than suggesting a fundamental shift in Mao Tse-tung's perspective on revolution. At this time the Chinese were under considerable pressure from the Soviets to play down the role of revolutionary violence, and for reasons of their own were seeking to improve relations with a number of 'national bourgeois' regimes in Asia. As relations with the USSR worsened in the late 1950s, and this constraint on Chinese candour was removed, Chinese spokesmen resurrected the position that in countries ruled by imperialist or bourgeois forces, peaceful liberation and transition to socialism were impossible. This line appeared first in documents of limited circulation,[260] and then more publicly.[261] This was coupled with expressions of support for movements engaged in armed struggle, such as the Algerian FLN, which were far more open and enthusiastic than contemporaneous Soviet statements.[262]

As the dispute deepened, the Chinese rejection of the applicability of the principles of peaceful coexistence to relations between oppressed nations and imperialism became even more blunt. By this time it was clear that differences over revolutionary violence were a significant ideological aspect of the Sino-Soviet dispute.[263] The view that violence was a necessary aspect of the national liberation revolution persisted through the Cultural Revolution[264] and into the early 1970s,[265] though the frequency of its expression decreased as the People's Republic once again embarked on a more active state-to-state diplomacy in the Third World. The Chinese voiced support of specific instances of armed struggle in the early 1970s only where they involved remaining struggles for independence (where the Chinese participated in a broad Third

World consensus, for example, Portuguese Africa), against 'imperialism' in the Middle East (for example, the Palestinian struggle), and against regimes with which the PRC had chronically poor relations (for example, Indonesia, Malaysia, Thailand). When relations improved, as with the latter two countries, support for these armed struggles was no longer prominently voiced. The same was true in situations where the Chinese sought to improve relations with regimes involved in the suppression of 'liberation movements' (for example, Iran in Dhofar). In this case, as relations with Iran improved, the Chinese no longer declared their support for and apparently ceased military assistance to the Popular Front for the Liberation of the Occupied Arab Gulf. As a result of these trends, by mid-decade, Chinese commentary on armed struggle for national liberation focused more and more narrowly on Southern Africa and the Palestinian question.

Among other liberation movements, the Vietnamese not surprisingly held that mass armed struggle was the only way to liberation, both in Vietnam and in general.[266] Ferhat Abbas, one of the more moderate members of the provisional government formed by Algeria's FLN, declared similarly that the colonial regime was born from violence, that its continued viability rested upon arbitrariness and force, and there-fore that 'par nature, il ne cede que devant la violence'.[267] Che Guevara in like fashion dismissed the possibility that peaceful coexistence could exist 'between the exploiters and the exploited, the oppressor and the oppressed' and therefore 'we cannot harbour any illusions, and we have no right to do so, that freedom can be obtained without fighting'.[268]

Turning to the Lusophone African literature, Amilcar Cabral and his colleagues also took the view that the intransigence of colonial rule meant that armed struggle 'was the only way out' for Guine-Bissau.[269] He later universalized this argument in terms which recall Fanon, suggesting that as 'imperialist domination' implied a 'state of permanent violence against the nationalist forces', no people could attain independence 'without victims'.[270] SWAPO, ZANU and the ANC shared a similar view with respect to their own struggles, but unlike those considered above, did not universalize the argument that violence was necessary in the struggle for liberation.[271]

The reasons for the widespread emphasis on the necessity of armed struggle are not difficult to find. In the first place, there is much truth in the oft-repeated contention[272] that other forms of struggle were tried first and proved ineffectual. By and large, these radical nationalists were faced by adversaries who were unwilling to abdicate their powers unless forced to do so. The French, for example, apparently were set on re-establishing their rule in Vietnam after the Second World War and were unwilling to accept the Viet Minh's claim to meaningful independence. In Algeria, the 25 years prior to the outbreak of war in 1954 had displayed clearly the incapacity of successive French governments to deliver on promised reforms, and, more profoundly, the unwillingness of the French nation to accommodate itself to the aspirations of the Algerian national movement. In Guine-Bissau, the Portuguese responded to non-violent means of struggle by massacring dock workers at Pidjiguiti in 1959. In Mozambique, it was the brutal suppression of peaceful protest at Mueda in 1960 which conditioned FRELIMO's commitment to the use of force. In South Africa, there is little to argue with in Mandela's assertion that 50 years of non-violent protest in defence of black rights had brought 'nothing but more and more repressive legislation and fewer and fewer rights'.[273] In short, the common assertion by these groups of the necessity of violence in the struggle for national liberation followed more or less logically from the severity of the resistance they faced in striving to attain their objectives.

The tendency among some of them to universalize this postulate reflects perhaps more than anything else the common proclivity to generalize from one's own experience. It may also reflect a desire to convince oneself, the members of one's movement, and the population at large that no alternative to war exists. If one accepted that violence could be avoided elsewhere, one faced the question of why it was unavoidable in one's own situation.

Beyond asserting the necessity of force for essentially pragmatic reasons, many radical nationalists have ascribed to violence a number of additional advantages. Many have argued, for example, that violence has an important educative effect. It is a consciousness-raising device, mobilizing and revolutionizing the people and creating a new situation conducive to the completion of the process of liberation.[274] Moreover, many considered that armed struggle fosters national unity by breaking down tribal, ethnic, and racial barriers, and forging new bonds of solidarity.[275] Beyond this, several claimed that armed struggle, by weeding out the incompetent and the less than truly committed, favoured the emergence of effective leadership.[276]

Finally, a number of African writers in particular followed Fanon in arguing that the use of violence against the oppressor had a psychologically therapeutic effect. Taking up arms against foreign oppression restored the dignity and self-respect of indigenous peoples, undoing the emotional damage which resulted from life in a society where the people's humanity was systematically denied. As such, violence was a 'cleansing force', not only by which but in which the colonized man found his freedom.[277] Sartre encapsulated this aspect of the discussion in his famous remark to the effect that 'the rebel's weapon is the proof of this humanity'. Shooting a European killed two birds with one stone, destroying the 'oppressor and the man he oppresses at the same time; there remain a dead man and a free man . . .'[278]

As conclusions drawn from experience, these do not stand up terribly well. One suspects that they confuse fact with hope. Yet they do serve as supplementary justifications for the choice of violence as an instrument of struggle and perhaps may be best explained in such terms. The attribution of these additional advantages to the use of force constitutes a substantial departure from orthodox marxism-leninism and from the Soviet perspective on the use of force, as will be seen in the next chapter.

## Conclusion

In conclusion, it should be stressed first that there is no single Third World ideology of national liberation in the sense of a unified and internally consistent set of beliefs which accounts for the phenomenon of imperialism, provides a vision of a desired future, and prescribes a set of strategies and tactics for getting from the present to that future. It would be unrealistic to expect that such an ideology would develop and be generally accepted in conditions as diverse as those of the Third World, particularly when one of the distinguishing characteristics of this body of thought is the desire to express national specificity and creativity in revolutionary doctrine.

However, radical nationalist thought in the Third World does display a number of characteristics which are sufficiently widespread to allow comparison between a Third World conception of national liberation on the one hand and Soviet and American thinking on political and social change in the Third World on the other. These common characteristics result from three factors:

(1) a common intellectual heritage (European nationalist and social-ist thought);
(2) a process of cross-fertilization as different groups read each

other's writings and as later struggles were affected by earlier successes; and

(3) a number of basic common features of the historical development of Third World states (for example, the experience of colonial subjugation, economic domination, and the overwhelming cultural impact of the West).

With regard to the definition of national liberation, it is commonly accepted that the process involves not only political independence, but also economic independence and self-reliance, profound internal social change, and cultural regeneration. Social change was to be both 'anti-feudal' and 'anti-capitalist'. Its *denoument* was to be socialism. Cultural regeneration involved not only the elimination of corruptive and demoralizing aspects of Western culture, but was also directed against elements of traditional indigenous culture which impeded effective resistance to Western penetration and which prevented progress towards non-exploitative relations of production. In its political, economic, and cultural aspects, the concept is particularistic. This is reflected in the practice of states formed by these movements, which tends to be highly nationalistic.

One expression in foreign policy of this nationalism is the qualification of a generally accepted internationalist commitment with a stress on the primacy of Third World concerns evident in such concepts as Afro-Asianism and nonalignment, the acceptance of regionalist, pan-ethnic, pan-religious, or racial solidarity, and a preoccupation in practice and to some degree in doctrine with the defence of *national* autonomy and the pursuit of *national* interest.

The concern with autonomy and national self-expression appears also in the realm of theory-formulation. Third World writers by and large reject foreign models and stress heavily the importance of specific historical conditions in the development of nationally specific doctrines of revolution and socio-political development. Several themes recur in the adaptation of revolutionary theory to Third World conditions. There is a clearly voluntaristic tendency in much of the literature, combined with a concern to justify leadership by conscious intellectuals. Moreover, there is a pronounced stress on the maintenance of national unity and a subordination of the resolution of contradictions within the people to this unity. There also recurs among Third World radical nationalist writings a populist strain embodied in a stress on rural struggle and on the central role of the peasant in the national liberation revolution.[279]

Finally, reflecting the frustration experienced by many of these writers in the attempt to struggle peacefully for liberation, there is frequent emphasis on the necessity of armed struggle, particularly in the fight for national independence. Radical nationalists have often supplemented this argument from necessity with assertions that violence educates, mobilizes, and unifies the people, favours the emergence of effective leadership, and frees colonial populations from the debilitating psychological impact of Western domination.

With certain exceptions (for example, the arguments concerning the necessity and desirability of armed struggle), these recurring themes in the radical discussion of national liberation do not diverge dramatically from mainstream Third World nationalism. By contrast, as will become evident in the next two chapters, they set Third World theorization about national liberation apart from both Soviet and American treatments of political and social development in Asia, Africa, and Latin America.

## Notes

1. Sun Yat-sen, *San Min Chu-i*, Taipei, Taipei Publishing Company, 1963, p. 208.
2. Cf. E. Smith, *Turkey: The Origins of the Kemalist Movement and the Government of the Grand National Assembly (1919-1923)*, Washington, Judd and Detweiler, 1959, p. 155. See also Tekin Alp's advocacy of an economic revolution to accompany the political and social one. The purpose of this economic revolution was to prevent the subjugation of the Turkish state to foreign capital. He specifically rejected economic liberalism because, in his view, it would deliver the Turkish economy into the hands of foreigners. Tekin Alp, *Le Kemalisme*, Paris, Libraire Felix Alcan, 1937, pp. 196, 250.
3. J. Legge, *Sukarno: A Political Biography*, London, Allen Lane, 1972, p. 349.
4. Mao Tse-tung, 'The Struggle in the Chingkang Mountains' (1928), excerpt in S. Schram, *The Political Thought of Mao Tse-tung* (hereafter *PT*), NY, Praeger, 1969, p. 215.
5. *People's Daily*, as cited in *Peking Review* (hereafter *PR*) (1960), no. 29, p. 13. See also Chou En-lai, 'Report on the Results of [a] Visit to Africa' in *PR* (1964), no. 18, p. 8; Nan Han-chen, 'Speech to the Afro-Asian Economic Seminar', *PR* (1965), no. 10, p. 21; Hsu Nai-chiung, 'The Inter-relation between Political and Economic Independence', *PR* (1966), no. 5, pp. 12-13; Chiao Kuan-hua, 'Speech at the 26th Session of the UN General Assembly', *PR* (1971), no. 47, p. 8; and Teng Hsiao-ping, 'Speech at the UN Special Session', *PR* (1974), no. 15, pp. 2, 4.
6. Truong Chingh, 'The August Revolution' (1946) in Truong Chinh, *Primer for Revolt*, NY, Praeger, 1963, pp. 55, 57.
7. Cited in A. Mandouze, *La Revolution Algerienne par les Textes*, Paris, Maspero, 1961, p. 38. See also F. Fanon, 'Face to Face with the French Torturers' (1957) in F. Fanon, *Towards the African Revolution*, Harmondsworth, Penguin,

1970, p. 96.

8. G. Chaliand, *Revolution in the Third World*, NY, Viking, 1977, pp. 109-10.

9. Che Guevara, 'Speech at the United Nations' (1964) in J. Mallin, ed., *'Che' Guevara on Revolution*, Coral Gables, University of Miami Press, 1969, p. 19.

10. C. Blasier, *The Hovering Giant: US Responses to Revolutionary Change in Latin America*, Pittsburgh, University of Pittsburgh Press, 1976, pp. 183-9.

11. PAIGC, 'Major Programme' (n.d.) in R. Chilcote, ed., *Emerging Nationalism in the Portuguese Colonies*, Stanford, Hoover Institution Press, 1972, pp. 361, 363.

12. Cf. for example, A. Cabral, 'Presuppositions and Objectives of National Liberation in Relation to Social Structures' (1966 speech given at the Tricontinental in Havana) in A. Cabral, *Unity and Struggle*, London, Heinemann, 1980. p. 130; and A. Cabral, 'To Start from the Reality of Our Land — To be Realistic' (1969 seminar to party cadres) in ibid., p. 48.

13. M. Dos Santos,'Resistance and Struggle for Independence' (1962) in Chilcote, *Emerging Nationalism*, p. 496.

14. As cited in E. Alpers, 'The Struggle for Socialism in Mozambique' in C. Rosberg and T. Callaghy, eds., *Socialism in Sub-Saharan Africa: A New Assessment*, Berkeley, Institute of International Studies, 1979, p. 279.

15. E. Mondlane, 'The Movement for Freedom in Mozambique', *Presence Africaine* (1965), no. 53, p. 36. See also Eduardo Mondlane, *The Struggle for Mozambique*, Harmondsworth, Penguin, 1969, p. 82.

16. MPLA, 'Programme' (1962) in Chilcote, *Emerging Nationalism*, pp. 228, 229, 232.

17. A.Neto, 'Who Is the Enemy? What Is Our Objective?' (1974) in J. Marcum, *The Angolan Revolution*, Vol. 2, Cambridge, MIT Press, 1978, p. 310. See also MPLA Central Committee, 'Programme of Action' (1976) in *Documents of the MPLA Plenary*, London, Mozambique, Angola, Guine-Bissau Information Centre, 1976, p.30.

18. Cf. references to economic independence and self-reliance in SWAPO, 'Political Programme' (n.d.) in *Namibia: SWAPO Fights for Freedom*, Oakland, LSM Press, 1978, p. 98; ZANU, 'Mwenje No. 2: ZANU's Political Programme' (1972) in C.Nyangoni and G. Nyandoro, eds., *Zimbabwe Independence Movements, Select Documents*, London, Rex Collings, 1979, p. 257; and ANC, 'The Strategy and Tactics of the ANC' (n.d.) in *Forward to Freedom: Documents on the National Policies of the ANC of South Africa*, Dar Es Salaam, n.p., 1971 (?) p. 14.

19. C. Young, *Ideology and Development in Africa*, New Haven, Yale University Press, 1982, p. 10.

20. A. Bennigsen and E. Wimbush, *Muslim National Communism in the Soviet Union*, Chicago, University of Chicago Press, 1979, pp. 38, 39, 44. Sultan-Galiev and his colleagues differed from many later theorists of national liberation, as seen below, in arguing that social revolution had to be postponed well into the future, given the backwardness of Muslim Tartar society and the primacy in the prevailing conditions of national rather than social tasks.

21. M. Rodinson, *Marxism and the Muslim World*, NY, Monthly Review Press, 1981, pp. 225-9, 234-7. The Syrian-Lebanese Communist Party under Khalid Bakdash sustained this course through the 1940s. The Maghrebian communist parties, by contrast, were constrained in their embrace of national tasks by their close ties to the French Communist Party and by the latter's reluctance (reflecting that of the USSR) to support Algerian independence. In the Algerian case, the focus of 'proletarian nationalism' shifted to the Etoile Nord-Africaine, which in the late 1930s and 1940s advocated a similar mixture of national independence

and substantial social change, and subsequently to the FLN.

22. Tekin Alp, *Le Kemalisme*, pp. 1918. See also Smith, *Turkey*, pp. 20, 97.

23. Alp, *Le Kemalisme*, pp. 198. 200.

24. H. Schiffrin, *Sun Yat-sen and the Origins of the Chinese Revolution*, Los Angeles, University of California Press, 1970, p. 88.

25. Ibid., pp. 136-7; and Sun Yat-sen, *San Min Chu-i*, pp. 170, 177, 198.

26. A. Sukarno, 'Nationalism, Islam, and Marxism' (1926), Ithaca, Cornell Modern Indonesia Project, 1969, pp. 3, 5, 42. See also B. Dahm, *Sukarno and the Struggle for Indonesian Independence*, London, Cornell University Press, 1969, p. 55.

27. Mao Tse-tung, 'The Struggle in the Chingkang Mountains', p. 215.

28. Cf., for example, Mao Tse-tung, 'The Chinese Revolution and the CCP' (1940) in Schram, *PT*, p. 232.

29. On this point, see A. Dirlik, 'National Development and Social Revolution in Early Chinese Marxist Thought', *China Quarterly* (henceforward *CQ*) (1974), no. 58, p. 287.

30. Central Committee of the CCP, 'Resolutions of the Emergency Conference' (1927) in K. Brandt *et al.*, *A Documentary History of Chinese Communism*, Cambridge, Harvard University Press, 1952, p. 119. See also Central Committee of the CCP, 'Report of the 2nd Plenum of the Central Committee' (1929) in ibid., where it was asserted that 'the overthrow of imperialist rule and the thorough accomplishment of the agrarian revolution are inseparable tasks'.

31. Lin Yi-chou, 'The Peasant Question in the Democratic Revolution', *Red Flag* (1961), no. 3 in *PR* (1961), no. 13, p. 5. See also Lin Piao, *Long Live the Victory of People's War*, in *Peking Review* (1965), no. 36, pp. 10-11.

32. Cf., for example Truong Chinh, *The August Revolution* (1946), pp. 16, 44-5, 56, 57, 58; Ho Chi Minh, 'Report to the National Assembly' (1953) in B. Fall, ed., *Ho Chi Minh on Revolution: Selected Writings*, NY, Prqeger, 1967, pp. 264-5; Ho Chi Minh, 'The Path Which Led Me to Leninism' (1960) in ibid., pp. 6-7; Vo Nguyen Giap, *People's War, People's Army*, NY, Praeger, 1962, p. 22. Both Ho and Giap pointed out on numerous occasions that the point of the social revolution was not only the ending of exploitation, but the rupturing of the link between the landowning traditional elite and the French colonial regime. Moreover, they maintained that the expropriation of this elite would engender mass support for the struggle against imperialism. Both of these arguments were used to justify the initiation in 1953 of a radical land reform programme in areas controlled by the Viet Minh while the struggle against the French continued. Giap, *People's War, People's Army*, pp. 22, 27; Ho, 'Report to the National Assembly', pp. 264-5. On land reform by the Viet Cong in South Vietnam, see G. Chaliand, *Revolution in the Third World*, pp. 92, 93.

33. Truong Chinh, 'The August Revolution', p. 58.

34. FLN, 'Platform', as cited in Mandouze, *Revolution Algerienne*, p. 29; and in A. Horne, *A Savage War of Peace*, London, Macmillan, 1977, p. 15.

35. F. Abbas, *Guerre et Revolution d'Algerie*, Paris, Rene Julliard, 1962, p. 11. Fanon concurred, affirming that 'there is no anti-imperialist revolution in any colonial country that does not mean overthrowing capitalism at the same time'. In his view, independence without social revolution would only result in a different system of exploitation. Frantz Fanon, *Studies in a Dying Colonialism*, NY, Monthly Review Press, 1965, p. 18.

36. A. Ben Bella, 'On the Anniversary of the Algerian Revolution' (1963) in H. Sharabi, *Nationalism and Revolution in the Arab World*, NY, Van Nostrand, 1966, p. 115.

37. D. and M. Ottaway, *Afrocommunism*, NY, Africana, 1981, pp. 61. 63.

38. Cf. Che Guevara, 'To Create a Second, A Third Vietnam' (1967) in Mallin,

*Guevara on Revolution*, pp. 157, 159; R. Debray, Castroism: The Long March in Latin America' (1965) in R. Blackburn, ed., *Strategy for Revolution*, London, Jonathan Cape, 1970, pp. 75-7; and C. Marighela, *For the Liberation of Brazil*, Harmondsworth, Penguin, 1971, p. 38. Marighela, a dissident Brazilian communist, formed an urban guerrilla group in Sao Paulo in the late 1960s known as Action for National Liberation.
  39. For figures on nationalization and collectivization of Cuban economic activity, see J. Dominguez, *Cuba: Order and Revolution*, Cambridge, Harvard University Press, 1978, p. 202. For an account of the agrarian reform process, see ibid., pp. 435-63.
  40. Cf. A. Cabral, A Brief Analysis of Social Structure in Guine' (1964) in R. Handyside, Ed., *Revolution in Guine*, London, Stage 1, 1969, pp. 49, 52; A. Cabral, 'The Options of the CONCP' (1965) in Cabral, *Unity and Struggle*, p. 254; Cabral, 'Presuppositions and Objectives', pp. 130, 133; A. Cabral, 'Not Everyone Is of the Party' (1969) in Cabral, *Unity and Struggle*, p. 86.
  41. A. Cabral, 'Destroy the Economy of the Enemy and Build Our Own Economy' (1965) in Cabral, *Unity and Struggle*, p. 241.
  42. Cf. First National Conference of the MPLA, 'The MPLA in the Fight for the National Liberation of Angola' (1962); and 'The Programme of Action of the MPLA' (1962), both in Chilcote, *Emerging Nationalism*, pp. 254, 258-9; Neto, 'Who Is the Enemy?', pp. 309, 310, 316; A. Neto, 'Long Live the People's Republic of Angola' (1975) in Liberation Support Movement, *Road to Liberation*, Oakland, Liberation Support Movement Press, 1976, pp. 4; 6; Central Committee of the MPLA, 'Ideological Questions' (1976), in *Documents of the 1976 Plenary*, p. 6.
  43. Cf. the programme of the 2nd FRELIMO congress, cited in Alpers, 'The Struggle for Socialism in Mozambique', p. 287; Mondlane, *Struggle for Mozambique*, p. 219; S. Machel, 'Leadership is Collective, Responsibility is Collective' (1975) in S. Machel, *Sowing the Seeds of Revolution*, London, Committee for Freedom in Mozambique, Angola, and Gine-Bissau, 1975, p. 19; J. Slovo, 'Interview with Marcelino dos Santos', *African Communist* (1973), no. 55, pp. 48-9; FRELIMO, 'Economic and Social Directives', *People's Power* (1977), no. 7/8, pp. 30, 36.
  44. Cf. ANC, 'Strategy and Tactics', p. 14.
  45. ZANU, 'Political Programme', pp. 256, 257-9; Chitepo, 'Address to the 6th PanAfrican Congress', pp. 286-9; and R. Mugabe, 'Interview', *Tempo* (26 March and 2 July 1978) in Liberation Support Movement, *Zimbabwe: The Final Advance*, Oakland, LSM, 1978, p. 31.
  46. SWAPO, 'Political Programme', p. 99.
  47. In this context, Kenneth Jowitt recently remarked that: 'The recent adoption of Marxist-Leninist facades by Ethiopia, Angola, and Mozambique may be partially interpreted as survival efforts by regimes faced with the threat of political extinction from powerful opponents.' K. Jowitt, 'Scientific Socialist Regimes in Africa' in Rosberg and Callaghy, *Socialism in SubSaharan Africa*, p. 137.
  48. This demonstrates some awareness of the point made by Joel Migdal that 'peasant participation in complex political organizations is realized in return for material inducements that are offered to individuals seeking to solve their economic crises'. Migdal, *Peasants, Politics and Revolutions*, pp. 21, 228-40.
  49. Smith, *Origins of the Kemalist Movement*, pp. 99, 102.
  50. A. Sukarno, *Indonesia Accuses* (1930), Kuala Lumpur, Oxford University Press, 1975, p. 51.
  51. Ibid., pp. 91, 92. See also Legge, *Sukarno*, p. 351; and D. Weatherbee, *Ideology in Indonesia*, New Haven, Yale South East Asian Studies Programme,

1966, p. 26.

52. On Li Ta-chao's voluntarism, see M. Meisner, *Li Ta-chao and the Foundations of Chinese Marxism*, NY, Atheneum, 1977, pp. 93, 112, 135, 147-9. Stuart Schram has argued that Mao's work also displays a persistent voluntarism. Schram, *PT*, p. p. 135.

53. Mao Tse-tung, 'On New Democracy' (1940) in *Selected Works*, Vol. 2, Peking, Foreign Languages Publishing House, pp. 340-1.

54. Cf., for example, *People's Daily*, 'Root out the Imperialist Forces in Africa', *PR* (1966), no. 17, p. 26, where it is asserted that 'the task confronting the African countries which have gained independence is to eradicate thoroughly all imperialist, colonialist, and neo-colonialist influences in the political, economic, military, and *cultural* spheres . . . Only by doing so can complete independence be won.' See also Chen I. 'Speech to the Afro-Asian Journalists' Association Emergency Meeting', *PR* (1966), no. 27, p. 34.

55. As cited in *PR* (1965), no. 45, p. 28. One wonders whether Marx's concept of the Asiatic mode of production and his assessment of the contributions of colonialism fall into Liu's category of Eurocentric falsification.

56. Mao Tse-tung, 'On the New Stage' (1938), excerpt in Schram, *PT*, pp. 171-3.

57. Ho Chi Minh, 'Political Report at the 2nd National Congress of the VNWP' (1951) in Fall, *Ho Chi Minh on Revolution*, p. 224. See also Truong Ching, 'The August Revolution', p. 74, where he calls for a cultural revolution to accompany the political and economic revolution and to achieve the reformation of thought and customs. See also ibid., pp. 133-4, where he specifies that this cultural revolution involves the 'wiping out' of the 'cowardly and parasitic ways of the French time' and the 'smashing' of the 'moral and intellectual fetters used by the French colonialists'.

58. Ho, 'Political Report', p. 224.

59. Truong Chinh, 'The August Revolution', p. 55. See also p. 136, where he calls for the elimination of all that is contrary to 'national, scientific, and popular principles'.

60. F. Fanon, 'Racism and Culture' (1956) in Fanon, *Toward the African Revolution*, pp. 44-5.

61. Cf., for example, Ferhat Abbas, cited in Mandouze, *Revolution Algerienne*, p. 25.

62. As Fanon put it, 'the thing which has been colonized becomes man during the same process by which it liberates itself'. F. Fanon, *The Wreteched of the Earth*, Harmondsworth, Penguin, 1967, p. 28.

63. Fanon, *Toward the African Revolution*, p. 114.

64. Cf. Fanon's argument with respect to the emancipation of slaves, summarized in I. Gendzier, *Frantz Fanon: A Critical Study*, London, Wildwood, 1973, pp. 27, 150.

65. Cf., for example, Mondlane, *The Struggle for Mozambique*, p. 59.

66. Neto. 'Who Is the Enemy?', p. 314. See also A. Cabral, 'The Facts about Portugal's African Colonies' (1960) in Cabral, *Unity and Struggle*, p. 27; and A. Cabral, 'National Liberation and Culture' (1970) in ibid., pp. 141-3.

67. 'Interview with E. Katjivena' (SWAPO representative in Algiers), *Namibia News*, II (1970), nos. 7-12, p. 10.

68. MPLA, 'Declaration' (1976) in *People's Power* (1976), no. 5, p. 18.

69. Cf. B. Davidson, *In the Eye of the Storm: Angola's People*, NY, Anchor, 1973, pp. 16-17; G; Chaliand, *Armed Struggle in Africa*, NY, Monthly Review Press, 1969, pp. 26, 63, 93, 94; A. Humbaraci and N. Muchnik, *Portugal's African Wars*, London, Macmillan, 1974. pp. 138, 152. See also D. Martin and P. Johnson, *The Struggle for Zimbabwe*, NY, Monthly Review Press, 1981, p. 82.

In some cases, however, movements used traditional beliefs in order to gain legitimacy in the eyes of the rural populaton. See, for example, the discussion of ZANU's use of spirit mediums in ibid., pp. 75-8.

70. Cabral, 'National Liberation and Culture', pp. 145, 147.

71. FRELIMO, 'Education Policy in the People's Republic of Mozambique' (1976), *People's Power* (1976), no. 3, p. 15; S. Machel, 'Educate Man to Win the War, Create a New Man, and Develop Our Country' (1970) in Machel, *Sowing the Seeds of Revolution*, p. 39.

72. It is appropriate to note here that this nationally specific cultural dimension is far less evident in the doctrinal statements (though not in the policy) of Latin American movements than elsewhere despite the anti-Americanism prevalent in this region. This may be explained in terms of the different historical circumstances from which the Latin American movements emerged. Spanish colonialism succeeded in large measure in imposing its culture in Latin America through settlement and the extermination of the indigenous population. The elites of these societies, since independence, have been drawn not from the Indian population (where it remains), but from white Spanish and Portuguese, and, later, Italian, German, and Anglo-Saxon settler stock. This applies not only to the oligarchies which have frequently been the targets of struggles for liberation, but to the leading cadres of the liberation movements themselves. As such, there is not among them the same sense of humiliation and inferiority, nor the same heritage of valued and violated tradition which catalyse the commitment to cultural liberation. However, both secular guerrillas and theologians of liberation in Latin America have placed considerable stress on the subjective component of liberation. In the latter case, Gustavo Gutierrez, for example, saw liberation as in part 'the creation of a new man' who 'assumed conscious responsibility for his own destiny', who '[made] himself throughout life and throughout history' (G. Gutierrez, *A Theology of Liberation*, Maryknoll, NY: Orbis, 1973, pp. 36-7).

73. Barrington Moore goes further in maintaining that for twentieth-century anti-colonial revolutions, 'throwing off the colonial yoke' is a means to the establishment of a 'new form of society with substantial socialist elements' (Moore, *Social Origins of Dictatorship and Democracy*, p. 113).

74. Cf., for example, J. Nehru, *A Discovery of India*, London, Meridian, 1951, pp. 273, 277, 357; and J. Nehru, *An Autobiography*, London, The Bodley Head, 1953, p. 434.

75. Cf., Sekou Toure, *Experience Guineene et Unite Africaine*, Paris, Presence Africaine, 1959, p. 337; Sekou Toure, *The Doctrine and Methods of the P.D.G.*, Conakry, 1963, p. 5; Tom Mboya, *Freedom and After*, London, Andre Deutsch, 1963, pp. 178, 192; J. Nyerere, 'Economic Nationalism' (1967) in J. Nyerere, *Freedom and Socialism: Uhuru na Ujamaa*, London, Oxford University Press, 1968, pp. 262-6; and J. Nyerere, 'Speech at the University of Ibadan' (1977) in *African Currents* (1977) no. 8, pp. 3, 4; K. Nkrumah, *I Speak of Freedom*, London, Heinemann, 1961, pp. 134, 153; and C. Legum, *Pan-Africanism: A Short Political Guide*, London, Pall Mall, 1962, pp. 214, 229, 238, 254.

76. Cf. United Nations General Assembly, 'Charter of Economic Rights and Duties of States' (Resolution 3281-XXIX); and 'Declaration on the Establishment of a New International Economic Order' (Resolution 3201-S-VI). Both as reproduced in *United Nations Yearbook* XXVIII (1974), pp. 324-6 and 403-7.

77. Nehru, *Discovery of India*, pp. 269, 329, 339, 346-7, 371, 384. Gandhi's populism displays similar concerns. He combined an advocacy of a return to traditional village life with a stress on economic equality and calls for a redistribution of resources in favour of the poor (cf. Mahatma Gandhi, *All Men Are*

*Brothers*, Paris, UNESCO, 1958, pp. 129, 131, 135).

78. Nehru, 'Whither India?' (1933) in J.Nehru, *India and the World*, London, George Allen and Unwin, 1936, pp. 44, 57, 59, 60, 62, 63; and J. Nehru, 'Presidential Address to the National Congress' (1936), in bidi., p. 80.

79. G.A. Nasser, *The Philosophy of the Revolution*, Cairo, Dar-al-Maaref, 1954, pp. 23, 24, 26.

80. Rodinson, *Marxism and the Muslim World*, pp. 216, 229, 244, 247.

81. Cf., for example, K. Nkrumah, 'The Circle' (1945) in E. Kedourie, *Nationalism and Nationalist Movements in Asia and Africa*, NY, New American Library, 1970, p. 391; K. Nkrumah, *Africa Must Unite*, London, Heinemann, 1963, pp. 118-21;K. Nkrumah, *Consciencism*, London, Heinemann, 1964, pp. 68, 74, 98; K. Nkrumah, *A Handbook of Revolutionary Warfare*, NY, International Publishers, 1968, p. 24; S. Toure, *Guinean Revolution and Social Progress*, Cairo, SOP Press, n.d., pp. 18, 114, 322, 361-2; Toure, *Doctrine and Methods*, p. 26; J. Nyerere, 'Ujamaa – The Basis of African Socialism' (1962) in J.Nyerere, *Freedom and Unity: Uhuru na Umoja*, London, Oxford University Press, 1967, pp. 162, 171; J. Nyerere, 'The Arusha Declaration' (1967) in Nyerere, *Freedom and Socialism*, pp. 231-5; Nyerere, 'Speech in Ibadan', p. 4; N. Sithole, *African Nationalism*, London, Oxford University Press, 1968, pp. 173-4, 185, 189-96.

82. G. Gutierrez, *A Theology of Liberation*, p. 36. For the 'Document on Justice' (1968), see J. Gremillion, ed., *The Gospel of Peace and Justice*, Maryknoll, NY, 1976, particularly pp. 455-7, and the excerpt reproduced in D. D. McCann, *Christian Realism and Liberation Theology*, Maryknoll, NY, 1981, p. 131.

83. Nehru, *Discovery of India*, p. 40. For a similar earlier Indian analysis, see Dipin Chandra Pal, 'Hinduism and Indian Nationalism' (1910) in Kedourie, *Nationalism in Asia and Africa*, p. 349.

84. Rodinson, *Marxism and the Muslim World*, p. 26.1. See also H. Sharabi, *Arab Intellectuals and the West: The Formative Years, 1875-1914*, Baltimore, Johns Hopkins Press, 1970, p. 135.

85. M. Garvey, 'The Resurrection of the Negro' (1922)in A.J. Garvey, ed., *The Philosophy and Opinions of Marcus Garvey*, London, Frank Cass, 1967, p. 67.

86. L. Senghor, 'L'Esprit de la Civilisation ou les Lois de la Culture Negro-Africaine', *Presence Africaine* (1956), nos. 8, 9, 10, p. 51; and L. Senghor, 'Negritde and the Concept of Universal Civilization', *Presence Africaine* (1959), no. 24, 25, pp. 105-6.

87. Toure, *Experience Guineene*, p. 253; Toure, L'Action *Politique du P.D.G.*, pp. 209, 211-12; Toure, *Guinean Revolution and Social Progress*, pp. 114-15; S. Toure, 'Le Leader Politique Considere comme le Representant d'une Culture', *Presence Africaine* (1959), nos. 24, 25, pp. 105-6.

88. Cf. Steve Biko, *Black Consciousness in South Africa* (M. Arnold, ed.), NY, Vintage, 1979, pp. xiv, xvii-xviii, xx, xxv, 22-3, 33; and G. Carter, *Which Way Is South Africa Going?*, Bloomington, Indiana University Press, 1980, pp. 54, 55, 57-8.

89. Some qualification is necessary here for doctrines of Islamic liberation, which are, in a number of respects, rooted in a theoretical tradition indigenous to the Third World, although such writers as Ali Shari'ati, to judge from their work, were profoundly influenced by trends in Western thought.

90. On this theme, see Kedourie, *Nationalism in Asia and Africa*, p. 35.

91. As Rupert Emerson put it, '19th century liberalism and laissez-faire capitalism have given way as the dominant creed to planning, social welfare, and collective controls, all of which expand the range of the nation-state and make it indispensable to its members'. R. Emerson, *From Empire to Nation*, Cambridge, Harvard University Press, 1962, p. 385.

92. This is not to say that all such groups mounted a steady critique of colonialism. The vacillations of the various metropolitan communist parties, for example, dictated largely by the exigencies of Soviet foreign policy (cf. Chapter 5), are a case in point. However, many luminaries of left-wing politics in the metropolitan countries (for example, Jean-Paul Sartre in France and Fenner Brockway in the UK) were quite consistently supportive of anti-colonial nationalism and vociferous in their condemnation of the institutions of empire. They were joined in specific periods (1923-7, 1928-35, 1939-41, and post-1953, the latter period excepting the French Communist Party) by the metropolitan communist parties.

93. Jowitt, 'Scientific Socialism', p. 136.

94. On the role of the Bolshevik Revolution in directing radical Chinese nationalists towards socialism and communism, see S. Schram, *Mao Tse-tung*, Harmondsworth, Penguin, 1977, pp. 47-8; and M. Meisner, *Li Ta-chao and the Foundations of Chinese Marxism*, p. 66.

95. Nehru, for example, notes his own attraction to the Soviet experience in the late 1920s in *An Autobiography*, pp. 166, 362.

96. A. Ulam, *Expansion and Coexistence*, NY, Praeger, 1974, pp. 132-3.

97. Cf. R. Kanet, 'The Comintern and the "Negro Question": Communist Policy in the US and Africa, 1921-1941', *Survey* XIX (1973), no. 4, for an account of the 'Negro International' and its activities.

98. Cf., for example, Lucio Lara's (a leading MPLA ideologue) emphasis on the importance of Vietnamese theory and practice in the definition of MPLA doctrine, cited in Young, *Ideology and Development*, p. 85. K. Brown ('Angolan Socialism' in Rosberg and Callaghy, *African Socialism*, pp. 301-3) notes in addition to the Vietnamese influence on the MPLA, that of Amilcar Cabral and Castro's Cuba. See also Alpers' comments on the influence of the Algerian struggle on Marcelino Dos Santos ('The Struggle for Socialism in Mozambique', p. 269).

99. Cabral, 'Independence of Thought and Action' (1969) in Cabral, *Unity and Struggle*, p. 80.

100. Hans Kohn focused on this political aspect in his definition of colonialism as a relationship in which 'one nation establishes and maintains political domination over a geographically external political unit inhabited by people of any race at any stage of cultural development'. H. Kohn, 'Reflections on Colonialism' in R. Strausz-Hupe and H. Hazard, *The Idea of Colonialism*, NY, Praeger, 1958, p. 4.

101. It is not being argued here that this economic aspect of colonial expansion always and necessarily took forms as extreme as these. Nor does this discussion of the economic aspect of colonialism constitute an acceptance of economic explanations for colonialism as a world historical phenomenon. What is being argued here is that practices perceived to be exploitative were sufficiently widespread for such explanations to be appealing to new Third World elites and for economic independence to be perceived as an essential aspect of national liberation.

102. Jowitt, 'Scientific Socialism', pp. 140-1.

103. For examples, see Kedourie, *Nationalism in Asia and Africa*, pp. 81-99.

104. As Roy put it:

To determine more especially the relations of the Communist International to the revolutionary movements in the countries dominated by capitalist imperialism, for instance, in China and India, is one of the most important questions before the 2nd Congress of the Third International. The history of the world revolution has come to a period when a proper understanding of this relation is indispensable. The Great European War and its result have shown that the masses of the non-European subjected countries are inseparably connected with the proletarian movement in Europe. (As reprinted in ibid., p. 547)

105. For excerpts, see ibid., pp. 562-9.
106. Meisner, *Li Ta-chao*, pp. 144-5, 191, and *passim*.
107. Cf., for example, his interview with Edgar Snow in the mid-1930s, as recounted in E. Snow, *Red Star over China*, Harmondsworth, Penguin, 1977, p. 439. See also Mao Tse-tung, 'On New Democracy', pp. 343, 346; and Mao Tse-tung, 'The Chinese Revolution and the CCP', p. 230.
108. Ho Chi Minh, 'Appeal Made on the Occasion of the Founding of the Communist Part of Indochina' (1930) in Fall, *Ho Chi Minh*, p. 127.
109. Che Guevara, 'To Create a Second, A Third Vietnam' (1967) in Mallin, *Guevara on Revolution*, pp. 159-61.
110. R. Bedeski, 'The Tutelary State and National Revolution in KMT Ideology', *CQ* (1971), no. 46, pp. 327-8.
111. D. Weatherbee, *Ideology in Indonesia*, pp. 25. 27.
112. As cited in Mandouze, *Revolution Algerienne*, pp. 54, 60.
113. F. Fanon, 'The Algerian War and Man's Liberation' in Fanon, *Towards the African Revolution*, p. 154. See also Gendzier, *Fanon*, p. 225.
114. A. Cabral, 'The Death Pangs of Imperialism' (1961) in Chilcote, *Emerging Nationalism*, pp. 301-3; and Cabral, 'Options of the CONCP', p. 253. See also FRELIMO's 1968 programme, as cited in Alpers, 'The Struggle for Socialism in Mozambique', p. 287.
115. Nehru, 'Whither India?', pp. 57, 60; Nehru, *Autobiography*, p. 161.
116. Toure, *Doctrine and Methods*, p. 44.
117. See note 47.
118. Sun Yat-sen, *San Min Chu-i*, pp. 2, 5. See also Schriffin, *Sun Yat-sen*, pp. 44, 50, 88, 212.
119. Sun Yat-sen, *San Min Chu-i*, pp. 16, 17, 20, 25. An analogous unreserved embrace of the national ideal is evident in the writings of Ziya Gokalp, the Turkish nationalist ideologue, who maintained that 'a land that is not the home of a nation is like a public garden where everyone merely feeds oneself'. Ziya Gokalp, 'The Ideal of Nationalism', as excerpted in Kedourie, *Nationalism*, p. 201.
120. Sukarno, 'Nationalism, Islam, and Marxism', p. 39.
121. For example, Teng Hsiao-ping's 1957 diatribe:

Bourgeois nationalism is an expression of the bourgeois world outlook. Starting from the selfish interest of the exploiting class, the bourgeoisie either places its own nation above others under the banner of big nation chauvinism in order to achieve the aim of oppressing and exploiting the other nations; or pits its own nation against the course of human progress by spreading the ideology of narrow nationalism . . . The imperialists and reactionaries have always exploited national sentiments to spread the virus of bourgeois nationalism as an important means of undermining the cause of the proletarian revolution and disrupting the unity of the various nations of the world.

Teng Hsiao-ping, 'The Great Unity of the Chinese People and the Great Unity of the Peoples of the World', *Peking Review* (1959), no. 39, p. 19. It is germane to note that the article was written for *Pravda*.
122. Ho Chi Minh, 'Political Report', p. 223.
123. Gendzier, *Fanon*, pp. 225-6.

124. R. Debray, 'Problems of Revolutionary Strategy in Latin America' (1965) in Blackburn, *Strategy for Revolution*, p. 122.

125. Slovo, 'Interview with Dos Santos', p. 44.

126. Nehru, 'Whither India?', p. 61.

127. Cf. Toure, *Experience Guineene*, p. 236; G. Padmore, *Panafricanism or Communism?*, London, Dennis Dobson, 1956, pp. 152, 340; J. Nyerere, 'African Unity', *Presence Africaine* (1961), no. 39, p. 12.

128. Cf., for example, Central Committee of the MPLA, ' Report to the 1st Congress' (1977) London, Mozambique, Angola, Guine-Bissau Information Centre, 1977, pp. 25-6; FRELIMO, 'Economic and Social Directives', p. 36, where the leading role of the USSR and the socialist camp in the world revolutionary process is acknowledged. Such statements appear in the literature of these movements only in the aftermath of independence, when both have had to depend to a great degree on Eastern bloc military, economic, and technical assistance.

129. M.N. Roy, 'Supplementary Theses' (1920-unamended), as reprinted in H. Carrere d'Encausse and S. Schram, *Marxism and Asia*, London, Allen Lane, 1969, p. 160. This was softened at (Lenin's insistence) by the 2nd Comintern Congress to: 'Without the control of the extensive market and vast fields of exploitation in the colonies, the capitalist powers of Europe cannot maintain their existence even for a short time.' As reprinted in Kedourie, *Nationalism in Asia and Africa*, p. 547.

130. As cited in Carrere d'Encausse and Schram, *Marxism and Asia*, p. 94.

131. Mir Said Sultan-Galiev, 'Social Revolution and the East' (1919) in Kedourie, *Nationalism in Asia and Africa*, p. 566.

132. Meisner, *Li Ta-chao, passim*, and in particular pp. 59, 65, 67, 126, 188. See also Li Ta-chao, 'Marx's Point of View on the Chinese Revolution' (1926) in Carrere d'Encausse and Schram, *Marxism and Asia*, p. 224. For Mao's later assertions on the advantages of backwardness, see Mao Tse-tung, 'On the Ten Great Relationships' (1956), and 'Speech at the Surpeme State Conference' (1958), both in S. Schram, *Mao Tse-tung Unrehearsed*, Harmondsworth, Penguin, 1979, pp. 83, 92; and J. Gittings, 'New Light on Mao — His View of the World', *China Quarterly* (1974), no. 60, p. 762. One might also cite in this context Li Li-san's 1930 'Resolution on Present Political Tasks' in Brandt, *et al., Documentary History*, p. 185.

133. Cf. Mao's 'Interview with Anna Louise Strong' (1946) in *Selected Works*, Vol. 3, pp. 99-100. See also Liu Ting-i (later a prominent spokesman on Third World issues), as quoted in Y. Schichor, *The Middle East in China's Foreign Policy 1949-1977*, London, Cambridge University Press, 1979, p. 12; and J. Gittings, *The World and China, 1922-1972*, London, Eyre Methuen, 1974, p. 219.

134. Liu Shao-ch'i, 'Speech to the WFTU' (1949) in Carrere d'Encausse and Schram, *Marxism and Asia*, p. 270.

135. 'Long Live Leninism', *Red Flag* in *PR* (1960), no. 17, p. 32.

136. Yu Chao-li, 'Excellent Situation for the Struggle for Peace', *Red Flag* in *PR* (1960), no. 1, p. 16; and Yu Chao-li, 'Imperialism — the Source of War in Modern Times', *Red Flag*, in *PR* (1960), no. 15, pp. 22, 23. For the link between Yu Chao-li and Mao Tse-tung, see Gittings, *China and the World*, p. 219.

137. Cf. *Red Flag*, 'More on the Differences between Comrade Togliatti and Us' in *PR* (1963), nos. 10 and 11, p. 19.

138. Peng Ch'en, 'Speech at the Aliarcham Academy' in *PR* (1965), no. 24, p. 12.

139. Lin Piao, 'Long Live the Victory of People's War', pp. 24-6.

140. Shih Chun, 'Again on Studying World History', *PR* (1972), no. 45, p. 12; Teng Hsiao-ping, 'Speech at the UN Special Session', *passim*.

141. More recently, however, China seems to have shifted back to the Third World focus characteristic of earlier doctrine and foreign policy. This presumably reflects a certain disillusionment with the results of China's opening to the West in the mid-1970s, and, in particular, unhappiness with the present American position on Taiwan. See C. Hamrin, 'China Reassesses the Superpowers', *Pacific Affairs* LVI (1983), no. 2,pp. 209-31.

142. And, more specifically, to the Indochinese war. Guevara, 'To Create a Second, A Third Vietnam', p. 151.

143. A. Sukarno, 'Speech' (1961) in *Conferences of Heads of State of the Nonaligned Countries*, Belgrade, n.p., 1961.

144. Fanon, *Wretched of the Earth*, p. 83.

145. Cf., for example, Cabral, 'The Death Pangs of Imperialism', in Chilcote, *Emerging Nationalism*, pp. 301, 303.

146. H. Chitepo, 'Address to the 6th PanAfrican Congress', p. 288.

147. Sukarno, *Indonesia Accuses*, p. 780; Padmore, *Panafricanism*, p. 95.

148. H. Mast, 'Revolution out of Tradition: The Political Ideology of Tai Chi-t'ao', *Journal of Asian Studies* XXVIII (1974), no. 1, p. 85; A Bennigsen and C. Quelqujay, *Le Sultan-galievisme au Tatarstan*, Paris, Mouton, 1960, p. 133.

149. As cited in 'Our Future', *Presence Africaine* (1960-1961), no. 37, p. 6. It is significant that the remark was cited with approval by the editors of a journal that was a leading forum for African intellectuals. See also J. Nyerere, 'Policy on Foreign Affairs' (1967) in Nyerere, *Freedom and Socialism*, pp. 368-9.

150. Sukarno, 'Nationalism, Islam, and Marxism', p. 39.

151. Ho Chi Minh, 'Political Report', p. 223.

152. Debray, 'Castroism', pp. 75-8.

153. Slovo, 'Interview with Dos Santos', p. 44.

154. Mao Tse-tung, 'Mobilzation of All the Nation's Forces' (1937), *Selected Works*, Vol. 2, p. 24; Mao Tse-tung, 'On New Democracy', p. 380.

155. C. Dorris, 'Peasant Mobilization in North China: Origins of Yenan Communism', *China Quarterly* (1976), no. 68, p. 719. See also C. Johnson, *Peasant Mobilization and Communist Power*, Stanford, Stanford University Press, 1962, pp. viii-xi, 4-5, 11, 72, 184 for the importance of nationalist appeals in Chinese communist mobilization of the rural population.

156. Sun Yat-sen, *San Min Chu-i*, pp. 2, 5; See also Sukarno, *Indonesia Accuses*, pp. 78, 83, 86.

157. R. Debray, 'Marxism and the National Question', *New Left Review* (1977), no. 105, pp. 33-5.

158. For example, Slovo, 'Interview with Dos Santos', pp. 43-4.

159. Nehru, *Autobiography*, pp. 365, 383; Nehru, *Discovery of India*, p. 36; Sukarno, *Indonesia Accuses*, pp. 78, 83, 86; Gendzier, *Fanon*, pp. 226, 229; Debray, 'Marxism and the National Question', p. 38.

160. Khrushchev quotes Mao's reaction to this request in his memoirs: 'We don't want them here. We've had the British and other foreigners on our territory for years now, and we're not ever going to let anyone use our land for their own purposes again.' N. Khrushchev, *Khrushchev Remembers*, Harmondsworth, Penguin, 1977, p. 503.

161. Schram, *Political Thought*, pp. 42, 135; Gittings, *The World and China*, p. 27.

162. Fall (*Ho Chi Minh*, pp. viii-x) points to the evidence of Ho's nationalism in the latter's choice of pseudonym,s (Nguyen O Phap meaning Nguyen who hates the French and Nguyen Ai Quoc meaning Nguyen who loves his country).

163. Cf. Brown, 'Angolan Socialism', p. 313; and J. Marcum, 'Angola' in
G. Carter and P. O'meara, eds., *Southern Africa: The Continuing Crisis*, Bloomington, Indiana University Press, 1980, pp. 193-4.

164. Cabral, in a discussion of the PAIGC's view of African unity, clearly
suggested such a hierarchy of priorities in asserting that:

> We are ready to unite with any African people, *with only one conditon*
> (author's emphasis), that the conquests, the gains of our people in the national
> liberation struggle, the economic and social gains, the gains of justice that we
> pursue . . . that none of this should be compromised by unities with other
> peoples . . . We are struggling in the first place for our peoples.

In Cabral, 'Options of the CONCP', pp.254-5.

165. Mao Tse-tung, 'Resolution of 5.x.28' in Schram, *PT*, p. 267.

166. Mao Tse-tung, 'Strategic Problems of China's Revolutionary War',
Schram, *PT*, pp. 276-9.

167. Mao Tse-tung, 'On Practice' (1937) in ibid., p. 194. See R. Wylie, 'Mao
Tse-tung, Ch'en Po-ta, and the "Sinification of Marxism", 1936-1938', *CQ*
(1979), no. 79, pp. 454-6.

168. Mao Tse-tung, 'On the New Stage' (1938) in Schram, *Political Thought*,
pp. 171-3.

169. Cf., for example, Mao Tse-tung, 'On New Democracy', p. 381; and Liu
Shao-ch'i, 'Report to the 7th Congress' (1945) in Carrere d'Encausse and
Schram, *Marxism and Asia*, pp. 251-2. Somewhat paradoxically, this coincided
with an escalation of Chinese claims that Mao's 'new democracy' constituted a
model applicable throughout the colonial and semi-colonial world. Cf S. Goldstein,
'The Chinese Revolution and the Colonial Areas: The View from Yenan', *CQ*,
(1978), no. 75, pp. 602-11; and Liu Shao-ch'i, 'Speech to the WFTU', pp. 271-2.

170. Mao Tse-tung, as cited in *PT*, pp. 82-3; Chou En-lai, 'Report to the
Chinese People's Consultative Conference' (1957) in Carrere d'Encausse and
Schram, *Marxism and Asia*, p. 297; and Mao Tse-tung, 'Speech to the Supreme
State Conference' (1958) in Schram, *Mao Unrehearsed*, pp. 91-5.

171. Mao Tse-tung, 'Talk to Music Workers' (1956) in ibid., p. 84; and
*People's Daily*, 'Give Full Play to the Revolutionary Spirit of the 1957 Moscow
Declaration' (1960) in *PR* (1960), no. 48, p. 8.

172. Mao Tse-tung, 'Speech at the Group Leaders' Forum of the Enlarged
Meeting of the Military Affairs Committee' (1958) in Schram, *Mao Unrehearsed*,
p. 129; and Gittings, 'New Light on Mao', p. 763.

173. Cf., for example, Lin Piao, 'Long Live the Victory of People's War',
pp. 23-5.

174. Cf. *Red Flag, People's Daily, Liberation Daily*, 'Long Live the Dictatorship of the Proletariat', *PR* (1971), no. 12, pp. 8-9.

175. Ho. Chi Minh, 'Political Report', p. 207; and 'Speech Opening the First
Theoretical Course of the Nguyen ai Quoc Party School' (1957) in Fall, *Ho Chi
Minh*, pp. 319, 31; See also Vo Nguyen Giap, 'People's War, People's Army',
pp. 41b, 41c, 63, 127. Truong Chinh also dwelt at length on the specifics of the
Vietnamese revolutionary war and the need to take account of them in the
development of strategy in 'The Resistance Will Win' (1947), in *Primer for
Revolt*, pp. 139-45.

176. Guevara, 'To Create a Second, A Third Vietnam', p. 154. Elsewhere, he
underlined the importance of conditions peculiar to colonial and semi-colonial
societies in the elaboration of a theory of revolution specific to the Third World.
Che Guevara, 'Prologue to *People's War, People's Army*' (1964) in Mallin,
*Guevara on Revolution*, pp. 105. 109.

177. Debray, 'Problems of Revolutionary Strategy', p. 128; R.Debray, *Revolution in the Revolution?*, NY, Monthly Review Press, 1967, pp. 21, 23, 60, 61, 64, 67; Debray, 'Castroism', p. 74.

178. S. Machel, 'Sowing the Seeds of Revolution' (1971) in Machel, *Sowing the Seeds*, p. 59.

179. Neto, 'Who Is the Enemy?', p. 311.

180. Central Committee of the MPLA, 'Report to the 1st Congress', p. 27.

181. Brown, 'Angolan Socialism', p. 299.

182. In this vein, Jowitt ('Scientific Socialism', p. 139) suggests that the selectivity of those in Africa espousing 'scientific socialism' *vis-à-vis* the content of marxism-leninism reflects a concern to maintain distance from the 'powerful and prestigious regimes they in some cases identify with'.

183. Sun Yat-sen, *San Min Chu-i*, pp. 160-4, 172. He did accept, however, that it was important to take into account the revolutionary experience of other countries. Sun Yat-sen, *A Programme of National Reconstruction for China*, London, Hutchinson, 1927. p. 120.

184. Weatherbee, *Ideology in Indonesia*, p. 24; Legge, *Sukarno*, p. 283. Sutan Sjahrir, a rival Indonesian nationalist, prefigured Debray in emphasizing practice as a source of theory rather than the inverse, theory being 'not absolute, but quite relative'. Sutan Sjahrir, *Out of Exile*, NY, John Day, 1949, pp. 37, 90.

185. Horne, *Savage War of Peace*, p. 133.

186. FLN, 'Programme' (1964) in Sharabi, *Nationalism and Revolution in the Arab World*, p. 122.

187. Fanon, *Wretched of the Earth*, p. 78; and 'Face to Face with the French Torturers', p. 75.

188. A. Cabral, 'To Start from the Reality of Our Land, To Be Specific' (1969) in Cabral, *Unity and Struggle*, pp. 45-51; and 'Presuppositions and Objectives', p. 122.

189. P. Chabal, 'The Social and Political Thought of Amilcar Cabral: A Reassessment', *Journal of Modern African Studies* XIX (1981), no. 1, p. 31. Nelson Mandela, the imprisoned leader of South Africa's ANC, in 1964 maintained analogously that the ANC was not a marxist movement and advocated an eclectic and practical approach in the development of theory. N. Mandela, 'Speech at the Rivonia Trial' (1964) in M. Benson, ed., *The Sun Will Rise*, London, IDAFSA, 1981, p. 20.

190. ANC, *Excerpts from Policy and Programme*, Dar Es Salaam, n.p., 1965, p. 4. See also ANC, *ANC – South Africa: A Short History*, London, ANC, 1971, p. 13. where it is stated that: 'Historical experience has clearly demonstrated that any struggle, whether violent or non-violent, will end in failure if it does not conform to objective and concrete conditions in the country in which it is fought.' That said, as the USSR and the South African Communist Party consolidated their positions of influence with the ANC in the early and mid-1970s, ANC doctrinal pronouncements came to approximate more closely the 'scientific socialist' position on Third World revolution. Whether this trend will survive the resurgence of black nationalism within the movement in the late 1970s and early 1980s remains to be seen.

191. Nehru, 'Presidential Address', p. 82.

192. Nehru, *Discovery Of India*, p. 16.

193. Nehru, *Autobiography*, pp. 362, 407.

194. E. Blyden, 'The Idea of an African Personality' (1881) in Legum, *Panafricanism*, p. 264.

195. Toure, *Guinean Revolution and Social Progress*, pp. 108, 111. See also L. Adamolekun, 'The Socialist Experience in Guinea' in Rosberg and Callaghy, *African Socialism*, p. 63.

196. Ibid., pp. 64-5.

197. Padmore, *Panafricanism*, p. 345.

198. Ibid., p. 342.

199. Nyerere, 'Ujamaa Is African Socialism', pp. 546, 547.

200. Cf. J. Slovo, 'Interview with Lucio Lara', *African Communist* (1978), no. 74, p. 65.

201. Brown, 'Angolan Socialism', pp. 299, 304.

202. Subandrio, cited in Weatherbee, *Ideology in Indonesia*, p. 29.

203. Meisner, *Li Ta-chao*, pp. 147-9.

204. Cf. B. Schwartz, *Chinese Communism and the Rise of Mao*, Cambridge, Harvard Univesity Press, 1952, p. 167; and B. Schwartz, *Communism and China: Ideology in Flux*, Cambridge, Harvard University Press, 1968, pp. 16, 20.

205. Che Guevara, 'Socialism and Man In Cuba' (1967) in Mallin. *Guevara on Revolution*, p. 129

206. For example, F. Castro, 'Speech at Pinar del Rio' (1976) in F. Castro, *Cuba's Internationalist Foreign Policy*, NY, Pathfinder, 1981, p. 112.

207. Debray,'Castroism', p. 33; *Revolution in the Revolution?*, pp. 21, 97, 106, 111-12; Debray, 'The Role of the Intellectual' (1966)inBlackburn, *Strategy for Revolution*, pp. 155, 156. See also C. Marighela, *For the Liberation of Brazil*, pp. 24. 57.

208. Fanon, *Wretched of the Earth*, pp. 53, 87, 96-7, 101.

209. Cabral, 'Presuppositions and Objectives', pp. 132, 134, 135-6; 'Unity and Struggle', pp. 35, 36; 'A Brief Analysis of Social Structure', pp. 57-9.

210. Jowitt notes that one distinguishing characteristic of 'African populist' thought is its strrong emphasis on ethics in development and change (Jowitt, 'Scientific Socialism', pp. 151-2). This factor distinguishing African thought from more orthodox forms of marxism has parallels elsewhere in the Third World. One is reminded in this context of Ali Shari'ati's criticism of realist (materialist and naturalist) philosophers who 'with their merciless and unfeeling pseudo-scientific analysis corrupt the essential sanctity and virtue of values and vivisect them as one cuts apart a living delicate system into dead substance and elementary material components.' A. Shari'ati, *Marxism and Other Western Fallacies: An Islamic Critique*, Berkeley, Mizan, 1980, p. 27. Liberation theologians also, not surprisingly, lay considerable stress on the subjective ethical component of ideologies of liberation. See, for example, the thought of Father Henrique de Lima Vaz, who, while emphasizing strongly the desirability of major social change, stressed that his conception of man's 'liberty and ethical duty to reshape his destiny sharply differentiates his Christian viewpoint from Marx's historical determinism'. Cf. F. C. Turner, *Catholicism and Political Development in Latin America*, Chapel Hill, University of North Carolina Press, 1971, pp. 21-2.

211. Brown, 'Angolan Socialism', p. 300.

212. C. Blasier, *The Giant's Rival: The USSR and Latin America*, Pittsburgh, University of Pittsburgh Press, 1983, pp. 107, 137.

213.A. Bennigsen and C. Quelquejay, *Le Sultangalievisme au Tatarstan*, Paris, Mouton, 1960, pp. 101, 104, 105, 135. 138.

214. Mao Tse-tung, 'The Great Union of the Popular Masses' (1919) in *CQ* (1971), no. 45, pp. 76, 83.

215. Li Ta-chao, 'The October Revolution and the Chinese People'(1922)in Carrere d'Encausse and Schram, *Marxism and Asia*, p. 215.

216. On the reluctance to accept organizational alliance with the KMT in the mid-1930s, see G. Benton, 'The "2nd Wang Ming Line" (1935-1938)', *CQ* (1976), no. 61, pp. 61-6. For the appeal to KMT soldiers, see Mao Tse-tung, Ho Lung *et al.*, 'A Letter to Our Brothers, The Soldiers of the White Army' (1931) in

Schram, *PT*, pp. 217-19.

217. Cf. the Maoerkhai Declaration (August 1935), which was directed to 'men and women in all walks of life', as cited in L. Van Slyke, *Enemies and Friends: The United Front in Chinese Communist History*, Stanford, Stanford University Press, 1967, pp. 55-6. At the Waiyaopu Conference in December 1935, Mao called for an anti-Japanese alliance taking in 'any armed force' and which was open not only to the petty and national bourgeoisie but also to 'even a part of the compradores and landlords'. Schram, *Mao Tse-tung*, p. 194.

218. Mao Tse-tung, 'On New Democracy', pp. 349-50. See also Central Committee of the CCP, 'The Organization and Work of United Front Bureaux' (1940); and 'On Policy' (1940), both in Van Slyke, *Enemies and Friends*, pp. 268, 272.

219. Cf. the 1948 'May Day Appeal', cited in ibid., p. 201.

220. Mao Tse-tung, 'On the People's Democratic Dictatorship' (1949), excerpt in Schram, *PT*, pp. 234-5.

221. Schwartz, *Communism and China*, pp. 59-60.

222. Cf., for example, Mao Tse-tung, 'On Democratic Centralism' (1962) in Schram, *Mao Unrehearsed*, pp. 169-70; and Li Wei-han, 'The United Front', *PR* (1961), no. 33, p. 13, and no. 34, p. 18.

223. Cf. Ho Chi Minh, 'The Party's Line in the Period of the Democratic Front' (1939) in Fall, *Ho Chi Minh*, p. 130; Ho Chi Minh, 'Letter from Abroad' (194?) in ibid., pp. 132-3; and Ho Chi Minh, 'Political Report', p. 211. See also Giap's references to the 'broadest possible united front' in *Big Victory, Great Task*, NY, Praeger, 1968, p. 47; and Truong Chinh's stress on the unity of all social classes or the whole people in 'The August Revolution', pp. 34, 40, 68, and in 'The Resistance Will Win', pp. 205-11.

224. Mao Tse-tung, 'On the Ten Great Relationships' (1956) in Schram, *Mao Unrehearsed*, pp. 76-7.

225. Sun Yat-sen, *San Min Chu-i*, p. 172.

226. Mast, 'Revolution out of Tradition', pp. 92, 98.

227. A. Sukarno, 'Marhaen and Proletarian' (1957), Ithaca, Cornell Modern Indonesia Program, 1960, pp. 7, 10.

228. Sukarno, *Indonesia Accuses*, pp. 97, 101.

229. Cf. the FLN presentation to the 1957 Cairo Conference of the AAPSO, cited in Mandouze, *Revolution Algerienne*, p. 30. A comparable list of participants in the Algerian revolution found in the 1964 party programme is so broad that it is difficult to conceive of a social group which was excluded. FLN, 'Program', p. 124.

230. Debray, *Revolution in the Revolution?*, pp. 82-7, 103.

231. Cabral, 'Brief Analysis of Social Structure', pp. 53, 56; Cabral, 'Unity and Struggle', pp. 28, 29, 35, 39; and Cabral, 'Not Everyone Is of the Party', p. 89.

232. MPLA, 'Programme', p. 228; and Neto, 'Who Is the Enemy?', p. 314.

233. Dos Santos, 'Resistance and Struggle for Independence', p. 496; Mondlane, *Struggle for Mozambique*, p. 166; FRELIMO, 'Constitution' (1962) in Chilcote, *Documents*, p. 430. In 1968, this was tightened to focus to a greater extent on political consciousness and the willingness to submit to military discipline as prerequisites for membership. The point remains that anyone, no matter what his class in objective terms, was eligible if he possessed the appropriate subjective characteristics. Alpers, 'The Struggle for Socialism in Mozambique', p. 286.

234. Nehru, *Autobiography*, pp. 198, 283.

235. Toure, *Doctrine and Methods of the PDG*, pp. 26, 43; and as cited in I. Wallerstein, 'The Political Ideology of the PDG', *Presence Africaine* (1962), no. 40, p. 31. See also Adamolekun, 'The Socialist Experience in Guinea',

pp. 72-3.

236. Nkrumah,, *Handbook*, p. 25; Nkrumah, *Neocolonialism*, p. xvii. For the emphasis on national unity, see also Padmore, *Panafricanism*, p. 171; and Nyerere, 'Speech in Ibadan', p. 3.

237. R. Jackson and C. Rosberg, 'Why Africa's Weak States Persist: The Empirical and Juridical in Statehood', *World Politics* XXXV (1982), no. 1, p. 6.

238. Meisner, *Li Ta-chao*, pp. 75, 81, 82, 239.

239. Cf. Mao's comment to Edgar Snow in Snow, *Red Star over China*, pp. 185-6; and Schram, *Mao Tse-tung*, p. 81.

240. Several authors have cited this work as a unique departure from orthodox marxism-leninism and as the starting point in Mao's 'evolution towards a genuinely original position'. Schram, *PT*, p. 51. See also Schwartz, *The Rise of Mao*, pp. 73-5; and Brandt, *Stalin's Failure in China*, Cambridge, Harvard University Press, 1958, p. 109. Mao's focus on the peasantry at this time reflected the view of a number of other party figures, such as P'eng Pai, who in 1926 established a Soviet among the peasants of the Haifeng district, and Kan Nai-kuang, who in 1925 had written that the peasantry was the 'main force' and the 'basic class' of the revolution, the working class being relegated to the role of 'most reliable ally of the peasants'. As cited in A. Cohen, *The Communism of Mao Tse-tung*, London, University of Chicago Press, 1964, pp. 44-5.

241. Li Li-san, cited in Schwartz, *Rise of Mao*, pp. 124-8, 133, 137, 139; and Li Li-san, 'Resolution on Present Political Tasks', pp. 190-2. Jerome Ch'en links Li's remarks specifically to Mao in J. Ch'en, *Mao and the Chinese Revolution*, London, Oxford University Press, 1965, p. 139.

242. Mao Tse-tung, 'On New Democracy', p. 367.

243. Cf., for example, Li Wei-han, 'The Peasant Question in the Democratic Revolution', *PR* (1961), no. 13, pp. 5-6.

244. Lin Piao, 'Long Live the Victory of People's War', p. 24.

245. Ho Chi Minh, 'The October Revolution', p. 332.

246. *L'Ouvrier Algerien*, as cited in Mandouze, *Revolution Algerienne*, p. 126.

247. Fanon, *Wretched of the Earth*, p. 47. For Fanon's view of the primacy of rural struggle, see ibid., p. 102.

248. Debray, 'Castroism', pp. 42, 63.

249. Debray, *Revolution in the Revolution?*, pp. 82-7, 103.

250. Cabral, 'Presuppositions and Objectives', p. 132.

251. In the case of African nationalists, see, for example, Mboya, *Freedom and After*, p. 50; Nkrumah, *I Speak of Freedom*, p. 175; Nyerere, 'Policy on Foreign Affairs', p. 374; J. Nyerere, 'Speech at Oxford University' (1975) in Nyangoni and Nyandoro, *Select Documents*, pp. 363-7; and Legum, *Panafricanism*, pp. 32, 38.

252. J. Nehru, 'Address to the Lahore Congress' (1929) in Nehru, *India and te World*, p. 33.

253. Gandhi, *All Men Are Brothers*, pp. 102-5.

254. As cited in McCann, *Christian Realism*, p. 144. See also Turner, *Catholicism and Political Development*, pp. 144-6.

255. Sun Yat-sen, *San Min Chu-i*, p. 25.

256. As cited in Ch'en, *Mao and the Chinese Revolution*, p. 71. See also Mao Tse-tung, 'Report on Hunan', p. 253, where Mao defines revolution as 'an act of *violence* whereby one class overthrows the authority of another'.

257. Cf. CCP 6th Congress, 'Political Resolution', pp. 131, 141; Li Li-san, 'Resolution on Present Political Tasks', pp. 188-9, 194; and Mao's remark of 1938 that:

Experience in the class struggle of the era of imperialism has shown that the working class and the toiling masses cannot defeat the armed bourgeois and landlord except by the power of the gun; in this sense we can even say that the whole world can be remoulded only with the gun.

Mao Tse-tung, 'Concluding Remarks at the 6th Plenum' (1938) in Schram, *PT*, pp. 290-1.
258. E.g. Mao Tse-tung, 'Let Us Strive to Draw the Broad Masses into the Anti-Japanese United Front' (1937) in Schram, *PT*, p. 227.
259. Cf. Liu Shao-ch'i's 1949 speech to the WFTU, as cited in A. Halpern, 'The Foreign Policy Uses of the Chinese Model', *CQ* (1961), no. 7, p. 2. and Meng Hsien-chang, *The New Aspect of the War of National Liberation*, excerpt in Carrere d'Encausse and Schram, *Marxism and Asia*, p. 279.
260. Cntral Committee of the CCP, 'Outline of Views on the Question of Peaceful Transition' (1957) in J. Gittings, *Survey of the Sino-Soviet Dispute*, London, Oxford University Press, 1968, pp. 307-8.
261. For example, Liu Chang-sheng, 'On the Question of War and Peace', *PR* (1960), no. 24, p. 14; and Feng Chih-tan, 'The Awakening of Africa', *PR* (1960), no. 27, p. 15.
262. On the differences between the Chinese and Soviet positions on Algeria in the late 1950s, see Zagoria, *The Sino-Soviet Dispute*, pp. 253-6, 270-4. For a general expression of Chinese support for wars of liberation, see Yu Chao-li, 'Imperialism – the Source of War in Modern Times and the Path of the People's Struggle for Peace', *Red Flag* in *PR* (1960), no. 15, p. 23.
263. *People's Daily*, 'The Differences between Comrade Togliatti and Us' in *PR* (1963), no. 1, p. 15. See also 'The Proletarian Revolution and Khrushchev's Revisionism', *PR* (1964), no. 14, pp. 7, 17.
264. Cf. Tung Ming, 'The Invincible Weapon That Guarantees Victory in People's Revolutionary War', in *PR* (1967), no. 1, p. 22; and Afro-Asian Journalists' Association, 'General Resolution on the Current Political Situation', *PR* (1967), no. 26, p. 44.
265. Cf. *Red Flag et al.*, 'Long Live the Victory of the Dictatorship of the Proletariat' in *PR* (1971), no. 12, pp. 5-6, 10.
266. Giap, *People's War*, p. 62. See also Truong Chinh, 'The Resistance Will Win', pp. 102-6.
267. Abbas, *Guerre et Revolution d'Algerie*, pp. 190, 208, 225. Abbas' position was echoed by Fanon, who argued that since violence was the essential nature of colonialism and yielded only in the face of superior force, 'violence was a necessary aspect of the struggle'. Fanon, *Wreteched of the Earth*, pp. 27, 28, 48, 56.
268. Guevara, 'Speech at the UN', p. 114; and 'To Create a Second, a Third Vietnam', p. 160.
269. Cabral, 'Options of the CONCP', p. 253.
270. Cabral, 'Presuppositions and Ojectives', p. 134; and 'New Year's Message' (1973) in A. Cabral, *Return to the Source*, London, Monthly Review Press, 1973, p. 97. Similar MPLA and FRELIMO perspectives may be found in A. Neto, 'Angola in Historical Perspective', p. 215; A. Neto, 'Long Live the People's Republic of Angola', p. 2; Neto, as cited in 'MPLA: A Brief History', p. 33; and Mondlane, *Struggle for Mozambique*, pp. 116-18, 123, 125.
271. Cf. Mugabe, 'Interview with Tempo', p. 29, where he argued that no other tactic brought results and therefore that the choice of armed struggle was inevitable. See also SWAPO, 'Political Programme', p. 102; N. Mandela, 'Speech at the Rivonia Trial', pp. 15-16.
272. For example, Nyerere, cited in G. Yu, *China's Africa Policy – A Study of Tanzania*, London, Praeger, 1975, p. 24; Truong Chingh, 'The Resistance Will

Win', pp. 95-101; Cabral, 'Options of the CONCP', p. 253; Mondlane, *Struggle for Mozambique*, pp. 116-18; Mugabe, 'Interview with Tempo', p. 29; Mandela, 'Speech at the Rivonia Trial', pp. 15, 16.

273. Ibid.

274. Cf. Mao Tse-tung's views on this subject in the 1930s and 1940s, as outlined in Gittings, *The World and China*, pp. 58-65, 99. Similar notions were aired during the Cultural Revolution (see 'The Raging Tide of the Arab people against US Imperialism Is Irresistible', *People's Daily* in *PR* (1967), no. 26, p. 39; and 'Palestinian People's Armed Struggle and New Awakening of the Arab People', *PR* (1969), no. 45, p. 19). See also Giap, *People's War, People's Army*, p. 62; and Giap, *Big Victory, Great Task*, p. 110; Fanon, *Wretched of the Earth*, pp. 114, 118; Guevara, *Guerrilla Warfare*, p. 47; Gott, *Rural Guerrillas in Latin America*, Harmondsworth, Penguin, 1973, p. 50; Cabral, 'Options of the CONCP' p. 253; Cabral, 'National Liberation and Culture', p. 151; and Mondlane, *Struggle for Mozambique*, pp. 129, 145-6, 219-20. See also Nehru's view of the impact of the Second World War on the Indian people in Nehru, *Discovery of India*, p. 443.

275. Fanon, *Wretched of the Earth*, pp. 37, 73, 74; Guevara, *Guerrilla Warfare*, p. 47; Cabral, 'The National Fight for Liberation' (1962) in Chilcote, *Emerging Nationalism*, pp. 374-5; Cabral, 'National Liberation and Culture', p. 152; Mario de Andrade (at the time a leading MPLA cadre), as cited in B. Davidson, *The Liberation Of Guine*, Harmondsworth, Penguin, 1969, p. 90; A. Neto, as cited in *MPLA, A Brief History*, p. 33; Slovo, 'Interview with Dos Santos', p. 42.

276. A. Ben Bella, as cited in Marcum, *Angolan Revolution*, p. 141; Che Guevara, 'To Create a Second, a Third Vietnam', p. 158; A. Cabral, 'Our Party and the Struggle Must Be Led by the Best Sons and Daughters of Our People' (1969) in Cabral, *Unity and Struggle*, p. 68; and Cabral, 'National Liberation and Culture', p. 152.

277. Fanon, *Wretched of the Earth*, pp. 68, 74; Cabral, 'The National Fight for Liberation', pp. 364-5; de Andrade, as cited in Davidson, *Liberation of Guine*, p. 90; ZANU, 'Mwenje #2', p. 261.

278. Jean Paul Sartre, 'Preface' in Fanon, *Wretched of the Earth*, p. 19.

279. A recent reading of Kenneth Jowitt's 'Scientific Socialist Regimes in Africa' has brought to my attention the similarity of a number of the generalizations in this paragraph to his illuminating discussion of what he refers to as 'African populism'. Jowitt, 'Scientific Socialist Regimes in Africa', pp. 151-4.

# 5   THE SOVIET UNION AND NATIONAL LIBERATION

## Introduction

How do these widely shared Third World attitudes match up to Soviet doctrine and policy concerning political and social change in the Third World? To what extent does there exist an ideological affinity between national liberation movements and the governments they create on the one hand and the Soviet bloc on the other? What differences are there between Soviet and Third World perspectives on national liberation and how do these impinge upon Soviet foreign policy?

This chapter addresses these questions in terms of the structure established in Chapters 3 and 4: definitions of national liberation; views concerning nationalism and the role of national liberation in the world revolutionary process; perspectives on universal and particular in theories of revolution and social change in the Third World; and the treatment of class and the use of force in the national liberation struggle. It focuses on Soviet thinking and action since the death of Stalin, since it is only since 1953 that the USSR has actively sought to affect political developments in areas of the Third World removed from its immediate periphery. None the less, some attention is devoted to the history of Soviet involvement in the Third World and to the evolution of Soviet thought concerning national liberation prior to 1953, since post-stalinist theory and practice draws in important ways upon the stalinist and pre-stalinist legacies. The analysis relies on several differnt types of source material: party doctrine as set out, for example, in party congress reports and resolutions and in *Kommunist* and *Pravda*; government policy statements on Third World affairs; and more scholarly discussions, such as those which appear in the journals *Voprosy Istorii* (*Questions of History*), *Voprosy Ekonomiki* (*Questions of Economics*), *Voprosy Filosofii* (*Questions of Philosophy*), and *Narody Azii i Afriki* (*Peoples of Asia and Africa*). The analysis does not address stematically the question of whether differing schools of thought exist on specific aspects of the issues covered here. To do so would involve substantial digression from the basic subject matter of this book. Instead, the attempt is made to sketch the broad general outlines of doctrine, the parameters within which debate over specific questions takes place.

## The Historical Background

It is useful, before beginning the analysis, to give a brief historical account of Soviet policy towards the national liberation movement and towards independent states in the Third World, of developments in the Soviet domestic and external environment which affected Soviet attitudes and policy towards these groups and states, and of how the needs of policy were reflected in doctrine. The latter will be treated only in the most general way here, as it is dealt with in considerably more depth in the sections which follow.

Although Lenin had written extensively on the problem of colonial revolution prior to 1917, the October Revolution and the intervention of the Entente powers in the Russian Civil War stimulated even greater Bolshevik interest in the colonial periphery. In the early days, any ally was a welcome one, no matter what his social origins or political beliefs. Soviet strategy concerning oppressed peoples was aimed in the first place at soliciting the support of national minorities on the periphery of Soviet Russia and in the second place at sowing confusion in the rear of the colonial powers by fomenting revolution in the colonies and semi-colonies. The main criterion of acceptability as an ally was opposition to imperialism. Thus, the Soviets courted such notables as Reza Khan of Persia, Aminullah of Afghanistan, and Kemal Pasha of Turkey, all of whom had highly dubious class credentials and none of whom had any particular sympathy for communism.[1] The enthusiasm of the Bolsheviks for colonial revolution at this time also stemmed from their belief in the imminence of the world revolution which would bring communism to Europe.

The Bolsheviks systematized their approach to anti-imperialist movements in the East (as the Third World was referred to at this time) in the theses of the Second Comintern Congress in July 1920. Their early interest in colonial revolution perhaps reached a climax at the Baku Congress of Toilers of the East later in the summer. However, although the Bolsheviks, and Lenin in particular, were intensely interested in the national liberation revolution at this time, their main focus was on developments in Europe, and in Germany in particular.[2] Moreover, soon after the Second Congress, the Comintern significantly moderated its activity in the Middle East and the colonies as part of a Soviet attempt to establish trading and diplomatic relations with the European powers and particularly with Great Britain.[3]

With the failure of communist attempts to provoke a proletarian revolution in Germany in 1919, 1921 and 1923, the destruction of the Soviets in Budapest, Vienna, and Munich, the general stabilization of the European situation, and the end of the Russo-Polish War, the prospects for revolution in the advanced capitalist countries looked bleak. The option of revolutionary agitation in the colonies was not an attractive one, given the apparent resilience of the colonial regimes and the desire of the Soviet government to rely on trade with and credits from the West to speed its economic recovery from the Civil War. This left China as an attractive venue for revolution. It bordered on the Soviet Union and had a dynamic and growing nationalist movement with which by 1923 the Soviet government had reasonably good ties. It was not a colony and there was therefore less risk of alienating an imperial power than there would have been in Soviet involvement in the internal affairs of such a colony. Finally, its domestic instability favoured revolutionary activity. In 1923, the Soviet Union and the Comintern began to involve themselves in a significant way in the affairs of the Kuomintang and of China.

The Soviet experience with China from 1923 to 1927 was not a happy one. Initially, the USSR's China policy met with considerable success: infiltration of the Kuomintang by the CCP, the placement of Soviet advisers in highly influential positions within the Kuomintang, the national government, and the nationalist army; and the rapid northward expansion of nationalist power and establishment of Kuomintang rule in the Yangtze Valley in preparation for the final thrust northwards towards Peking. However, this did not last. The USSR met with a number of reversals in 1926-8. These culminated in the Kuomintang's attack on the CCP and trade union movement in Shanghai in April 1927. This was followed by the split between the left Kuomintang government in Wuhan on the one hand and the CCP and the Comintern on the other in the summer of the same year, the subsequent return to Russia of Soviet advisers, and, finally, the failure of the Autumn Harvest, Nanchang, and Canton uprisings by the CCP later in 1927. Soviet designs for China lay in ruins.

This disastrous outcome was followed by a certain disenchantment with bourgeois nationalist liberation movements, reflected in the resolutions of the Sixth Comintern Congress in July 1928. This change in line coincided with the final triumph of Stalin over the 'left opposition' in 1927-8. This victory freed Stalin to turn his attention to consolidating power within the Soviet Union and to the pursuit of socialism in one country. This amounted to a preoccupation with the domestic development of the USSR and the assurance of its security rather than with the furtherance of revolutionary activity abroad. The Soviet Union turned inwards and displayed little interest in national liberation struggles in the Third World. Even had the will been there, given the capabilities of the USSR at this time, it could provide little tangible support to anti-colonial revolution.

Activity in China was not the only aspect of Comintern activity with regard to the 'national and colonial question' in 1923-8. In 1927, as was seen in the previous chapter, the Comintern was instrumental in the formation of the League against Imperialism, while the Profintern (Trade Union International) sponsored the creation of the International Trade Union Commitee of Negro Workers.[4] Soon after the formation of the league, the Comintern, influenced by the Chinese experience and reflecting the line adopted at the Sixth Congress, drew back from collaboration with non-proletarian forces in the Third World. The bulk of the period between the Sixth and Seventh (1935) Comintern Congresses was characterized by a radically sectarian approach to the problem of national liberation, as will be seen below.

Events in the early 1930s, however, necessitated a rethinking of Soviet doctrine concerning national liberation. The 1931 invasion of Manchuria marked the beginning of a rapid Japanese expansion on the Asian continent. This led eventually to a number of large scale armour and infantry engagements between the Soviets and the Japanese in 1938-9. The rise of a Japanese threat in the Far East was paralleled by that of Nazi Germany in the West. While the Soviets had not taken the Nazi Party seriously during its rise to power, the threat posed by a resurgent, militarized, avowedly anti-communist Germany soon became evident.

The development of serious security problems at both ends of the USSR induced the party leadership once again to search for allies. As part of this search, they re-established relations with the Kuomintang government in 1932, exchanged representatives with the United States in 1933, joined the League of Nations in 1934 (becoming one of the most avid proponents of collective security), and concluded a treaty of mutual assistance with France in 1935. As part of this effort at winning friends among the Western powers, doctrine on national liberation was considerably moderated. Organizations such as the League against Imperialism and the 'Negro International' were disbanded or transformed into anti-fascist organizations.[5] The CCP was once again pressured into a compromise with the Kuomintang. In practice, the Soviet

Union assiduously avoided involvement in colonial struggles, while commentary on colonial questions in the Comintern press was minimal.

The attempt at a collective security solution to the combined threat of Germany and Japan foundered in the face of Western indecision. In response to this setback, the USSR concluded the Nazi-Soviet Pact in August 1939 in the hope of directing the imminent war westward. In the colonies and semi-colonies, this period was charcterized by a far more active posture with regard to colonialism and the struggle for national independence on the part of local communist parties.[6] But Soviet policy-makers remained uninterested in the struggles of the national liberation movement at this time. The eyes of the USSR were on Germany and Europe. All else paled into insignificance.

Not surprisingly, Soviet passivity with regard to questions of national liberation persisted through the period of alliance with the Western democracies which followed Germany's attack on the Soviet Union in June 1941. In the Soviet view, the struggle against colonialism was to be deferred until the battle against the greater evil — Germany — had been won. This implied disapproval of and lack of support for efforts which weakened the colonial powers. The anti-colonial activities of indigenous communists, as in India, were replaced by enthusiastic support for the war effort. At the height of the war, representatives of the USSR remained aloof from the inter-allied discussions on colonialism and on the application of the Atlantic Charter to colonial peoples, matters which disturbed relations between their English and American partners.

In the first years following the war, Soviet writers on national liberation displayed considerable moderation, contemplating collaboration between communists and non-proletarian nationalists in the struggle for independence and accepting the revolutionary credentials of the 'national bourgeoisie'. However, as relations with the Western allies deteriorated, attitudes towards collaboration with other classes changed. The return to militant hostility towards Western capitalism brought with it a re-emergence of radical sectarianism with regard to questions of national liberation. Communist-led or inspired insurrections broke out in South and South East Asia. Soviet publicists burst forth with vitriolic propaganda denouncing the Western presence in the Third World and advocating violent struggle against it. Their hostility extended to the 'bourgeois nationalist' regimes which assumed power in a number of ex-colonies such as India and Pakistan in the early postwar years.

This hardening in Soviet attitudes towards the leaders of bourgeois national movements can be attributed to a number of factors. The willingness of the British in particular to deal with moderate leaders up to the point of granting them independence in certain cases removed, as far as these leaders were concerned, the need for militant violent or non-violent action against the colonial regime. Moreover, the moderate Soviet strategy with respect to bourgeois nationalists was becoming more and more questionable with regard to one of the main arenas for which it had been designed — China. The CCP had abandoned it soon after the end of the Second World War and had by 1947-8 grown considerably in strength.[7] Finally, it may be that the return to a radical sectarian line justified, in a way, the lack of involvement in and support for the national liberation movement during a period in which Soviet attention was turned towards the task of reconstruction and the consolidation of Eastern Europe. One cannot be faulted for failing to provide support when there is no one worthy of it. Countries which had acquired independence peacefully were not considered to be independent. Their leaders were held to be stooges of the colonial power or of American imperialism. The latter was presented as a force replacing European colonialism in Asia and Africa. In the stalinist view, the form taken by imperialism might have been changing, but its essence (subjection, dependence, and exploitation) remained unchanged.

The posture of unrestrained hostility towards the West and towards the new governments in the Third World was not particularly successful. It led to confrontation and retreat in Berlin and an expensive but inconclusive war in Korea. It induced the further consolidation of the Western alliance system. It provoked renewed American involvement on the Asian mainland. The violent insurrections in South and South East Asia were in the main unsuccessful or had ambiguous results. The behaviour of states such as India, particularly with respect to the Korean War, indicated that these states were not in fact puppets of the Western powers, but capable of pursuing independent foreign policies. Given that these states could and did act independently, the USSR, by rejecting contact with them, was forgoing an opportunity to expand its influence in an area which had previously been closed to it. In response to these factors, and perhaps reflecting a certain drift in foreign policy during Stalin's last years of life as well, the hostility of the USSR towards states such as India began to soften in the early 1950s.[8] Associated with this was a return to more moderate positions on the strategy and tactics of the struggle for national liberation.

This trend continued in the first years of the post-Stalin era. Khrushchev and Bulganin toured South Asia in 1955 and undertook significant trade and aid commitments with India, Afghanistan, and Burma. The Soviet Union arranged the sale of Czech arms to Egypt in 1955, the first major post-war arms agreement between a non-communist nation and a member of the communist bloc. This was followed in 1956 by a Soviet-Egyptian agreement on the construction of the Aswan Dam. The Soviets had awakened to the reality and significance of decolonization and attempted to make up for lost time with a large and sustained effort to increase their influence in the Third World. The CPSU leadership and Khrushchev in particular were highly optimistic about their ability to compete economically and militarily with the West, about the gradual shift in the 'correlation of forces' towards the socialist camp. and about the likely evolution towards socialism of much of the Third World. They committed themseves accordingly.

Coincident with this approach to the Third World was the adoption of doctrinal postures on issues such as leadership and membership in the united front, the global significance of the national liberation movement, national forms of socialism, and so on, which were consistent with close collaboration with non-communist regimes in the Third World. One might view such changes as a form of pandering to those leaders whom they sought to influence, or as a way to explain and to justify to the Soviet peoople, to CPSU rank and file, and perhaps to themselves, collaboration with class enemies. In somewhat less sceptical terms, these modifications, which are discussed at length below, may have been a sincere attempt to square theory with new perceptions of the changing reality that doctrine was meant to explain.

This moderate, optimistic, and positive perspective on national liberation lasted (with one or two falterings; in 1959-60 which resulted from the suppression of the Iraqi communists and the deterioration of relations with Egypt[9], and in 1961-2 when Soviet Ambassador Solod was expelled from the Republic of Guinea whose relations with the USA improved dramatically)[10] through the Khrushchev period. The USSR became intimately associated with a number of radical, or in Soviet terms, 'progressive' Third World regimes. Notable among these were the United Arab Republic, Indonesia, Algeria, Mali, Guinea and Ghana. Involvement in radical causes in the Third World was encouraged during this period by the emergence of China as a serious rival for influence among 'progressive' forces in Africa and Asia. This competition from the left may have induced the leadership of the CPSU to adopt more radical postures and to become more heavily involved with the Third World 'left' than they might otherwise have chosen.[11]

Khrushchev fell from power in 1964. Four years before this, the Soviet Union had been humiliated in its abortive and ill-conceived intervention in the Congo crisis.[12] In 1962, they had been humiliated once again in the Cuban missile crisis. Massive aid to countries such as Egypt, India and Indonesia had brought few significant gains. Although the spread of nonalignment might to some extent have been considered positive (see below), the benefits from this were limited. The major proponents of nonalignment (Nasser, Nehru and Sukarno) were wary of excessive involvement with the Soviet Union. Beyond this, there was no apparent drift towards 'scientific socialism' in the Third World. The economy of the USSR was faltering and it was becoming increasingly difficult to justify large diversions of scarce resources to the Third World, particularly when such diversions were by Soviet admission, wasteful and ineffective.[13] Several of the more prominent Soviet client regimes (Indonesia, Ghana, Algeria, and somewhat later Mali) fell from power soon after Khrushchev did, the victims of internal instability and the impatience and disillusionment of the military. This exposed the weakness of the radical regimes Khrushchev had been courting. Finally, the intensity of the American response to the communist-led liberation struggle in Vietnam made quite clear the potential dangers of what was perceived by the adversary to be an active communist challenge in the Third World.[14]

These factors set the stage for a further shift in Soviet attitudes towards the national liberation movement. Soviet writers became far less optimistic about the evolution of the Third World, and far more sceptical in their appraisals of left-wing non-communists. The USSR severely trimmed its aid programme. As the Soviets distanced themselves from radical regimes, they made serious efforts to broaden their base of contacts in the Third World, dealing with governments on the basis of mutual advantage rather than proferring concessionary aid. They placed particular emphasis on those countries of considerable strategic and economic importance in specific regions, rather than on those perceived to be ideologically preferable. Hence in the mid and late 1960s, Soviet policy-makers placed considerable emphasis on relations with Nigeria.[15]

This retreat from radicalism was easier than it might have been for at this time the People's Republic of China was experiencing serious internal upheavals. Its internal condition and pronouncements on foreign policy were so incomprehensible or noxious to most groups in the Third World that the USSR did not need to worry to any great degree about Chinese efforts to discredit the Soviet Union as a revolutionary force and to drive a wedge between the 'world socialist system' and the national liberation movement.[16]

Several factors in the Soviet domestic and international situation changed in the late 1960s and early 1970s, bringing about yet another swing in attitudes towards national liberation and Third World radicalism. The USA, as a result of the experience in Vietnam, became far less willing to compete with the USSR for influence in the Third World. This removed an important constraint on Soviet activism. Detente may actually have encouraged such activism; because the Soviets believed that the Americans would not wish to jeopardize the process as a whole by hostile reactions to Soviet activities in selected Third World arenas, moreover, the acceptance of a detente with America drew into question the revolutionary commitment of the Soviet regime. This induced them to take actions which would reaffirm this commitment. The latter factor was all the more important given China's re-emergence in 1969-70 as a major competitor for influence in the Third World.

Growing resentment of the West in the Third World — evident in the highly vocal radicalization of the foreign policies of many states and the apparently growing 'Southern' unity in anti-Western causes, particularly in North-South economic issues (the Group of 77 and UNCTAD), the Arab-Israeli dispute, and opposition to American involvement in South East Asia — encouraged renewed Soviet optimism about political trends in the less developed world. The increased perception of resource scarcity enhanced the significance of Third World states in the international capitalist economy, rendering influence over them all the more valuable in East-West competition. Finally, the rapidly deteriorating situation in Southern Africa, associated with the atrophy of the Portuguese presence there, provided an attractive opportunity for the entry of the Soviet Union into the affairs of a region of great strategic and economic importance.

These international factors favouring a more forward Soviet policy in the Third World emerged at a time of rapidly expanding Soviet military capabilities. This expansion greatly enhanced the USSR's capacity to take advantage of such openings as did appear in the international environment. Strategic parity with the USA was recognized by the Americans in 1972, eliminating American strategic superiority as a possible constraint on action by the Soviet Union. The build-up in strategic weapons was matched by a rapid increase in conventional capabilities. Expansion of the navy was coupled with a steady increase in Soviet air transport capabilities. The growing Soviet capacity to project force at points distant from Soviet frontiers was graphically and repeatedly displayed in the mid-1970s (for example; the resupply of Egypt and Syria in 1973; the support of Cuban intervention in Angola in 1975-6; and the involvement in the war between Ethiopia and Somalia in 1977-8).

In short, in the early and mid-1970s, the USSR faced an environment in the Third World in which important constraints limiting its activities had been removed or weakened, important stimuli for such activity had emerged or re-emerged, and its capabilities to undertake such activities had increased. These changes were reflected in CPSU doctrine on national liberation. The near unanimous pessimism and conservatism of the late 1960s softened and more optimistic views, many of which had been common in the later Khrushchev period, re-emerged. They were also reflected in a much more active Soviet posture in the Third World, and particularly in Africa, as is clear from the Angolan and Ethiopian interventions.

This new elan towards radical groups in the Third World did not, however, bring with it an abandonment of the effort to improve relations with more moderate or conservative governments in states of great intrinsic importance (for example, India and Nigeria), or where good relations brought valued returns to the USSR itself (for example, Argentina). Thus, in the early and mid-1970s, the Soviet Union was following a 'dual policy'; one aspect of which was radical and directed towards revolutionary movements in the Third World, and the other practical, responding more directly to the interests of the Soviet state, and focused on the governments of significant states, whatever their ideological coloration.

The late 1970s brought yet another shift in nuance in Soviet policy towards left-wing states and in doctrine towards non-communist leftists. Again, the shift may be attributed to changes in the historical reality that doctrine was intended to describe and explain. Egypt, the USSR's longest standing client in the Middle East broke with the Soviet Union in 1975-7, abrogating the treaty of friendship the two countries had signed, expelling Soviet advisers, turning to the USA for military and economic aid, and ultimately signing what the Soviets perceived to be a separate peace with Israel. Somalia, one of the USSR's earliest clients in East Africa and again a state which had benefited from considerable Soviet economic and military largesse, broke with the USSR in 1977 as a result of improvements in Soviet relations with Ethiopia and Soviet opposition to Somalia's irredentist ambitions. This led to the re-emergence of a more jaundiced view of what the Soviets perceived to be non-marxist-leninist leftists in the Third World. On a more positive note, a number of regimes subscribing to 'scientific socialism' emerged in the mid and late 1970s (for example, Angola, Mozambique, Ethiopia, South Yemen, and Afghanistan). The natural Soviet preference for governments formed and directed by 'vanguard parties' subscribing to scientific socialism was apparently being validated by history. This coupled with the problems in relations with more ideologically suspect regimes brought a return to more orthodox perspectives on national liberation, as shall be seen below.

## The Soviet Definition of National Liberation

The Soviet definition of national liberation resembles in a number of important ways Third World thought on the same subject. With regard to political sovereignty, early in the history of Soviet theorizing about national liberation[17] and during the late stalinist period[18] there was much scepticism about the value of political independence as an aspect of liberation. However, since the death of Stalin, Soviet writers have generally recognized the significance of political independence as an essential step along the path to 'true' liberation. As Khrushchev put it in 1956, 'The winning of political freedom by the peoples of the former colonies and semi-colonies is the first and a very important pre-requisite of their complete independence . . . '[19] Somewhat later, a prominent Soviet analyst writing in the leading party journal added an international dimension to the Soviet endorsement of political independence as a critical aspect of liberation by noting that it led to significant changes in the system of relations in the 'world capitalist economy', thereby weakening imperialism.[20]

However, like Third World writers, Soviet experts have argued that political self-determination — the achievement of state sovereignty — is insufficient. It is not an end in itself, but a means to more important ends. There is in the Soviet literature prior to Stalin's death little recognition of the importance of economic independence. Indeed, such a stance would have been inconsistent with Lenin's and Marx's opposition to the rupture of structures of interdependence which colonial regimes had fostered.

In post-Stalin literature, however, one sees growing attention to the significance of economic independence from the international capitalist system as an integral aspect of national liberation. Several explanations for this development are plausible. First, it may have been a response to dictates of Soviet diplomacy in the Third World. If new states felt strongly about economic independence, Soviet support for this objective enhanced the USSR's capacity to expand its influence at the expense of the West. Moreover, given that these new states were linked to the Western economies, the quest for economic independence, to the extent that it was successful, would weaken the USSR's main adversaries in world politics. The latter point had some doctrinal respectability in the context of the theory of imperialism; a denial of access to peripheral economies as sources of raw materials and as sinks for surplus capital would hasten proletarian revolution in the West. Beyond this, economic independence from the world capitalist system came to be seen as a prerequisite for the integration of new states into the international socialist division of labour, or, in more practical terms, for the economic expansion of the world socialist system. Finally, from a 'vulgar marxist' perspective, it is economic rather than political factors which are the essence of social phenomena. In a sense, therefore, it is logical for those operating from such a perspective, in considering the concept of independence, to argue that it is economic relations rather than political sovereignty that are the essential criteria in assessing degrees of independence.

Khrushchev stressed in his South Asian tour of the mid-1950s that the essence of 'real genuine freedom' (*sic*) was the elimination of economic dependence.[21] Many Soviet writers both during and after the Khrushchev period have affirmed that with the achievement of political independence, the character of the anti-imperialist struggle changes and shifts towards the economic. Its goal becomes the elimination of the system of 'neocolonialist' exploitation embodied in unequal trade, foreign investment, and 'enslaving aid'.[22]

Political independence in the Soviet view is also a means towards social revolution, the ultimate objective of which is the creation of a socialist society free from the 'exploitation of man by man'. As noted in Chapter 3, Lenin recognized that social progress in an anti-feudal and anti-capitalist direction was an essential attribute of the overall process of liberation. The Soviet stress on social objectives of the struggle for freedom has been a steady refrain ever since, from the Baku Congress (1920),[23] through various Comintern discussions of colonial liberation,[24] to the post-Second World War discussions of Indian independence.[25]

One might have expected some moderation of the doctrinal emphasis on the social revolutionary character of the struggle for liberation during the Khrushchev period, when the USSR was seeking to forge ties with new states led by what the Soviets could only consider to be exploitative social groups. As shall be seen below, the dilemma created by the Soviet attachment to anti-feudal and anti-capitalist revolution in their attempt to cultivate what were at first glance counter-revolutionary groups caused Soviet writers much difficulty in their discussion of class and liberation in the Third World. But despite this tension between the imperatives of ideology and interest, there was little change in this aspect of the Soviet definition of national liberation. The 1961 CPSU programme, for example, stated that: 'A national liberation revolution does not end with the winning of political independence. This independence will be unstable and will turn into a fiction if the revolution does not lead to radical changes in *social* and economic life.'[26] V. Tyagunenko, writing in 1964, noted that the full realization of the tasks of the national liberation revolution necessitated an eventual turn against capitalism and towards socialism.[27]

If anything, the Soviet stress on the social aspect of liberation grew stronger as the Brezhnev period progressed and the Soviets were repeatedly confronted with the weakness of many sympathetic Third World regimes (for example, Ghana, Mali and Indonesia) and the unreliability of other allies, such as the Egyptians and Somalis. Hence, references to the inevitable anti-capitalist turn in the national liberation struggle (prescriptive here mixing with descriptive), to the elimination of social oppression as the fundamental end of national liberation, to the trend towards socialism of the national liberation movement, and to the social aspect of national liberation revolutions growing ever more pronounced, dot the literature with increasing frequency.[28]

This is reflected in the apparent shift in Soviet policy in the middle and late 1970s towards emphasis on relations with regimes, particularly in Africa (for example, Angola, Mozambique and Ethiopia) committed to and pursuing profound social changes in an anti-capitalist direction – the so-called states of 'socialist orientation', led by 'vanguard revolutionary parties of the working people'.[29] It is also seen in Soviet pressure upon these governments to adopt internal policies which the Soviets believe would institutionalize and render irreversible such changes (for example, Soviet pressure on Ethiopia to form a vanguard marxist-leninist party[30]).

In terms of policy, these views on national liberation clearly have not had a determining impact on Soviet foreign policy in the Third World. However, the Soviet preference for detachment from the world capitalist economy – for economic independence – is reflected in qualified endorsement of Third World demands for a new international economic order.[31] Their preference for non-capitalist, 'socialist-oriented' relations of production shows itself in the character of Soviet assistance programmes in new states, which stress heavily the state sector of the economy and investment in heavy industry. Such policies, in the Soviet view, lay the material basis for the transition to socialism.

Thus far, there is much common ground between Soviet and Third World conceptions of the nature and objectives of the process of national liberation. Each conceives of it as a process involving political self-determination, economic independence, and profound social change leading in the direction of socialism. With regard to the fourth (cultural or subjective) dimension, however, the two diverge. There is little discussion in the Soviet literature of the necessity of cultural liber-liberation, little concern for the restoration of the dignity and self-respect of the colonized individual and for the regeneration of a distinct national culture.

There are a number of reasons for this divergence. Operating from a marxist-leninist perspective, the Soviets would, as a matter of course, underestimate and be unsympathetic to the drive for a particularistic national identity. Moreover, the crude determinism of orthodox Soviet marxism favours a devaluation of subjective factors. Thirdly, this oversight may reflect the experiential difference between Soviet and Third World writers. Russia and the Soviet Union have not experienced prolonged colonial rule and its cultural impact. Soviet writers do not have the experience of 'deculturation' and humiliation which informs much Third World discussion of national liberation. Finally, from a policy perspective, the encouragement of cultural specificity would have conflicted with the Soviet quest for influence in the Third World, given that national particularism tends to be undiscriminating in its international implications. It is the construction of an identity in contradistinction to outsiders as such.

The failure to take into account the particularistic cultural aspect of national liberation is the first of a number of aspects of the Soviet undervaluation of nationalist and autonomist aspirations in Third World liberation movements. To their credit, there is evident in the recent Soviet literature a recognition of the importance of subjective aspects of national liberation. Karen Brutents, for example, in a recent work stresses the importance of 'ideological, cultural and psychological factors' in the 'origination and development of national liberation movements', citing their role in awakening national consciousness.[32] This presumably reflects a growing Soviet awareness of the power of national and cultural aspirations among Third World elites, and of shortcomings in earlier Soviet doctrine and policy which failed to take these aspirations sufficiently into account (see below). But there appears to be little recognition even now of the intrinsic value to Third World elites of cultural identity. Instead, these factors are important in the Soviet view because of their role in expediting the anti-colonial struggle.

In closing, it is worth noting that Soviet writers since the death of Stalin have tended to view these three aspects of national liberation — political independence, economic independence, and social revolution — as more or less sequential. A broad national struggle for state power and the success of this effort are prerequisites for the movement to achieve economic independence. Moreover, it is in the post-independence phase of 'social differentiation' and growing conflict of class interests that social revolutionary tasks become salient.[33] This attitude towards stages of revolution in the Third World recalls Soviet criticisms of trotskyite notions of 'telescoping' the proletarian revolution. It distinguishes Soviet thinking from that of many Third World radicals who have taken the view that class struggle is necessary *during* the battle for state power in order to involve the masses in the struggle.

## The World Revolutionary Process

Soviet attitudes concerning the role of national liberation in the world revolutionary process also display considerable continuity. Since Lenin's death, Soviet political figures, academic commentators, and journalists have steadily recognized the significance of anti-Western revolution as a component of the general struggle of 'progressive forces' against imperialism.

The Second Comintern Congress' theses on the national and colonial question called for the 'closest alliance with Soviet Russia of all the national and colonial liberation movements'.[34] Stalin in 1924 argued that the road to the victory of revolution in the West lay 'through a revolutionary alliance with the liberation movement of the colonies and dependent countries against imperialism'.[35] The Sixth Comintern Congress declared that the national liberation revolution was integrally linked to the security of the Soviet Union and that this revolution was one of the two main forces of the world revolutionary movement.[36] Just after the Second World War, Evgenii Zhukov, a leading Soviet commentator on Third World issues, reiterated the importance of national liberation to world revolution, calling for the binding together of the struggle of oppressed peoples with that of the world proletariat.[37]

It was only with the death of Stalin, however, that this aspect of Soviet doctrine was translated into policy. The elan of Soviet policy into the Third World during the Khrushchev period was informed by Khrushchev's personal sense of the importance of the Third World in the global struggle between capitalism and socialism, particularly when competition at the centre was constrained by the danger of nuclear war. The national liberation movements were implicitly included among progressive forces in Khrushchev's 1956 division of the world into a zone of peace and a zone of war.[38] The 1960 'Statement of Communist and Workers' Parties, stated that: 'The breakdown of the system of colonial slavery under the impact of the national liberation movement is a phenomenon ranking second in historical importance only to the formation of the world socialist system.'

Writers closely associated with Khrushchevian optimism concerning socio-political trends in the Third World argued that the forces of national liberation were merging with those of world socialism into a single stream.[39] Even those writers who displayed considerable scepticism about Third World revolution in the aftermath of Khrushchev's fall from power acknowledged that national liberation was, in its objective impact, anti-imperialist.[40] As Soviet commentators regained their optimism concerning developments in the Third World in the early 1970s (in response, as noted above, to shifts in the perceived international correlation of forces and particularly the Soviet attainment of strategic parity, and to the American debacle in Vietnam), it was commonly argued that the national liberation movement was an inseparable part of the world revolutionary process and a constructive factor of fundamental importance in world politics.[41] This perception has persisted through the 1970s and into the 1980s more or less independently of the fortunes of Soviet policy in the Third World.[42]

The perception that the socialist countries and the national liberation movement were allies in a joint struggle against imperialism was shared by the bulk of the movements and writers considered in Chapter 4. There is, however, good reason to doubt that they would accept that their interests were *inseparably* linked. The policies adopted by these groups suggest that they had a more selfish perception of their basic objectives and a narrower definition of the scope of the alliance with world socialism.

Even clearer divergences emerge in the consideration of who was to lead the world revolutionary process, what the principal contradictions in world politics were, and the extent to which particular interests were to be subordinated to general ones. These divergences reflected an unwillingness on the part of Third World revolutionary movements to accept Soviet assertions that Third World struggle and those involved in it were subordinate to the Soviet Union.

With regard to leadership of the world revolutionary movement, one can cite numerous Comintern resolutions to the effect that this role belonged to the international communist movement, with the USSR at its head.[43] During the stalinist period, the USSR's claim to leadership often slid into assertions that Stalin himself led the world revolutionary process.[44] Throughout the Khrushchev period, the Soviet literature was laden with references to the USSR and the socialist camp as the leading force or 'main bulwark' of the overall struggle against imperialism. To argue that the national liberation movement had supplanted the USSR and the world socialist system as the leading force in the world revolutionary process was 'wrong-headed and anti-marxist'. Soviet claims of this sort grew particularly strident during the open polemics with the CCP in 1963-5.[45]

In the post-Khrushchev period, Soviet writers continued to underline with great consistency the primacy in world revolution of the USSR and the world socialist system.[46] Contemporary sources claim that the October Revolution opened the way for victory in the anti-colonial struggle, while the 'consolidation of the world socialist system' made it possible for the anti-colonial challenge to spread throughout the Third World. Moreover, the growing weight of the USSR in world affairs makes possible the radicalization of the national liberation movement, its turning to the questions of economic independence, non-capitalist development, and social revolution by:

(1) deterring imperialist agression;
(2) providing alternative sources of assistance;
(3) providing a compelling example of non-capitalist or socialist oriented development.[47]

There is, by constrast, little readiness among Third World sources to accept Soviet leadership or explanations of their success which rest upon the emergence of the Soviet state or the world socialist system, or upon assistance rendered by the latter two to national liberation movements.

It is important to stress that the contemporary Soviet vision of their own concrete contribution to the success of the national liberation revolution is primarily permissive rather than active. The USSR, through expanding its strength and that of its closest allies, creates the conditions for successful revolution in the Third World and protects these revolutions from external interference. While it renders some assistance, the USSR does not make these revolutions. As a recent Soviet commentator put it:

> The question of how real socialism can best increase its influence on world development and help deepen the world revolutionary process has nothing to do with the notorious accusations citing the 'hand of Moscow' or the 'hand' of any other socialist state. These states are opposed in principle to exporting revolution to non-socialist countries.[48]

Beyond this, Soviet writers have persistently argued that it is the confrontation between the USSR and its allies on the one hand and the developed capitalist world on the other which is of fundamental importance in international politics. All others pale by comparison. They have refuted claims by Third World nationalists and national communists that the focus of world revolution has shifted to the colonial and semi-colonial countries and that the principal contradiction in world politics is that between imperialism and the national liberation movement. Such concerns were evident in Lenin's refutation of Roy's position at the Second Comintern Congress[49] and in Stalin's criticism of Sultan-Galiev's ideas.[50] Zhdanov's 1947 elaboration of the 'two camp' view of word politics underlined the centrality of the contradiction between socialism and capitalism and relegated the question of national liberation to a distinctly secondary and instrumental role.[51]

During the Khrushchev period, the issue of where the main contradiction in world politics lay became entangled in the Sino-Soviet dispute, with the Chinese arguing that the focus of 'world storms' had shifted to Asia and Africa. The debate on this subject became part of the Soviet attempt to beat off the Chinese challenge to Soviet leadership of the international communist movement. In this context, it is not surprising that Soviet statements on this subject became increasingly vehement. In 1964, for example, Suslov specifically rejected the notion of the primacy of the national liberation movement, calling it revisionist and maintaining that while attaching great significance to the national liberation movement, Marxist-Leninists at the same time consider that the world socialist system determines the chief content, the chief direction, and the chief features of the historical development of human society in the contemporary era . . . the prime role of the world revolutionary process belongs to the socialist countries.[52]

The fall of Khrushchev and the retrenchment in Soviet policy in the Third World in the mid and late 1960s did not result in any significant alteration in the Soviet assessment of the comparative importance of national liberation and world socialism. However, writing on the subject reflected a more pessimistic evaluation of the direction likely to be taken by the new states and a concern to justify an increasing Soviet preoccupation with domestic economic concerns. Hence, it was argued in 1965 that each wing of the world revolutionary process had to focus on its own specific tasks. The principal responsibility of the socialist countries was the construction of socialism and communism. This was the *decisive* contribution to global revolutionary transformation. This in turn determined the vanguard role of these states in the world revolutionary process.[53]

Soviet writers in the mid-1970s and early 1980s continued to assert the primacy of the struggle on a world scale between socialism and capitalism and the secondary role of the national liberation revolution. They criticized those 'left opportunists' and 'national ideologists of the Third World [who] have clearly overrated the importance and revolutionary role of the national liberation movement'.[54] The concept of 'vostochnotsentrizm' (eastern-centredness − the view that the focus of world contradictions had shifted to the Third World) was termed 'twisted' and 'chauvinist'.[55] This view contrasts starkly with the dominant perception of Third World revolutionaries, who viewed the struggle for national liberation as the most important aspect of world revolution and who stressed the primacy of the contradiction between the peoples of the Third World and imperialism.

It is not difficult to fathom the reasons for these Soviet positions. With regard to leadership, there is a certain logic to Soviet claims from an orthodox marxist-leninist perspective. In marxist thought, the world socialist utopia was to emerge from the confrontation of the proletariat and bourgeoisie in the advanced industrial economies. The transition from capitalism to socialism was the principal task of the epoch. Third World non-industrial societies emerging from 'feudal' and 'prefeudal' relations of production could not, by their 'objective' nature, assume a leading role in such a transition. Their contradiction with capitalism, therefore, could only be of secondary importance. In the Soviet view, Russia was the first state in which this confrontation between the bourgeoisie and the proletariat had produced a 'proletarian' regime. It was the USSR which was the principal agent in spreading socialism to the other members of the world socialist system and which guaranteed that the socialist revolution in these countries would not be overpowered by domestic or international 'reaction'. Moreover, the Soviet Union was by far the most powerful member of the socialist camp. As such, it was natural for Soviet spokesmen to claim a leading role for themselves.

Leaving aside questions of ideology, such a position has clear political advantages for the Soviet leadership. Externally, it legitimizes Soviet attempts to manipulate revolutionary movements in other countries in the service of Soviet interests. To the extent that others accept this Soviet position, they become willing instruments of Soviet policy. Internally, the legitimacy of party rule in the Soviet Union rests in part on its much-touted status as the vanguard of a revolutionary process of world historical significance. To the extent that the party succeeds in convincing the populace of this role, it becomes easier to justify the hardship and privation of everyday life in the USSR and the lack of basic freedoms which characterizes Soviet society.

## Nationalism, Regionalism and Nonalignment

Further divergences between Soviet and Third World conceptions of the role of the national liberation movement in the world revolutionary process emerge in the Soviet discussion of general and particular in the interests and loyalties of national liberation movements. Soviet discussions display a tendency to stress the universal anti-imperialist rather than specifically national character of the movement. This is implicit in the Soviet proclivity throughout the periods under consideration to speak of *the* national liberation movement rather than of specific national liberation movements, national liberation being seen as a rather amorphous anti-imperialist force involving the entire Third World.

Recent writers have attempted explicitly to dissociate national liberation from nationalism. One source, for example, while admitting that nationalism was the chosen ideology of the national liberation movement, denied that there was any *necessary* connection between the two, for 'even the tactical principles of nationalism are not always adequate methods of and means for anti-imperialist struggle'.[56] Another argued that the peoples of the new states were increasingly convinced that the 'national liberation movement, by its very nature, cannot take on a nationalist character', and stressed that the movement, while it could be national in form, was internationalist in essence.[57] Likewise, Karen Brutents has argued that because of the international character of imperialism, the main target of the struggle for national liberation, 'national liberation revolutions in our day tend at root to transcend the national framework and to be internationalized'. The conflicts which generate them now appear not only as a part of the general contradiction 'between all the subjugated peoples and imperialism, but also as part of the worldwide antagonism between the forces of democracy and socialism on the one hand, and the forces of oppression and reaction on the other.'[58]

A similar perspective informs Soviet commentary on nonalignment, neutralism and Third World solidarity. In theory, from the Soviet perspective, the essence of nonalignment, or positive neutralism, is its anti-imperialist aspect. As such, the nonaligned movement is viewed as a contributor to the world revolutionary process. 'Real' nonalignment or 'positive' neutralism, in the Soviet view, corresponds to alignment with 'world socialism'. The socialist countries and the world communist movement are the natural allies of the nonaligned.[59] By contrast, Soviet writers ignore or condemn the attempt to define nonalignment in terms of equidistance from the two blocs and non-commitment to either one as evidence of national chauvinism, imperialist penetration, or (as in 1961-5 and 1969-76) Chinese anti-Soviet machination. V. Ovchinnikov's recent comment is typical:

Attempts to lead the nonaligned movement up the blind alley of 'equidistance' are meant to drive a wedge between the liberated governments and their natural allies — the socialist countries — so as to narrow the common front of opposition to the forces of imperialism and war.[60]

The idea of a self-reliant Third World holding itself apart from the socialist as well as the capitalist systems was criticized as an instrument of ideological struggle against communism. Soviet writers referred to the lumping together of the USSR and the other socialist countries along with the Western powers on the rich Northern side of a rich-poor, North-South dichotomy in international politics as 'bourgeois sophistry'.[61]

The degree of Soviet enthusiasm for the Afro-Asian and nonaligned movements has varied since the Bandung (1955) and Belgrade (1961) conferences according to the degree to which these movements have conformed to this Soviet vision of neutralism and Third World solidarity, with the intensity of the Chinese challenge to Soviet influence among members of these movements, and with the degree of overall Soviet optimism or pessimism *vis-à-vis* trends in Third World politics. But this basic notion of nonalignment and Third World solidarity as constituting, in objective terms, alignment with progressive forces led by the USSR in the struggle against international capitalism has changed little since the mid-1950s.

Again, these perspectives on the transnational character of national liberation and the 'progressive' character of nonalignment may be explained with reference both to the marxist-leninist world view and to the interests of the Soviet state. As a form of advocacy, it serves Soviet interests. If others accept it, they subordinate their own specific objectives to those of the USSR as leader of this broad international movement. As empirical analysis, however, it ignores the fact that for movements seeking national liberation, anti-imperialism is only one side of the coin, the other being a positive desire to create a nation-state which is an autonomous actor in world politics.

One expression of this desire is the idea of nonalignment. The colonial legacy and the continuing depth and noxious (to much Third World opinion) character of Western involvement throughout much of the Third World (for example, Vietnam, the Middle East, and Southern Africa) have favoured a concentration on the part of the nonaligned movement on the threat from the West. This bias has been strengthened further by Soviet support for and Western diffidence towards causes which are embraced by large numbers of Third World actors (for example, Palestinian rights and the anti-apartheid movement). Yet to the extent that the USSR itself threatens the objectives of autonomy, it too runs afoul of the principles of nonalignment as they are conceived by the bulk of Third World opinion. This is evident in the Third World response to the Soviet invasion of Afghanistan and in growing African concern in the aftermath of Soviet-Cuban intervention in Angola about a Soviet threat to Africa.[62] As such, the Soviet perception of the international character of national liberation and the necessarily aligned character of nonalignment would appear to be a confusion of 'is' with 'ought'.

Similar dissonances between Soviet and Third World thinking about national liberation are evident in the treatment of national particularism. It will be recalled that there is in the Third World radical literature and practice little tendency to subordinate nationally specific objectives to broader internationalist ones. Since Lenin's death, Soviet attitudes towards Third World national, regional, or ethnic particularism have displayed considerable ambivalence. Several threads appear and reappear with great regularity as Soviet writers have attempted to square marxist-leninist hostility to nationalism *per se* and awareness of the threat of minority nationalism within the USSR itself with their appreciation of the fact that nationalism, when directed primarily against adversaries of the USSR, can rebound to Soviet advantage.

Soviet writers have quite steadily recognized that doctrines such as nationalism, Pan-Africanism, and Pan-Islamic solidarity are potential obstacles to the development of an internationalist consciousness and to the unity of the anti-imperialist movement. Internally, they may impede progressive change by diverting the attention of the masses from class struggle. In the early years of Soviet power, their criticism of national or religious exclusivity which threatened the cohesion of the Soviet state was particularly strong. Stalin, for example, in a 1924 criticism of Sultan-Galiev, affirmed the

> necessity of fighting against the national insularity, narrowness, and aloofness of the socialists in the oppressed countries, who do not want to rise above their national steeple and who do not understand the connection between the liberation movement in their various countries and the proletarian movement in the ruling countries.[63]

As time passed, this kind of criticism was extended to manifestations of nationalism elsewhere in the colonial and semi-colonial world. In 1926, a Comintern document referred to attempts on the part of the 'big bourgeoisie' to recapture the KMT by 'using the ideology of bourgeois nationalism to counter the idea of class struggle'.[64] In the aftermath of the Second World War, Evgenii Zhukov dismissed Third World nationalism as an imperialist ploy to disunite the peoples of the colonies and semi-colonies and to neutralize the national liberation movement by diverting the masses from revolutionary objectives.[65]

Soon after Stalin's death, the same author, by then the doyen of Soviet writers on national liberation, noted the profound contradiction between nationalism and the internationalist class perspective of the proletariat.[66] The 22nd Congress Party Programme noted that nationalism was the chief ideological and political weapon of international and domestic reaction against socialism.[67] In 1964, the leading Soviet africanist roundly condemned 'negritude' as 'anti-racist racism'.[68] More or less contemporaneously, Georgii Mirskii warned against the reverse racism of racial solidarity which set non-white against white. Such postures undermined the unity of the world revolutionary movement.[69] Mirskii's admonitions, although consistent with the main thrust of Soviet argument on nationalism, also reflect Soviet concern at this time about Chinese attempts to manipulate the race issue in order to exclude the USSR from the Afro-Asian movement.

This negative assessment of national and racial particularism persisted into the Brezhnev period. Soviet writers characterized Third World nationalism as a reactionary ideological weapon used by the bourgeoisie against the working class, diverting the latter from class struggle by substituting the illusion of intra-national harmony and international conflict for the reality of intranational conflict of class interests and community of interest within transnational class groups.[70] Alternatively, they described it as a tool used by the imperialists to divide the world revolutionary movement by 'falsely setting anti-imperialism and alliance with the socialist states in opposition to a misguided understanding of patriotism'.[71]

At a more abstract level, one Soviet commentator judged nationalism to be pernicious in its very essence, in that:

> The basic idea of nationalism is exclusivity – the extolment of the merits of one's own nation to the utmost, the attribution to it of a special historical mission, a belief in its superiority and its right to manifest intolerance towards other nations . . . However nationalism appears, as open or covert, as progressive or reactionary, as a source of the ideology of egoism it is always bad.[72]

That is to say, at the root of Soviet criticism of nationalism was the latter's *particular* aspect, which constituted an impediment to the emergence of the collective universal consciousness which was the subjective precondition of effective struggle against the West. In more concrete terms, this position reflects not only the principled opposition which bearers of a universalist messianic faith must display towards all forms of particularism, but also the recognition that nationalism and other forms of exclusive ethnic, religious, and regional doctrines constitute obstacles to the spread and consolidation of Soviet influence.

That said, from quite early in Soviet history, and particularly since the death of Stalin, this negative assessment of Third World nationalism has frequently been balanced by the realization that, in practice, anti-Western nationalism, despite its particularistic character, had an objectively anti-imperialist impact. As such, during the struggle against the colonial and neocolonial powers, it was constructive. The degree to which Soviet spokesmen and scholars have emphasized the progressive potential of Third World nationalism has varied over time with the success or failure of attempts to broaden relations with groups espousing it, with the degree of sectarianism characterizing Soviet relations with non-communist groups in general, with the priority placed on good relations with the capitalist states in the West, and with the degree of prominence accorded the Third World in overall Soviet foreign policy.

In the mid-1920s, during the period of close relations with the KMT, Soviet writers displayed considerable optimism concerning the progressive character of nationalism in the colonial and semi-colonial countries. This largely disappeared after the break with the KMT in 1927. One might have expected Soviet endorsement of the progressive impact of nationalism to reappear once the USSR reverted to the popular front line in the mid-1930s in order to contain the spread of European fascism and Japanese militarism. But the endorsement of anti-colonial nationalism would have interfered with Soviet attempts to cultivate closer relations with France and Britain. Hence there was little movement in this direction. For similar reasons, Soviet writers refrained from any sustained consideration of the progressive aspect of Third World nationalism during the Second World War. A more positive assessment in the aftermath of the break with the Western power after the war was precluded by the sectarian introversion of Soviet policy from 1947 to 1952.

It was only with the death of Stalin that the way was cleared for a return to a 'leninist' appreciation of the potential contribution of Third World nationalism to world anti-imperialist revolution, as Soviet policy-makers began actively to seek influence with new states in the Third World. In the mid and late 1950s, awareness of the alien character of nationalism was matched by a stress on its anti-imperialist impact. As Zhukov put it:

> . . . it should not be forgotten that the national bourgeoisie plays an active part in the struggle against imperialism. Its ideology is bourgeois nationalism. To the extent that the national bourgeoisie shows itself to be an active participant of the anti-imperialist struggle, its nationalist ideology may not be an insuperable obstacle barring the

working masses from cooperation and alliance with it against imperialism. In this case nationalism is opposed to imperialism.[73]

The 1961 Party Programme maintained that the nationalism of oppressed peoples, because it was anti-imperialist, had a 'general democratic content' and was 'historically justified at a given stage'.[74]

With the disappointments of the mid-1960s, the fall of Khrushchev (with whom the attitude of optimism *vis-à-vis* the progressive character of non-proletarian forces in the Third World and of their ideologies had been most closely associated), and the reduction in Soviet involvement in the Third World after his fall, reference to the progressive character of Third World nationalism again grew rare.

As the USSR approached parity in nuclear weapons and began to see the results of its decisions to expand conventional force projection capabilities, and as the extent of damage to American foreign policy caused by the Vietnam involvement became increasingly evident, Soviet optimism concerning Third World revolution returned. With it came a renewed emphasis that anti-Western nationalism could play a constructive role in world social development. Commentators frequently cited Lenin's various remarks on the democratic, anti-imperialist content of the nationalism of oppressed peoples, and on self-determination as a step towards eventual federation. They stressed nationalism's historically progressive role during the process of decolonization, and its anti-imperialist character in the present stage of state formation in the Third World.[75]

More recently, there is evidence of a more differentiated attitude towards Third World nationalism, the recognition of its progressive role being complemented by the view that as the anti-colonial phase of struggle passes into history and as the new states take on more distinct personalities, the exclusive, egoistic character of nationalism grows in significance. Ul'yanovsky, for example, in 1978 noted that while 'anti-imperialist nationalism today is a dominant force in the former colonial and semi-colonial countries', nationalism in the Third World was a highly complex phenomenon, its evolution 'full of contradictions', and capable or being 'progressive at one stage and conservative and reactionary at another'.[76] He stressed that under

bourgeois or petty bourgeois control of the anti-imperialist struggle national elements tend to become, to their own detriment, nationalist, isolationist, separatist, exclusive, messianic, and, in the final analysis, chauvinist, which consequently opposes the national to the international.[77]

He maintained that the 'reactionary elements in bourgeois nationalism' grew as internal social contradictions sharpened in the aftermath of independence. This, and similar assessments by other writers late in the 1970s reflect the unhappy Soviet experience with Egyptian and Somali nationalism, two cases in which local clients were willing to foresake their internationalist orientations in order to pursue particular national objectives.

These 'reactionary elements' were balanced, however, by the growing strength of the democratic (that is, anti-imperialist and inter-nationalist) aspect of the nationalism of 'politically oppressed and economically exploited strata'.[78] One might dismiss this formulation simply as a *pro forma* statement of faith, but it does reflect a third aspect of the Soviet treatment of Third World nationalism which has important policy implications. Nationalism, as a superstructural manifestation of capitalist relations of production, was destined in Soviet eyes, to disappear as societies made the transition to socialism. It was an epiphenomenon of little intrinsic importance when compared to the internationalism of anti-imperialist forces in world politics. In essence, Soviet writers have steadily translated their dislike of national, religious, and ethnic chauvinism in the Third World into an undervaluation of its significance as a political phenomenon. As with their assertion of the non-national essence of national liberation, they have confused fact and value. This is evident in doctrine in the attachment of nationalism exclusively to either the national or petty bourgeoisie, but is even clearer in the string of Soviet setbacks in relations with what were, from their point of view, progressive Third World regimes, setbacks which stemmed at least in part from a Soviet failure to recognize and to adapt to the class-transcendent character of Third World nationalism.

The break with China resulted in part from insufficient Soviet sensitivity to the nationalist orientation and aspirations of the CCP leadership, as when Stalin insisted on and Khrushchev requested basing rights for Soviet forces in the PRC. One might also cite Khrushchev's attempt to subordinate Chinese irredentism to the dictates of East-West peaceful coexistence, when he failed to back the Chinese on the Taiwan issue. Khrushchev's comments on altercations with the Chinese on the matter of bases betray a striking naiveté in his complete lack of comprehension of the nationalist animus of Chinese policy-making on this issue.[79]

The break with Egypt in 1972, and more definitively in 1975-7, suggests a similar insensitivity to the particular concerns of Egypt as a

Arab state partially occupied by a foreign power and possessing an intense desire to solve or at least to mitigate considerably its security problem in order to be able to get on with the business of national development. To put it another way, it reflects a Soviet overestimation of the degree to which Egypt could be treated as an instrument of superpower diplomacy in the Middle East.

The Soviet approach to the Ethiopia-Somalia conflict, as was noted above, also displayed a Soviet incapacity to comprehend the intensity of the confrontation between Pan-Somali expansionism and Ethiopian nationalism. The proposal floated in March 1977 by Castro, apparently at the behest of his Soviet patrons, that Somalia and Ethiopia should join with an autonomous Eritrea and South Yemen in a marxist-leninist federation again suggests an amazing lack of realiism. This originates at least in part from this Soviet tendency to underplay the significance of nationalism. Their attempts to pressure the Ethiopian government to negotiate with the Eritreans on autonomy suggest a similar perceptual failure in their incomprehension both of the Dergue's vision of Ethiopia and the Eritreans' devotion to the objective of independence.

It is also plausible that this distortive aspect of Soviet doctrine concerning Third World politics contributed to what was clearly a Soviet underestimation of the probable nationalist response to their invasion of Afghanistan. Finally, the persistent Soviet demand upon its African, Middle Eastern, and South Asian clients for bases shows a Soviet propensity to assume that these states share a conception of nonalignment identical to that of the USSR. That they do not is evident in Angolan, Mozambican, Ethiopian, and Indian resistance to or refusal of Soviet requests. This kind of pressure has, moreover, perturbed relations between the USSR and these clients.

## National Forms of Socialism

Soviet attitudes towards national forms of socialism display similar dilemmas. On the one hand, the universalist claims of marxism-leninism imply a strong prejudice against the attempt to develop new theories adapted to particular historical circumstances. Moreover, to the extent that the CPSU perceives its domestic and international legitimacy to be bound up with its status as the guardian of this universal truth, its apologists have a strong interest in denying the validity of attempts to adapt or supersede it.

However, for purely practical reasons, it makes sense to adapt doctrinal prescriptions to differing situations. The failure to do so invites failure and is, therefore, an impediment to the progress of the world revolutionary movement. Beyond this, to the extent that potential allies have pretensions of their own to theoretical originality, criticism or rejection of such creativity can impede diplomatic efforts to secure influence. Both of these considerations suggest that some flexibility towards particularism in revolutionary theory is desirable. Soviet perspectives on national forms of socialism since the revolution have reflected the tensions between these competing imperatives.

In this instance, the balance between dictates of ideology and interest has varied over time in relation to a number of factors:

(1) the degree of importance attached to the Third World as an arena of struggle and to relations with an influence over non-proletarian groups in Asia, Africa, and Latin America;
(2) the degree of Soviet optimism concerning the evolution of the Third World towards socialism;
(3) the extent to which rival groups in the world revolutionary movement were making competing universalist claims.

Though Lenin warned of the 'attempt to paint bourgeois democratic liberation trends in the backward countries in communist colours',[80] he also accepted that there were many different paths to socialism, and insisted on adapting marxist theory to specific Third World conditions. This perspective was shared by Stalin during the period of KMT-CCP collaboration, and was in fact a justification for this alliance.[81]

The debacle in China favoured revision in the Soviet attitude towards national forms of socialism. Despite the continuing recognition at the 6th Comintern Congress in 1928 that 'the construction of socialism will assume different forms in different countries',[82] there was evident at the Congress and in its aftermath a much heavier emphasis on universal principles (such as the leadership of the proletariat — see below), and a corresponding intolerance of diversity in the application of revolutionary theory in specific situations. As the Third International put it in 1933:

There is no way out of the general crisis of capitalism other than the one shown by the October Revolution . . . Only [the example of the USSR] shows the way out and the way to save the exploited and oppressed in all the imperialist *and colonial* countries.[83]

Such a perspective was consistent with the sectarian refusal to collaborate with non-communist forces which characterized Soviet doctrine and practice fom 1928 to 1935.

Growing concern over the rise of Germany and Japan favoured a new quest for allies among non-communist forces in the Western world, and, consequently, a new tolerance of diversity in doctrine. One aspect of this was a re-evaluation of the balance between universal and particular in theories of revolution and the transition to socialism. In an almost Orwellian reversal, member parties attending the 7th Comintern Congress were cautioned explicitly against the 'mechanical transportation of ready made forms and methods' and were encouraged to experiment with new tactics adapted to nationally specific conditions of struggle.[84] A similar degree of latitude was implicit in Soviet attitudes immediately after the Second World War, as is clear in their stress on peaceful and evolutionary tactics, both in Europe and in the East. However, the deterioration in East-West relations into the Cold War, and the intense suspicion with which Soviet policy-makers came to regard collaboration with non-proletarian forces – evident in Zhdanov's speech to the Cominform in 1947[85] – led once again to a sectarian emphasis on the universal character of revolutionary theory and a corresponding downplaying of doctrinal creativity in specific historical circumstances.

While Soviet writers in the late 1940s, impressed by the success of the CCP, recognized China as a 'vast treasury of revolutionary experience' and as a potential model for revolution throughout the Third World,[86] this did not constitute any great concession. The Chinese revolutionary experience was seen in its essentials as a reaffirmation of the Bolshevik model, a creative application of strategy and tactics developed by Lenin and Stalin and of the 'enormous experience' of the CPSU. Stalin, moreover, had 'brilliantly predicted the course of the Chinese revolution and indicated the conditions in which it would succeed'.[87]

As the nature of Chinese claims to status as a centre of Third World revolution and as a model peculiarly appropriate to the colonial and semi-colonial countries became clear at the beginning of the 1950s, Soviet writers sought to deflate this implicit challenge to the Soviet position in the world revolutionary movement without directly criticizing the CCP. This, ironically, led to a renewed emphasis on the significance of the peculiarities of each revolutionary situation. As Zhukov put it in 1952, because of the 'principle of the obligatory consideration of the particularly and specifically national elements in each individual country, it would be risky to regard the Chinese model as some kind of stereotype for people's democratic revolution in other countries of Asia'.[88]

With Stalin's death and the subsequent Soviet opening to non-proletarian regimes in the Third World, the Soviets came to have a concrete foreign policy incentive for allowing diversity in theorizing about the transition to socialism. Most of the countries with whom they were dealing sought to adapt socialism to particular national conditions. To have rejected out of hand these efforts would have been offensive. Policy in Eastern Europe – where the Soviets were calling for destalinization and for greater responsiveness to national sensitivities in the transition to socialism – also favoured greater flexibility in doctrine with respect to the balance between universal and particular in national forms of socialism. Hence, Khrushchev stressed in his 20th CPSU Congress speech (1956) that forms of the transition to socialism would become 'more and more varied'.[89]

Some retreat was evident, however, later in the year when Khrushchev, perhaps chastened by the Hungarian and Polish experiences in the autumn of 1956, noted that 'undue emphasis on national peculiarities could 'harm both socialist construction and the whole family of socialist nations'.[90]

The subject came up again at the 1957 Conference of Communist and Workers' Parties, the Soviet desire to maintain some degree of cohesion in and control of the movement and to satisfy the 'leftism' of the Chinese running up against Eastern European pressures towards autonomy and 'polycentrism' and the Soviet recognition that some concession to particularistic tendencies in the satellite states was politically expedient. The final document attempted to reconcile these conflicting pressures by calling on the one hand for the creative application of marxism-leninism and rejecting 'the mechanical imitation of the policies and tactics of the communist parties of other countries'. That presumably spoke to the Poles and Yugoslavs. On the other hand, the document warned against the 'exaggeration of the role of peculiarities or the departure under the pretext of national peculiarities from the universal Marxist-Leninist truth of the socialist revolution and building socialism'.[91] As is seen below, the document went on to spell out in more than usual detail just what this universal truth was. This presumably was a bow in the direction of the CCP and of more orthodox elements within the CPSU itself.

The discussion of the concept of 'national democracy' in the final doument of the 1960 Conference of Communist and Workers Parties reflected a similar attempt to recognize the importance of specifics (which legitimized close Soviet ties with emergent radical, but non-communist regimes such as those in Indonesia, Guinea, Cuba and Ghana) while underlining the universality of basic principles of marxism-leninism (see below).

In subsequent years, as the claims of African and Arab clients to have developed specific types of socialism which were different from and superior (in local conditions) to marxism-leninism, the tension between the dictates of the quest for influence and those of ideological legitimacy grew sharper. Increasingly open Chinese criticism of Soviet 'revisionism' rendered the Soviet situation even less comfortable. The difficulties in reconciling these desiderata were evident in considerable incoherence in the Soviet discussion of 'national forms of socialism' between 1960 and 1964.

The 1961 CPSU programme relected the pressure of the Chinese and, more importantly, of more conservative groups within the party in stating that Arab and African socialisms were as a rule 'petty bourgeois illusions'. It stressed that revolution and the dictatorship of the proletariat were necessary aspects of the transition to socialism.[92] The literature of the next two years is littered with criticisms of African and Arab variants of socialism as 'demagogic attempts' by the national bourgeoisie to divert the masses and to win their loyalty and as evidence of a profound misunderstanding of socialism and a persistence of utopianism.[93] Ivan Potekhin in early 1964 criticized ideological particularism in Africa as an impediment to the spread of real socialism, and one which strengthened the position of bourgeois ideology. He explicitly denied the proposition that marxism was inappropriate in the African context.[94]

In essence, the Soviet criticism of African socialism amounted to an assertion that it departed from what Potekhin called marxism's 'general laws for the development of any society, including pre-capitalist ones'.[95] Among more disturbing aspects of this departure were the denial of the existence of classes in African society and of the necessity of class struggle, the assertion that precolonial society had been socialist in character, and the rejection of the dictatorship of the proletariat and, indeed, of marxism as a theoretical construct relevant to African reality.

On the other hand, there was ample evidence, particularly in the last year of Khrushchev's rule, of considerably greater flexibility towards national forms of socialism in the Third World. This appeared first in the writings of commentators such as Igor Belyayev and Georgii Mirskii on Algeria and the United Arab Republic in early and mid-1963. That official attitudes on the subject were changing dramatically was evident at the end of 1963, in Khrushchev's interview with Third World journalists, which could be construed as a relatively unambiguous endorsement of national forms of socialism.[96] In mid-December of the same year, Kosygin referred to Algeria's following the socialist path. In early 1964, Khrushchev himself referred approvingly to Algeria's determination to 'embark upon the socialist path', and in May, during a visit to the United Arab Republic, referred to that country's having embarked on socialist construction.[97] These departures from orthodoxy may be explained in terms of a Soviet desire to curry favour with influential Third World regimes at a time of intense Sino-Soviet competition for influence in the Afro-Asian bloc, and perhaps by Khrushchev's own desire, after a number of conspicuous failures in foreign policy for quick and substantial gains in the Third World.[98]

Khrushchev's eclecticism on this subject was by no means unanimously endorsed.[99] Nevertheless, it opened the way for far more optimistic assessments of national forms of socialism in the academic and party press. Scholars at the Institute of World Economy and International Relations and elsewhere attacked the dogmatism of previous views on the subject, stressed the possibility for developing countries to make the transition to socialism from the present stage, and approved the transition from the ideology of nationalism to that of socialism 'of the national type' which was held to be occurring in the 'revolutionary democracies' (see below). Many also maintained that despite their 'utopian' character, such doctrines reflected a desire resolutely to implement the national liberation process, paving the way for non-capitalist development. Moreover 'petty bourgeois socialism' (*sic*) was held to be on the borderline of scientific socialism. It reflected the transition of these societies towards socialist construction, the petty bourgeois elements disappearing with time.[100] This was a far cry from Lenin's warning about national bourgeois attempts to cloak their revolution in communist colours. It should be stresssed, however, that there was at this time no explicit statement that socialism could be *achieved* by non-proletarian groups. What had changed apparently was the assessment of whether non-proletarians could *begin* the transition to socialism. Khrushchev had said, effectively, that Nasser and Ben Bella were on the path to socialism, not that they ruled socialist societies, or that they could follow this path to its end without a considerable ideological evolution on their parts.

The suggestion that non-proletarian elements could begin the transition to socialism was an important qualitative shift in Soviet doctrine, undermining the position of indigenous communist parties in the Third World and, by implication, drawing into question the legitimacy of the leadership of the CPSU within the USSR itself. As such, it is not surprising that it did not survive the demise of the premier and his replacement by more orthodox personalities.

The natural conservatism of the new leadership, its reduced interest in revolutionary developments in the Third World, and the string of reversals in the mid-1960s affecting close Third World allies all favoured a return to a more orthodox position with respect to the balance of universal and particular in theories of Third World revolution. Soviet writers were careful to note that countries aspiring to socialism, such as Algeria and Burma, were on the non-capitalist path and not yet engaged in socialist construction, despite their ultimate objectives. The socialist revolution required a class displacement resulting in the hegemony of the proletariat. [101] This amounted to the assertion that the embrace of marxist-leninist scientific socialism was a precondition not only for the achievement of socialism, but also for entering the transition to it.

This may appear to be splitting hairs, but it had important implications from the Soviet perspective. A narrower more rigorous definition of the transition to socialism and the role of the proletariat in that transition re-established the necessary character of CPSU leadership in the *Soviet* transition to socialism. Second, it re-established the place of local communist parties in the Third World revolutionary process. Third, it facilitated the explanation of how progressive regimes in the Third World could be replaced by reactionary ones. Fourth, to the extent that recognizing that a regime was on the socialist path rather than in some prior stage implied a heightened Soviet commitment to that regime's survival, the distinction between these two categories allowed greater flexibility in Soviet policy. Moreover, it meant a lesser strain on Soviet resources and less risk to Soviet prestige in the event that the regime concerned fell victim to 'domestic reaction' or 'imperialist intervention'. At a time of considerable American military involvement in the Third World, such flexibility had substantial utility. This position clearly dominated Soviet discussion of the balance between universal and particular until the early 1970s, when a diversity of opinion emerged once again, the product of greater Soviet optimism and a correspondingly growing willingness to play an active role in the revolutionary process in the Third World.

Scepticism regarding the unscientific, eclectic, and immature, 'splittist' and mystifying character of 'national forms of socialism', and assertions to the effect that communist leadership was necessary for the transition to socialism persisted in some quarters.[102] Soviet commentators specifically criticized a number of the characteristics of Third World doctrines of socialism outlined in Chapter 4: the 'idealization' of the peasantry, the attempt to marry socialism with religion (as in some forms of Arab socialism), the voluntaristic disregard for objective factors in social development, and the 'utopian' appeal of some doctrines to tribal/communal traditions.[103] Coupled with this scepticism was frequent wishful thinking to the effect that marxism-leninism was gradually winning the day, its influence replacing that of 'national forms of socialism'.[104]

On the other hand, Soviet commentators continued to stress the undesirability of mechanically copying the experiences of other parties, given the dissimilarity of revolutionary conditions in different countries.[105] Beyond this, some of the writers cited in the previous paragraph entertained the possibility that the 'national democratic' variant of 'national forms of socialism' (for example, the doctrines of Nasser, Toure, Nkrumah and Keita), because of its emphasis on 'general conformity with the laws of social development' and on production relations rather than moral/ethical considerations, could evolve into marxism-leninism.[106] Others held that national socialist theories were progressive in their programmatic aspects and theoretical underpinnings despite their ideological shortcomings. They recognized that these theories shared the same basic objectives as scientific socialism – the end of all forms of exploitation and the embrace of a socialist path.[107] In this vein, Lenin's point that although all nations would become socialist, they would do so by different paths was recalled.[108] It is important to note, however, that the essence of this greater solicitude with regard to particular theories of socialism and towards regimes which Soviet writers deemed to be of 'socialist orientation' was a recognition of their universal aspect – their recognition of general principles, their devotion to a single objective, and their potential for transformation into marxism-leninism as the Soviets defined it.

Since the mid-1970s, there appears again to have been a degree of tightening up in the Soviet discussion of national forms of socialism and a more critical view of the latter. This has been coupled with some narrowing in the parameters of the category of 'states of socialist orientation', and may be ascribed to a number of factors:

(1) a number of more important Soviet clients in Africa (for example, Egypt and Somalia) defected into the camp of 'imperialism

and reaction', casting into doubt once more the depth of the progressive commitment of non-communist Third World regimes;
(2) several self-proclaimed marxist-leninist regimes (for example, Angola, Mozambique, Ethiopia and South Yemen) appeared in Africa and elsewhere;
(3) centrifugal pressures within the world communist movement intensified as a result of the challenge of 'Eurocommunism' and the impact of detente in Eastern Europe.

States which acknowledged the universality of marxism-leninism and which, in one way or another, sought to translate their understanding of this ideology into social reality, often relying on Soviet and Eastern European advice and assistance, were singled out for praise in Soviet writing and benefited disproportionately from Soviet economic and, to some extent, military largesse.[109] In contrast, Soviet writers have more frequently made the point that national types of socialism which reject marxism-leninism tend to degenerate into national chauvinism and leftist extremism.[110]

Within the marxist-leninist context, it was emphasized that while a certain amount of creativity in the adaptation of revolutionary theory was laudable, this effort had

nothing in common with the artificial, arbitrary breakup of marxism-leninism into 'variants' and 'models' that are actually covers for deviations from the uniform, genuinely scientific principles of internationalism. The thesis of the multivariant character of marxism-leninism and its inevitable 'division' into 'national' and 'regional' forms as different countries and peoples move towards socialism has no basis in fact.[111]

From a broader perspective, one Soviet commentator dismissed the suggestion that there could be a 'third way of development' peculiar to the Third World as reflective of the impact of bourgeois ideology.[112] With regard to Chinese attempts to modify marxism-leninism, Soviet official commentary continued to display great hostility. A 1981 Central Committee resolution, for example, condemned the notion of 'sinified marxism' as petty bourgeois nationalism, the characteristic feature of the CCP's platform being an exclusivist disregard for the 'general laws governing the construction of socialism'.[113] One of the greater sins of the CCP clearly continued to be that party's voluntaristic attempts to transcend objective conditions of development.[114]

The basic point is that underlying these shifts in the Soviet assessment of national variants of socialism is a far greater stress on universals and on 'objective laws of social development' in revolution and in the transition to socialism than is evident in much of the Third World literature discussed in the last chapter. Moreover, as a rule, to the extent that particularism in doctrine is endorsed, it is justified pragmatically in terms of the adaptation of universal theory to the demands of differing situations. There is little sympathy for the need to express national creativity and to create or strengthen national identity which the particularism of national forms of socialism in part reflects. There is also little understanding of the legitimizing function of the 'nationalization' of theory. Such concerns are, in Soviet eyes, indications of national chauvinism.

## Class and National Liberation

Three of the more obvious aspects of the Soviet tendency to stress the universality of revolutionary theory concern class and its relation to national liberation. The first — the Soviet discussion of leadership in national liberation revolutions — reflects a dilemma similar to those concerning nationalism and national forms of socialism. On the one hand, marxism-leninism dictates that the most reliable internationalists in any given population are the organized working class and its vanguard party. As such, it is this group which will most reliably carry through the anti-imperialist and social revolutionary aspects of national liberation. Moreover, Soviet discussions of the subject suggest a belief that of the various groups involved in national liberation revolutions, proletarians and communists are those most likely to accept the Soviet leading role in the world revolutionary process, and hence are likely to be those most susceptible to Soviet influence. The experience of the Soviet-Yugoslav, Sino-Soviet, and Soviet-Albanian splits does not seem to have affected substantially this view.

On the other hand, the Soviets have been faced since the beginnings of their involvement in the Third World with the 'objective reality' that — given uneven development and the fact that most non-European societies found themselves in precapitalist or early capitalist stages of development — the working class was pitifully small and communist parties virtually nonexistent and certainly politically marginal throughout much of the East. The politics of national liberation have generally been dominated by a motley group of what Soviet writers have loosely

referred to as 'national bourgeois' or 'petty bourgeois',[115] with an occasional salting of 'feudal reactionaries'. In such conditions, to insist on
proletarian leadership as a condition for Soviet involvement would be
unrealistic in historical terms and would impede severely attempts to
expand Soviet influence among anti-colonial and anti-Western groups in
the Third World. The tension between the preference for proletarian
hegemony and the need to take into account the balance of social
forces within Third World societies and dominant political groups within them has been evident in Soviet doctrine and policy towards national
liberation movements since the revolution and, more particularly, since
the death of Stalin and the beginning of sustained Soviet attempts to
play an active role in Third World politics beyond the periphery of the
USSR. Soviet writers have since the revolution accepted the possibility
of non-proletarian leadership of the national liberation revolution, with
the exception of a few brief periods of radical sectarianism (for example, 1928-34 and 1947-53).[116] What is more striking, however, is
their steady assertion of the temporary character of this leadership and
the necessity of its replacement by proletarian dictatorship in order for
the national liberation revolution to be carried beyond its first stages to
successful completion. This contrasts markedly with the mainstream of
Third World radical opinion discussed in the previous chapter.

　　The controversy between Lenin and Roy on the question of leadership of the national liberation revolution has already been discussed
(see Chapters 2 and 4). The Soviet acceptancy of the 'united front from
above' (collaboration with organizations dominated by the national
bourgeoisie, acceptance of bourgeois hegemony at that stage of the
national revolution, and the entry of communists as individuals into
the broader national organizations) between the CCP and the KMT reflected a pragmatic willingness to deal with and to seek influence over
what was clearly the most dynamic force in Chinese politics of the day.
Soviet spokesmen did little to hide the fact that they viewed this
arrangement with the KMT to be temporary and to be followed once
the KMT had established itself throughout China by a proletarian
challenge to bourgeois hegemony.

　　Soviet writers after the 6th Comintern Congress shifted to the advocacy of proletarian leadership at the current stage of the national liberation revolution, for reasons suggested in note 116. In the aftermath of
the 7th Comintern Congress, the Soviet line shifted back to a recognition of the possibility of national bourgeois leadership and the 'united
front from above'. This displayed the greater flexibility towards collaboration with non-communists in general during the pre-war period. It

is a fair guess that the recognition of the possibility that wars conducted by the national bourgeoisie of an occupied country could assume the character of wars of national liberation[117] reflected a Soviet desire to justify the resumption of relations with and assistance to the KMT government in China and pressure on the CCP to reconstitute the united front, all of this with a view to fostering a more effective Chinese resistance to Japanese expansionism. The basic principle that proletarian leadership was necessary for the completion of the national liberation revolution was not at issue.

Although discussion of this aspect of Third World revolution lapsed during the Second World War, in its immediate aftermath several Soviet writers stressed the progressive character of bourgeois nationalist movements in the colonies and advocated the continuation of the 'united front from above' approach, which amounted to an acceptance of bourgeois leadership.[118] The USSR's early post-war policy towards China, where Stalin initially opposed the CCP challenge to the KMT and apparently envisaged instead a long period of nationalist rule with CCP collaboration,[119] was a practical manifestation of this perspective.

As relations with the Western allies deteriorated, and as the Soviets moved gradually to consolidate their rule over Eastern Europe by squeezing out non-proletarian elements of ruling coalitions, the line on leadership in the anti-colonial revolution hardened once more. In 1946, by putting forward the October Revolution as a model for the East, one prominent Soviet commentator implied that leadership of the struggle should be vested in local communist parties.[120] During the 1947-8 anti-Varga campaign, the idea that the USSR should support movements dominated by the national bourgeoisie, such as the Indian National Congress, was condemned.[121] Zhukov, in an article discussing Zhdanov's 1947 Cominform speech, affirmed that proletarian and communist leadership was a necessary condition for alliance with the national bourgeoisie, which, in the face of growing mass involvement in the anti-colonial struggle, tended to side with imperialism.[122] The diplomatic reflection of this change in Soviet doctrine was the non-recognition of newly independent states in Asia, such as India, Pakistan and Burma.

Before going on to the period after Stalin's death, it is important to note that in those parts of the stalinist period when bourgeois leadership was accepted, this acceptance was limited only to the struggle for political independence (or, in the case of China, national unification and the ejection of the imperialist presence). Once the colonial presence had been removed, it was fully anticipated that the bourgeoisie would abandon the revolution and seek to consolidate its own class hegemony at the expense of the masses.

In the years after Stalin's death, improving relations with new states in the Third World were accompanied by the re-emergence of the view that the national bourgeoisie could lead in the national revolution. Evgenii Varga had the last word in the 'Varga Dispute' in 1955 when he stressed the falseness of the view that victory in the anti-colonial struggle was possible only when the communist party played the leading role.[123]

The necessity of justifying close ties with national bourgeois regimes in the period after independence led Soviet writers to accept a more durable constructive role for the bourgeoisie. Hence, at the 20th Party Congress it was argued that the bourgeoisie was not necessarily inconsequential in the post-independence stage as continuing pressure from imperialism led it to hold on to its progressive position. This justified not only Soviet ties with the national bourgeoisie, but also pressure on local communist parties to collaborate with non-proletarian regimes governing new states. The CPSU constrained local parties to abandon temporarily the theme of combat against the national bourgeoisie and to present themselves as national rather than proletarian parties.[124] Soviet leaders retained the view, however, that the leadership of the working class and its vanguard was the 'absolute and decisive requirement for all forms of the transition to socialism'.[125]

Later in the 1950s, however, a number of factors contributed to a less favourable view of national bourgeois regimes. The initial successes and obvious strength of the Iraqi Communist Party in the 1958 coup and subsequently suggested that Soviet analysts had underestimated the power of the organized proletariat. The attitude of Nasser towards developments in Iraq and his suppression of local communists in Syria and Egypt raised doubts about just how progressive the national bourgeoisie was. Moreover, it created problems for the CPSU within the world communist movement, the Chinese bringing increasing pressure to bear upon the Soviets to adopt a more class-oriented revolutionary posture towards the politics of national liberation. These concerns were reflected at a conference in Leipzig sponsored by the *World Marxist Review* in 1959, where Soviet and foreign communist specialists stressed the vacillating and exploitative character of the national bourgeoisie, its unwillingness to involve the masses in the revolution, and, consequently, the necessity for the proletariat to retain its organizational independence and to assume the leadership of the national liberation revolution.[126]

A similar perspective, though one slightly different in emphasis, was evident at the 1960 Conference of Communist and Workers' Parties which produced the first systematic attempt to square the theoretical circle of seeking close ties with progressive non-proletarian regimes in new states and at the same time favouring internal pressure on these leaderships to move further to the left and eventually either to step aside in favour of or to join a proletarian dictatorship. This was the concept of national democracy, a rather shaky compromise between the CPSU and the CCP on the one hand and between orthodox and opportunistic perspectives within the CPSU on the other.

For our purposes, perhaps the most important element of 'national democracy' was its dynamic aspect. The drafters of the final document of the conference recognized the possibility of national bourgeois leadership in the struggle for independence, and in the aftermath of its attainment. However, they also stressed the dual character of this class — its conflict of interest with imperialism being less strong than was that of other social groups, and being complemented by a fear of mass involvement in national politics, a fear which favoured the abandonment of the struggle for national liberation and compromise with imperialism. These tendencies towards vacillation deepened once independence was achieved, in the face of growing class differentiation and mass pressure for social change.

Its defection could be prevented and the continuation of the national liberation revolution through social reform and non-capitalist development could be assured only by a growing role for the organized proletariat (the decisive force in the united front) and by a progressive dilution of bourgeois leadership, leading to its ultimate replacement by the dictatorship of the proletariat. The state of national democracy — in which dictatorship was rejected and a conscious and sustained effort made to involve the masses and their organizations in politics — was a formula by which this transition could be achieved peacefully.[127]

This formula allowed the Soviet leadership to reconcile support for non-proletarian regimes conducting anti-Western foreign policies with continued commitment to proletarian revolution. It also allowed Soviet writers to go some distance towards acknowledging the socialist aspirations of a number of regimes in the Third World, without recognizing their socialist character. In this vein, the 1961 party programme stressed the necessity of proletarian dictatorship during the transition to socialism.[128]

To put it mildly, the concept of national democracy betrayed considerable lack of realism on the part of its formulators. Most notably, it ignored the claims of a number of Third World leaders (for example, Sekou Toure, Kwame Nkrumah, Sukarno and Nasser) that despite the non-communist character of their regimes and their opposition (at the time) to the idea of class struggle, and, indeed, in a number of instances, their sustained persecution of national communists, they were building socialism. Moreover, the CPSU was in effect asking these leaders to accept the proposition that the revolution in their countries could advance only to the extent that they allowed their power to slip away and that they should therefore establish the conditions for their own consignment to the 'dustbin of history'.

The attitude of at least one of these leaders towards the concept was evident in Sekou Toure's suppression in late 1961 of a teachers' strike in Conakry; his expulsion of the Soviet Ambassador Solod for interference in Guinea's internal affairs; and the subsequent thaw in relations between Guinea and the USA.[129] One might also cite in this regard the extremely negative Egyptian response to Khrushchev's attempt to convince them that the transition to communism in Egypt was inevitable and that they should therefore cease their obstruction of agitation by Egypt's communist party.[130]

The need to explain these anomalies and to justify continuing close relations with non-communist regimes in the Middle East, Africa and South Asia despite their failure to conform to the national democratic model fostered considerable debate in Soviet academic and policy-making circles over the extent to which non-proletarian regimes could transcend their class origins and embark on a socialist path in the aftermath of independence. Through much of 1962, perhaps in part as a result of problems in relations with Guinea and Egypt, the prevailing mood was one of pessimism and disillusionment with regard to non-proletarian regimes. This is evident, for instance, in Khrushchev's mid-1962 comments concerning the vacillating character and naivete of many 'fence-sitting' leaders in the Third World, and his criticism of their refusal to accept class struggle and the class structure of society.[131]

However, by late 1963, Khrushchev's concern to preserve and extend Soviet influence over anti-Western regimes in the Third World apparently won out over ideological orthodoxy. In December 1963, Khrushchev enunciated the notion of the 'revolutionary democrat', a leader who 'sincerely advocated non-capitalist methods for the solution of national problems and declared [his] determination to build socialism'.[132] This set the scene for the subsequent recognition of

Nasser's and Ben Bella's socialist credentials in early 1964 (see above).

The notion that non-proletarian elites could overcome their class background and build socialism was defended by a greater emphasis on subjective factors in the transition to socialism. Leaders of any class origin, provided that they possessed sufficient revolutionary consciousness, could overcome their class limitations and adopt progressive policies which were inconsistent with the interests of their original class.[133] In this way 'if the conditions for proletarian leadership have not yet matured, the historical mission of breaking with capitalism can be carried out by elements close to the working class', particularly in conditions where the world socialist system was capable of 'performing the functions of the proletarian vanguard in relation to the imperialist oppressed nations'.[134] In like fashion, it was possible for mass national parties to transform themselves into marxist-leninist parties. One sees in the last years of Khrushchev's rule a significant modification of the conventional Soviet weighting of subjective and objective factors in social development, a voluntaristic interlude in the evolution of Soviet doctrine concerning Third World revolution.

None the less, while this amounted to a considerable expansion in the Soviet view of the capacity of non-proletarian leaders to adopt and carry through 'progressive' measures, it did not constitute an abandonment of the Soviet commitment to proletarian leadership in the transition to socialism. What was being argued here was essentially that the 'revolutionary democrats' were *coming over* to proletarian marxist-leninist positions.

The concept of 'revolutionary democracy' was thus an attempt to satisfy a number of desiderata:

(1) to legitimize recognition of the progressive and, beyond this, the socialist credentials of non-communist leaders being courted by the USSR;

(2) to explain how what appeared to be the beginnings of a 'socialist transformation' (for example, nationalization of the principal means of production and of trading and finance sectors, and land reform and on occasion collectivization of agriculture) could occur in societies without a numerous working class and communist vanguard;

(3) and to do this without drawing into question the universality of marxism-leninism and, by extension, the legitimacy of CPSU rule in the USSR by denying the necessity of communist leadership in the transition to socialism.

A number of events prior to and closely following Khrushchev's ousting suggested that some of the premier's colleagues resisted this ideological innovation and the optimism concerning the capacity of subjective factors to overcome objective constraints which it reflected.[135] The removal of Khrushchev, and the overthrow of a number of prominent Third World progressive regimes which had been or were closely linked to the USSR (as in Indonesia and Algeria in 1965, Ghana in 1966, and in Mali in 1968) brought a return to orthodoxy on the question of leadership in the transition to socialism. Optimism with regard to the potential of 'revolutionary democrats' was severely tempered and far greater stress laid on their non-proletarian origins. Soviet writers maintained that these origins encouraged a utopian disregard of obstacles on the path to socialism, an underestimation of the strength of 'reactionary' elements in their societies (including Western-leaning elements of the military), a failure to mobilize the masses and to develop effective and durable party structures, all of which rendered revolutionary democratic regimes vulnerable to overthrow. They were also criticized for bureaucratization, vacillation in their anti-imperialist commitment, and extreme national egoism.[136] Soviet writers also returned to considerably greater pessimism with regard to the revolutionary potential of the national bourgeoisie.[137]

Soviet writers complemented these criticisms of their erstwhile favourites with a renewed emphasis on the necessity of working class leadership not only in the transition to socialism, but also in the phase of 'non-capitalist development'.[138] This leadership was to take the form of vanguard communist parties, reflecting growing Soviet doubts about the potential of mass nationalist parties.[139] Paradoxically, this was accompanied by an increasing realism with regard to the weakness of the working class and its vanguard in less developed Third World societies.[140] This seeming contradiction may perhaps best be explained in terms of a Soviet desire to justify the distancing from radical regimes during this period mentioned in the introduction to this chapter, and the reorientation in Soviet diplomacy in the Third World towards intrinsically important but ideologically suspect regimes. Since radical petty bourgeois regimes were incapable of making the transition to socialism and were weak and unstable, it made little sense to commit the USSR to them. If the one class capable of truly significant social progress was weak, then socialist transformation was a matter for the distant future, and not on the agenda of the moment. In such conditions, one was not sabotaging the proletarian socialist revolution by developing close ties with conservative national bourgeois regimes (for example, Nigeria, Iran, or Pakistan).

The growing optimism evident in Soviet commentary on national liberation in the early 1970s — an optimism which was grounded, as seen above, in the attainment of strategic parity and in the American defeat in Vietnam and subsequent neo-isolationism — was reflected to a degree in more sanguine appraisals of the progressive potential of non-proletarian regimes, of their capacity to undertake not only anti-imperialist but also anti-capitalist measures, and of the possibility that 'national democratic ideology may gradually evolve into scientific socialism'.[141]

Once again, however the stress was on these groups 'coming over' to the proletariat rather than replacing it in the transition to socialism. And much of the period's commentary on the potential of revolutionary democrats to begin the transition to socialism had an air of *faute de mieux* about it, one author pointing out that it was the absence of an effective proletariat which brought about the situation in which petty bourgeois coalition regimes were often, in practice, the 'basic leading force'.[142] Moreover, it was still heavily stressed, particularly by authors with close party ties (for example, R. Ul'yanovsky) that proletarian leadership by a vanguard party was a necessity for the consummation of socialist revolution.[143] The leadership of petty bourgeois revolutionary democrats remained a temporary expedient.

In the late 1970s, Soviet commentary shifted again towards greater orthodoxy, firmer stress being placed on the leading role of vanguard parties in carrying through non-capitalist development and beginning the transition to socialism.[144] This presumably reflected, as was noted above, Soviet disillusionment with non-proletarian client regimes which had in the mid-1970s distanced themselves from the USSR (for example, Egypt, Somalia and Iraq), and the emergence, particularly in Africa, of a number of self-avowed marxist-leninist regimes (Angola, Mozambique, Ethiopia, South Yemen and Afghanistan) or of regimes many of whose principals espoused marxism-leninism (for example, Nicaragua).

Karen Brutents, for example, clearly viewed proletarian leadership of the national liberation revolution to be preferable, since the proletariat was the only class whose aims 'fully accord with the ultimate aims of the national liberation movement, because it has an interest in national consolidation on a socialist basis'.[145] Although it was recognized that the leadership of 'intermediate social sections' (the 'intelligentsia' and 'urban petty bourgeoisie') had proved to be the 'most widespread [variant] in the present-day national liberation movement', this was perceived to be temporary. As social differentiation (that is, class formation) progressed, either the bourgeoisie or the proletariat assumed control, and the society concerned moved either in a capitalist direction (abandoning the national liberation revolution) or in a socialist one. The 'intermediate section' in such circumstances abandoned their effort to follow a third path and opted for one of these 'only two possible and socially antithetical variants'.[146]

In what was perhaps a reflection in theory of Soviet and Cuban practice in Third World conflicts in the mid and late 1970s, Brutents maintained further that: 'International class forces have a tremendous role to play in the shaping of the social orientation of the intermediate sections, acting something like a substitute for the absence of such factors at home or compensating for their weakness.'[147]

Soviet writers, in setting limits on the degree to which 'intermediate sections' could lead the movement towards socialism, clearly distinguished between non-capitalist development or socialist orientation in which the leadership of revolutionary democrats was possible on the one hand, and the building of socialism which required the hegemony of the proletariat guided by a marxist-leninist party on the other.[148]

The basic point in the above is that despite changes in emphasis which are largely explicable in terms of Soviet foreign policy and as responses to specific opportunities and set-backs, there has existed in Soviet doctrine and in the writings of Soviet scholars a basic preference for proletarian leadership, particularly in the later stages of the national liberation revolution, and, with very few exceptions, an insistence that such leadership is necessary in the transition to socialism. Although Soviet scholars have come to accept that non-proletarian elements can play a constructive leadership role after independence and that as a result communists should accept a subordinate position in national fronts, this role is limited and temporary. Such groups can maintain their progressive character only to the extent that they become marxist-leninists, abandoning any pretensions of developing a 'third way'. It is the working class, led by its communist vanguard, that is the most resolute fighter for national liberation.

In policy terms, although this position generally has not impeded the USSR from cultivating regimes which persecute local communists, it is reasonably clear that this preference, coupled with Soviet pressure on Third World clients to integrate communists into their regimes and to allow more open communist activity, and Soviet attempts to intercede in conditions of active persecution of communists, have aroused suspicion among Third World radical nationalist regimes. They have served as an irritant in Soviet-Arab relations in particular, and as such have impeded Soviet efforts to obtain influence.[149] The Soviet ideological commitment to local communists has also on occasion been exploited by clients of the USSR. As Freedman notes: 'Arab regimes had established party-to-party relations with the CPSU, established united fronts, and allowed communists into their governments – in nominal positions – primarily to extract more economic and military assistance from the USSR'.[150]

Closely linked to the question of leadership is that of the character of class relations between various component parts of the national liberation movements. Soviet writers, like their Third World counterparts, have as a rule taken the view that united fronts for national liberation are composed of a very broad and diverse array of class forces. It was noted in Chapter 4 that a great premium was placed by many Third World writers on consolidating these forces into one nation – on unity rather than conflict within the nation. Where they deemed class struggle necessary, it was to be limited in character and to take place within the bounds of an overarching national unity.

By contrast, Soviet discussions of national liberation emphasize the inevitability and, indeed, the desirability of struggle within the national front, particularly in the later stages of the national liberation revolution when social tasks began to outweigh 'anti-imperialist' ones on the agenda of the movement. It is through struggle against and pressure upon non-proletarian leading elements in the national liberation movement that the working class and its vanguard attain their position of hegemony which is necessary for the transition to socialism.

The emphasis on struggle within the liberation movement follows logically from the embrace of marxism-leninism, in that class conflict is the motor of all social development. To deny its necessity in the Third World context would be to draw into question the universality of basic marxist-leninist principles. However, to emphasize the desirability of conflict within societies ruled by regimes with whom the USSR seeks close relations runs the risk of undermining Soviet diplomacy. Such commentary may be viewed as divisive, if not subversive, especially when translated into action by local communists perceived to be linked to the USSR. It is not surprising, therefore, that while the theme of struggle is a constant thread in Soviet analysis, its prominence relative to its antithesis, alliance, varies in relation to Soviet policy objectives and practical experience. In general, emphasis on the necessity of struggle against 'bourgeois' or 'petty bourgeois' leading elements in the national liberation movements closely parallels that on the necessity of proletarian or communist leadership. Hence, when in 1928-34 and 1947-52, Soviet writers insisted on the necessity of proletarian leadership of the struggle against imperialism, they also stressed the necessity of active struggle against non-proletarian aspirants to hegemony in the national liberation movement. By contrast, when the USSR sought amicable relations with non-proletarian groups and regimes in the Third World and as a result accepted the possibility of leadership by groups other than the working class and its vanguard, Soviet writers toned down references to class struggle or maintained that struggle against the bourgeoisie was a matter for the future.

However, that alliance must be supplemented by struggle has been a steady theme of Soviet discourse on national liberation despite the twists and turns of Soviet policy towards national liberation movements and new states. The 7th Comintern Congress, for example, which resurrected the line of collaboration with movements led by the national bourgeoisie, maintained none the less that it was the task of local communists to carry on 'an irreconcilable struggle to safeguard the economic and political positions of the workers, toiling peasants, and national minorities . . . '[151]

In the early 1960s, a period of similar emphasis on collaboration, the formula of the 'national democratic state' accounted for the capacity of non-proletarians to pursue progressive policies in the aftermath of independence in terms of pressure exerted on them by the working class and its party. The transition to socialism was to be the outcome of a process whereby the power of the bourgeoisie was progressively supplanted by that of the proletariat. The 'revolutionary democrats' were characterized as allies of the proletariat in a struggle against vacillating and reactionary elements in the new states.

As social differentiation within the new states deepened, this class struggle intensified. Brutents in 1978 argued along these lines that there was occurring in these states a 'sharpening of class conflicts and their expansion on a nationwise scale'. Class struggle was becoming, in his view, a critical factor in the accomplishment of the tasks of national liberation.[152] The denial of class struggle by such figures as Toure, Nkrumah, and Nyerere was frequently criticized.[153] Nehru's view that class contradictions could be overcome through reform and co-operation was also rejected.[154]

Associated with this stress on the unavoidability and desirability of class struggle was a stress on the necessity of maintaining the independence of the party of the proletariat. With the partial exception of the mid and late 1960s, when for reasons of policy several Arab communist parties were urged to disband or to submerge themselves in broader national movements, Soviet writers have from the beginning of their theorizing about national revolution in the Third World called for organizational autonomy and freedom of propaganda for local parties. The proletariat and its party required freedom of action in order to fulfil their role of laying the subjective groundwork for the adoption of scientific socialism. Collaboration was to be complemented by separateness.[155] As an editor of the *World Marxist Review* once put it: 'The independence of the proletarian party in the political coalition is the most important factor that provides direction and organization to the association of democratic forces, a factor on which the revolutionary effectiveness of the coalition depends.'[156]

This position was consistent with the Soviet image of the proletariat as the most ideologically conscious and reliable force in the liberation movement and as the eventual hegemon within it, and their view that the other forces within the movement were susceptible to such heresies as national chauvinism and (paradoxically) compromise with imperialism in the face of growing challenges from the masses.

But it conflicted with the intolerance of internal division characteristic of radical and moderate nationalist circles in the Third World. When the principle of independence of the party of the proletariat was tied to those of the necessity of struggle within the nation and eventual proletarian hegemony within the national liberation movement, it was on more than one occasion viewed as subversive. Problems in Soviet relations with Arab regimes associated with the activities of local communists have already been noted. One might also argue that it was the package of eventual communist leadership, the necessity of struggle within the national front as the working class displaced the bourgeoisie, and the insistence on separate organization which, despite efforts to mollify Chiang, aroused his hostility towards the CCP and the USSR.

One last aspect of Soviet discussions of class and national liberation which distinguishes the Soviet conception of revolutionary struggle from those of their Third World counterparts is their treatment of the peasantry. It was noted in Chapter 4 that radical nationalist writers on national liberation in general emphasized the critical role of the peasantry in the revolution and the primacy of rural struggle.

Soviet writers have by no means denied the importance of peasant participation in revolutionary struggle in overwhelmingly rural Third World societies. They have quite steadily affirmed that the worker-peasant alliance is the basic driving force of the national liberation movement. Success in the anti-imperialist struggle depends largely on broad peasant participation.[157]

However, Soviet writers have also generally held that the peasantry is not capable of an independent revolutionary role, as it is scattered, often isolated, politically immature, displays petty bourgeois tendencies, and is susceptible to manipulation by traditonal elites espousing obscurantist religious and tribalist notions.[158] Moreover, they have stressed that the peasantry is not an undifferentiated whole, but is divided into exploiting and exploited sections.[159] Finally, they have repeatedly criticized Third World figures such as Gandhi and Fanon for an idealization of the peasantry and of peasant life,[160] and for tendencies to ignore or reject collaboration with the working class (in this instance, Khrushchev's drawing into question of Mao's marxist credentials is typical).[161] Severe criticism at the height of the Sino-Soviet dispute of the CCP's reliance on the peasantry and the Chinese predilection to redefine the proletariat subjectively in order to allow the inclusion of the peasantry within the proletariat suggest deep-seated resistance to the idea that proletarian status can be divorced from role in the productive process.[162]

## Violence

Turning finally to the utility of force in struggles for national liberation, the Soviet position is on the whole more restrained than that of Third World writers. Soviet writers, even at their most extreme, have not gone beyond the Clausewitzian view that force is merely one policy instrument among many, and one which is in certain circumstances more suited to the specific end in view than are others.

Early Soviet writers held the view that violence was a universal and necessary attribute of revolution.[163] Over time, and in response most notably to the peaceful acquisition of independence by a number of states in Asia and the Middle East, as well as to a desire to establish peaceful coexistence as the basis of East-West relations, writers in the post-Stalin period have recognized the possibility of peaceful liberation. They have played down the importance of armed struggle.[164] Since the 20th Party Congress, it has been maintained in doctrine that armed struggle may or may not be an appropriate approach to the problem of liberation, depending on the specific circumstances in question. The most important determinant of the appropriateness of violence is the degree of resistance to revolutionary change mounted by 'imperialism and reaction'. As such, violence is a regrettable last resort. It is not so much a choice of the revolutionaries, but results from the decisions of those who are resisting change.[165] The undifferentiated advocacy of armed struggle, common among Third World activists, as was seen in the previous chapter, has been condemned as adventurist or as 'left opportunism'.[166]

In practice, Soviet statements of support for armed struggle have tended to vary in relation to a number of factors which pull in different directons. First is the intrinsic importance in Soviet foreign policy of groups in the Third World engaged in armed struggle (for example, the PLO). Second is the degree to which the USSR has felt it necessary to polish its revolutionary credentials in the face of criticism from the left of the international communist movement. In this vein, Khrushchev's specific endorsement of wars of national liberation in 1961 and the contemporaneous airlift of equipment to the Pathet Lao were related to criticism from the CCP. Heavy Soviet involvement in the Angolan War in 1975-76 was in part a response to Chinese attempts to undermine Soviet influence among Southern African governments and liberation movements.[167] Third is the state of and trend in East-West relations. In periods when relations are bad and/or improvement is sought, Soviet support for wars of national liberation is played down (as in the late 1950s and very recently). Fourth is the internal situation of the USSR. When the USSR seeks to concentrate on solving domestic problems (as in the mid-1960s and perhaps at present), it seeks tranquillity in its international environment and hence mutes its support for revolutionary causes.[168] Fifth is the trend in the 'international correlation of forces'[169] and particularly in its military aspect. As the USSR approached and then attained strategic parity, and as its conventional force projection capabilities expanded in the late 1960s and early 1970s,[170] Soviet writers grew less cautious in their expressions of support for wars of national liberation.[171]

Yet the basic point remains. The Soviet view of the utility of force in wars of national liberation is basically practical and expediential. It may or may not be the most effective means of winning. That is the central issue in deciding whether or not to use it. Questions of the 'liberation of the spirit', the 'regaining of dignity', the selection of leadership, and the forging of the nation through armed struggle do not figure prominently, if they figure at all, in Soviet commentary. Moreover, Soviet writers since the death of Stalin, have not viewed it as a necessary aspect of the struggle for liberation. This too sets them apart from many of the radical nationalists considered in Chapter 4. Finally, since the death of Stalin, Soviet writers have displayed considerable caution in recommending violence. In their view, it is a last resort, forced upon liberation movements by the use of force again them.

## Conclusion

There seem to be substantial affinities between Soviet and Third World conceptions of national liberation and between their respective views on how this liberation is to be achieved. With regard to the definition of the process of national liberation, Soviet writers have generally shared the view that while political independence is an important step along the road, it is by no means a sufficient condition of national liberation. Instead it is a means to deeper and more important changes. Since Stalin's death, Soviet commentators have maintained that a further necessary condition of national liberation is economic independence – the severing of asymmetrical subordinate economic ties to the former colonial power and, more broadly, to the international capitalist system. Beyond this, given that in their terms liberation implies and end to all forms of exploitation, they concur that social revolution – both anti-feudal and anti-capitalist – is a necessary aspect of the process of national liberation. This process is completed only by the transition to socialism.

With regard to the significance of Third World anti-Western struggle for the global revolutionary movement, Soviet writers have generally recognized the national liberation movement as an important ally in the struggle between the forces of progress and those of reaction. They have also accepted that there are constructive aspects to Third World nationalism and to doctrines of regional, ethnic, and religious solidarity, to the extent that these ideological currents are directed against the West. They have shared the view that revolutionary theory must be adapted to suit local conditions, and in particular that in the Third World revolutionary movements must build broad inter-class alliances in the anti-imperialist struggle. Finally, they have commonly accepted that armed struggle is a legitimate and in certain circumstances a necessary form of opposition to foreign domination in Third World societies.

There are also a number of significant disparities however, between Soviet and Third World thinking concerning revolution. With regard to the definition of the process of national liberation, there was little attention in the Soviet literature to the cultural dimension and little sympathy for the particularistic tendencies which it reflected. Moreover,

Soviet writers have taken a view on the sequential character of the main tasks of the national liberation revolution which distinguishes them from many radical nationalist writers in the Third World who appear to merge anti-imperialist and social revolutionary tasks.

The Soviet conception of the world revolutionary movement also differed in a number of important respects from Third World views on the same subject. Soviet writers have quite consistently maintained that the USSR or the 'world socialist system' was the natural leader of this historical force, that the principal contradiction in world politics was that between socialism and capitalism, and that the national liberation movement, though important, played a secondary and subordinate role in the overall movement. The successes of the national liberation movement were explicable largely in terms of permissive conditions established by the rise of, and active support form, the USSR. All of these positions diverge rather dramatically from the Third World stress on the significance of their own struggle against the West, and their refusal (with a few exceptions which are largely explicable in tactical terms) to acknowledge outside leadership and to accept that their victories were made possible by the USSR.

The Soviet conception of the world revolutionary process and the Soviet role in it is universalist. Soviet writers have consistently opposed exclusive tendencies which impeded global revolutionary solidarity. They have dissociated nationalism from national liberation, stressing that the movement is internationalist in essence. While recognizing since the death of Stalin the potentially constructive impact of anti-colonial nationalism, they have expressed serious reservations about national particularism as an impediment to proletarian internationalism and to internal social revolution, particularly in the post-independence phase. Their opposition, in principle, and ambivalence towards practical manifestations of Third World nationalism, have favoured a tendency in Soviet foreign policy to underestimate the significance of this factor in world politics.

Regarding nonalignment, Soviet writers have argued that *true* nonalignment, rather than calling for the dissociation of the Third World from both East and West, is primarily anti-imperialist by nature. Ideas of opting out of struggle between the blocs and of Third World solidarity exclusive of the USSR are denounced as counter-revolutionary, the alliance between the socialist camp and the national liberation movement is therefore objectively determined. This of course runs against the grain of the conception of nonalignment as equidistance from East and West and pursuit of interests specific to the Third

World which appears to be widely entertained in the less developed countries.

Soviet commentators have shown similar discomfort over the particularism of radical Third World nationalists in the realm of theory. While generally willing to accept some diversity in the application of marxism-leninism to revolutionary conditions in the Third World, they have displayed considerable scepticism about national forms of socialism and as a rule have placed a greater stress on universals in revolutionary doctrine than have their Third World interlocutors. Moreover, Soviet writers have adamantly asserted the general applicability of marxism-leninism and have shown great hostility towards claims that this body of theory is irrelevant in Third World conditions. They have emphasized the uniqueness of socialism as a state and have derided what they consider to be a voluntaristic disregard of the 'objective laws of social development' in much Third World writing.

With regard to class, Soviet writers have consistently favoured proletarian leadership in the later stages of the national liberation revolution. Although they have come to accept that other classes, and notably the national and petty bourgeoisie, can play a constructive leading role not only prior to, but in the aftermath of independence, the Soviets take the view that if the national liberation revolution is not to go off the rails, such groups must either be displaced by or come over to the working class and its marxist-leninist vanguard. The consummation of the national liberation revolution in the transition to socialism is attainable only under the leadership of the communist party.

Given the necessity of such a displacement, Soviet writers, with certain exceptions, have maintained that class struggle within the nation is both inevitable and desirable. Class affinity across national lines is more important than national unity. A corollary of the emphasis on class struggle has been a sustained preference (with the exception of the late Khrushchev period of 1963-4, and a certain overhang into the early years of the Brezhnev period with regard to Arab communists) for the organizational independence of indigenous communist parties. Soviet commentators have defended the right of these parties to put forward their own programmes within the context of the united front. This position has on numerous occasions proven unpopular with radical nationalist movements and governments, a principal priority of which has been the consolidation of national unity and the suppression of independent centres of opposition.

A final point which distinguishes the Soviet view of social forces involved in the struggle for liberation from that of many Third World writers is the Soviet ambivalence about the peasantry. Although Soviet writers recognize the importance of the peasant contribution, their commentary emphasizes the limitations on that class's revolutionary role and its reactionary tendencies. Soviet doctrine instead tends to stress the revolutionary potential of *urban* social groups, such as the proletariat and, with qualifications, the bourgeoisie. In this sense, it is with the mainstream of orthodox marxism, which tends to disparage rural groups.

With regard to the use of force, post Stalinist Soviet writers have not deemed it a necessary attribute of struggles for national liberation. It is deemed a last resort and is viewed as a matter of expediency. It is to be adopted when no other instrument will do the job. Beyond the issue of how to win, they have not vested violence with positive psychological or political consequences. This sets Soviet commentators apart from those Third World writers who view armed struggle as a means of psychological liberation, mobilization, unification, or leadership selection.

In terms of the impact of doctrine on Soviet foreign policy, the most significant aspects of the divergence between Soviet and Third World approaches to national liberation are:

(1) the Soviet stress in the formulation of theory on universal marxist principles and their rejection of Third World doctrines which purport to provide an original 'third way' to socialism; and

(2) the advocacy of a transnational proletarian internationalism as the most important focus of revolutionary commitment and an ambivalence, if not an outright hostility towards national, regional, or religious particularism.

This amounts to a refusal to accept, if not an inability to understand Third World aspirations to autonomy.

Finally, though in order to reach a confident conclusion, much further research would have to be done, the evidence in this chapter does not appear to support the hypothesis that Soviet analyses of Third World problems, and the policies which presumably draw to some extent from these analyses display a Soviet 'learning curve' with regard to Third World politics. The basic outlines of Soviet doctrine on the Third World have remained quite stable since the death of Stalin. What variation occurs tends to be cyclical, and can be accounted for largely in terms of political exigency and shifts in Soviet attitudes between optimism and pessimism with regard to their own development, the

international correlation of forces, and the course of events in the
Third World.

## Notes

1. See E.H. Carr, *The Bolshevik Revolution, 1917-1923*, Vol. 3, Harmondsworth, Penguin, 1977, pp. 239-52.
2. Cf. R. Kanet, *The Soviet Union and the Developing Countries*, Baltimore,
Johns Hopkins Press, 1974, p. 9; and C. McLane, *Soviet Strategies in South East
Asia*, Princeton, Princeton University Press, 1966, p. 32.
3. Kanet, *The Soviet Union*, p. 9; Carr, *The Bolshevik Revolution*, p. 305;
and S. White, 'Communism and the East: The Baku Congress, 1920', *Slavic
Review* XXIII (1974), no. 4, pp. 503, 506.
4. R. Kanet, 'The Comintern and the Negro Question', *Survey*, XIX (1973),
no. 4, gives an informative account of the fortunes of the ITUCNW. See also
E. Wilson, *Russia and Africa*, London, Holmes and Meier, 1974, pp. 170-90.
5. Kanet, 'The Comintern and the Negro Question', pp. 111-12.
6. The point is illustrated with reference to India in J. Kautsky, *Moscow and
the Communist Party of India*, London, Chapman and Hall, 1956, P. 17.
7. M. Djilas notes Stalin's recognition as early February 1948 that the
moderate strategy was inappropriate in post-war China, in *Conversations with
Stalin*, London, Hart-Davis, 1962, pp.164-5.
8. McLane, *Soviet Strategies*, p. 450; H. Kapur, *The Soviet Union and the
Emerging Nations*, London, M. Joseph, 1968, p. 42.
9. K. Dawisha, *Soviet Foreign Policy towards Egypt*, London, Macmillan,
1979, pp. 24-6; A. Klinghoffer, 'The Soviet Union and Africa' in Kanet, *The
Soviet Union*, p. 56. See also N. Khrushchev, 'Vseocherednoi XXI S'ezd KPSS:
Doklad Tov. N.S. Khrushcheva', *Pravda* (28 Jan. 1959), p. 7.
10. W. Attwood, *The Reds and the Blacks*, London, Hutchinson, 1967,
pp. 59-66; and R. Legvold, *Soviet Policy in West Africa*, Cambridge, Harvard
University Press, 1970, pp. 123-9.
11. Cf. Adam Ulam, 'The Soviet Union and the Rules of the International
Game' in K. London, ed., *The Soviet Union in World Politics*, Boulder, Westview,
1980, p. 42.
12. Cf. Legvold, *Soviet Policy in West Africa*, p. 78; and W. Nielsen, *The Great
Powers in Africa*, London, Pall Mall, 1969, pp. 194-5.
13. E. Valkeneir, 'New Trends in Soviet Economic Relations with the Third
World', *World Politics* XXII (1970), no. 3, pp. 415, 416.
14. Dawisha, *Soviet Foreign Policy towards Egypt*, pp. 36-7.
15. Legvold, *Soviet Policy in West Africa*, pp. 222-3 and 252-8.
16. Ibid., p. 337.
17. For example, N. Pavlovic (cited in extracts from the debate at the 1920
Baku Congress, Carrere d'Encausse and Schram, *Marxism and Asia*, p. 76), who
argued that 'the establishment of national Eastern states in which power left the
hands of expelled aliens only to pass into those of indigenous capitalists and
landowners would not constitute a great step forward in trying to improve the
situation of the masses'.
18. It being argued at this time that political independence was merely a
façade masking continued economic dependence and social oppression (for
example, V. Balabushevich, 'Novyi Etap Natsional'no-osvoboditel'noi Borby
Narodov Indii', *Voprosy Ekonomiki* (1949), no. 8, pp. 32, 44-7; E. Zhukov,

'Voprosy Natsional'no-kolonial'noi Bor'by posle Vtoroi Mirovoi Voiny', *Voprosy Ekonomiki* (1949), no. 9, p. 58; and V. Maslennikov, 'O Rukovodyashchei Roli Rabochevo Klassa v Natsional'no-osvoboditel'nom Dvizhenii', ibid., pp. 57, 69.

19. N. Khrushchev, 'Otchotnyi Doklad Ts. K. KPSS XX S'ezdu Partii', *Pravda* 15 Feb. 1956), p. 3. For similar assessments from the Khrushchev period, see E. Zhukov, 'The October Revolution and the Rise of the National Liberation Movement', *International Affairs* (Moscow) (henceforward *IA*) (1957), no. 9, p. 41; N. Mukhitdinov, 'Prenia po Dokladu Tov. N.S. Khrushcheva', *Pravda* (31.i.59), p. 8; and S. Ogurtsov, 'Razvivayushchiesya Strany i Sotsial'nyi Progress', *Azia i Afrika Sevodnya* (1963), no. 7, p. 2.

20. V. Tyagunenko, 'Mirovoi Sotsializm i Natsional'no-osvoboditel'naya Revolyutsia', *Kommunist* (1973), no. 8, p. 43. See also G. Skorov 'Imperializm – Razvivayushchiesya Strany: Antagonizm Uglublyaetsya', *Kommunist* (1974), no. 18, pp. 98-9. For a more recent recognition of the political aspect of national liberation revolutions, see K. Brutents, *National Liberation Revolutions Today*, Part 2, Moscow, Progress, 1977, p. 47.

21. N. Khrushchev, 'Speech at Rangoon University' (1955) in *IA* (1956), no. 1, p. 235. See also Khrushchev, 'Otchotnyi Doklad XX S'ezdu', p. 3.

22. Cf. K. Ivanov, 'Present Day Colonialism and International Relations', *IA* (1962), no. 4, pp. 42-3; B. Ponomarev, 'O Gosudarstve Natsional'noi Demokratii' *Kommunist* (1961), no. 8, pp. 33, 36, 43, 44; R. Ul'yanovsky, 'Natsional-no-osvoboditel'noe Dvizhenie v Bor'be za Ekonomicheskuyu Nezavisimost", *Kommunist* (1975), no. 14, p. 117; Brutents, *National Liberation Revolutions Today*, Part 1, pp. 9, 29, 45, 47; and A. Gromyko and B. Ponomarev, *Soviet Foreign Policy Today*, Vol. 2 (1945-1980), Moscow, Progress, 1981, pp. 261, 491.

23. Cf. the comments by Zinoviev and Pavlovich at the congress to the effect that the point of revolution in the East was to get rid of *all* oppression, foreign and indigrenous (as cited in Carrere d'Encausse and Schram, *Marxism and Asia*, pp. 172, 176).

24. Executive Committee of the Comintern (ECCI), 'Instructions to the 3rd CCP Congress' (1923) in J. Degras, ed., *Documents of the Comintern*, Vol. 2, London, Oxford University Press, 1960, p. 25-6; ECCI, 'Theses of the 10th Plenum on China' (1929); and ECCI, 'Resolution on the Chinese Question' (1930), both in ibid., Vol. 3, pp. 44, 115, 118. Such statements were, however, comparatively rare in the 'popular front' period of 1935-9 and during the period of the Grand Alliance, for obvious tactical reasons.

25. Cf. the statement of Soviet Indian specialist V. Balabushevich to the effect that 'freedom in the period of imperialism implies freedom not only from oppression by the colonizers but also from oppression by 'one's own' native bourgeoisie, in 'Novyi Etap Natsional'no-osvoboditel'noi Bor'by Narodov Indii, pp. 30, 34-5, 45.

26. CPSU 'Programma KPSS', *Pravda* (2 Nov. 1961), pp. 2-4. See also Ponomaryev, 'O Gosudarstve National'noi Demokratii', pp. 36, 41-6; N. Khrushehv, 'Otchot Ts. K. KPSS XXII S'ezdu KPSS', *Pravda* (18 Oct. 1961), p. 3; and V. Guzevaty, ' "Third Way" or Genuine Freedom', *IA* (1963), no. 4, p. 46.

27. V. Tyagunenko, 'Zaklyuchitel'noe Slovo' in *MEiMO*, 'Diskussia: Sotsializm, Kapitalizm, Slaborazvitye Strany', *MEiMO* (1964), no. 6, p. 78.

28. Cf. Tyagunenko, 'Mirovoi Sotsializm', p. 51: G. Drambyants, 'Atkual'nye Problemy Nationsal'no-osvbooditel'novo Dvizhenia', *Kommunist* (1963), no. 18, p.112; G. Kim and P. Shastitko, 'Nekotorye Problemy Natsional'no-osvoboditel' noi Revolyutsii v Azii i Afriki', *Voprosy Istorii* (1973), no. 8, p. 83; V. Tyul'-panov, Tendentsii Razvitia "Tret'evo Mira"', *Kommunist* (1975), no. 3, p. 126; Brutents, *National Liberation Revolutions Today*, Part 1, pp. 26-7; K. Brutents,

'Imperializm i Osvobodivshiesya Strany', *Pravda* (10.ii.78), p. 3; A. Gromyko, 'Soviet Foreign Policy and Africa', *IA* (1982), no. 2, p. 31.

29. The term comes from Yu. Irkhin, 'Avangardnye Revolyutsionnye Partii Trudyaschikhsya v Osvobodivshikhsya Stranakh', *Voprosy Istorii* (1982), no. 4, pp. 55-67.

30. P. Henze, 'Communism in Ethiopia', *Problems of Communism* XXX (1981), no. 3, pp. 63-4.

31. For endorsement of Third World demands for control over their own resources, see Gromyko and Ponomarev, *Soviet Foreign Policy*, Vol. 2, pp. 493, 499-500. Soviet writers are adamant, however, in their criticism of attempts to characterize international politics in North-South terms and to lump the USSR in with other rich states in the North from whom the Third World is entitled to restitution for previous exploitation (see below).

32. Brutents, *National Liberation Revolutions Today*, Part 1, pp. 34-5. In his discussion of the nature of colonialism, Brutents points out that colonial oppression had four aspects — political, economic, social, and 'ideological/spiritual'. (ibid., p. 41).

33. For representative views on stages of revolution, see Khrushchev, 'Vseocherednoi XXI S'ezd: Doklad Tov. N.S. Khrushcheva', p. 7; and Ponomarev, 'O Gosudarstve Natsional'noi Demokratii', p. 36.

34. V. Lenin, 'Draft Theses on the National and Colonial Questions' (1920) in *CW* XXI, p. 146.

35. J. Stalin, *Fundamentals of Leninism* (1924) in J. Stalin, *Marxism and the National and Colonial Question*, p. 192.

36. 6th Comintern Congress, 'Programme of the Communist International' (1928) in Degras, *Documents*, Vol. 2, pp. 479, 509.

37. E. Zhukov, 'The Colonial Question after the Second War' (1947) in A. Rubinstein, ed., *The Foreign Policy of the Soviet Union*, NY, Random House, 1966, p. 399.

38. Khrushchev, 'Otchotnyi Doklad XX S'ezdu', p. 3. See also 'Deklaratsia Soveshchania Kommunisticheskikh i Rabochikh Partii Sotsialisticheskikh Stran', *Pravda* (22 Nov. 1957), p. 1.

39. Zayavlenie Soveshchania Predstavitelei Kommunisticheskikh i Rabochikh Partii', *Pravda* (6 Dec. 1960), p. 3. See also E. Zhukov, 'Zamechatel'nyi Faktor Nashevo Vremeni', *Pravda* (26 Aug. 1960), pp. 3-4; and (Peredovaya), 'Natsional'-no-osvoboditel'noe Dvizhenie — Neot'emlemaya Chast' Mirovovo Revolyutsion-novo Protsessa', *Kommunist* (1962), no. 2, p. 18.

40. N. Simonia, 'O Kharaktere Natsional'no-osvoboditel'nykh Revolyutsii', *Narody Azii i Afriki* (henceforward *NAiA*) (1966), no. 6, pp. 8, 13.

41. Cf. V. Tyagunenko, 'Nekotorye Problemy Natsional'no-osvoboditel'noi Revolyutsii v Svete Leninizma', *Mirovaya Ekonomika i Mezhdunarodnye Otno-shenia* (henceforward *MEiMO*) (1970), no. 5, p. 27; B. Gafurov, 'The Soviet Union and the National Liberation Movement' *IA* (1971), no. 7, p. 21; G. Kim and A. Kaufman, 'Leninskie Printsipy Soyuza Sotsializma s Natsional'no-osvoboditel'nym Dvizheniem', *NAiA* (1970), no. 2 p. 9; K. Brutents, 'Natsional'-no-osvoboditel'naya Revolyutisa' in *Bol'shaya Sovetskaya Entsiklopedia*, Vol. 17, Moscow, Izdatel'stvo Sovetskoi Entsyklopedii, 1974, p. 366.

42. Brutents, *National Liberation Revolutions Today*, Part 1, p. 51; Gromyko and Ponomarev, *Soviet Foreign Policy*, Vol. 2, p. 491.

43. For example, 6th Comintern Congress, 'Programme', p. 508.

44. ECCI Agitprop Dept., 'Theses on the 15th Anniversary of the Foundation of the Communist International' (1934) in Degras, *Documents*, Vol. 3, pp.325-6.

45. Cf. E. Alekseev, 'Natsional'no-osvoboditel'noe Dvizhenie — Sostavnaya Chast' Mirovovo Revolyutsionnovo Protsessa', *AiAS* (1963), no. 12, pp. 2-4;

G. Mirskii, 'Sotsializm, Imperializm, i Afro-Aziatskaya Solidarnost', *Izvestia* (16 July 1963), p. 2; and Central Committee of the CPSU, 'Letter to the Party Organization' (1963), as reprinted in *PR* (1963), no. 25, p. 25.

46. See, for example, 'Zadachi Bor'by protiv Imperializma na Sovremennom Etape i Edinstvo Deistvii Kommunisticheskikh i Rabochikh Partii, Vsekh Anti-imperialisticheskikh Sil', *Pravda* (18.vi.69), pp. 1, 3; Tyagunenko, 'Mirovoi Sotsializm', p. 54; G. Aliev, 'Oktyabr'skaya Revolyutsia i Natsional'no-osvoboditel'noe Dvizhenie', *Kommunist* (1977), no. 9, pp. 26-7; M. Suslov, 'Kommunisticheskoe Dvizhenie v Avangarde Bor'by za Mir, Sotsializm, i. Natsional'noe Osvobozhdenie', *Kommunist* (1975), no. 11, pp. 7-8; Gromyko and Ponomarev, *Soviet Foreign Policy*, Vol. 2, p. 410; R. Ul'yanovsky, *Present Day Problems in Asia and Africa*, Moscow, Progress, 1980, pp. 20. 27.

47. Cf. Brutents, *National Liberation Revolutions Today*, Part 1, pp. 61-5; Gromyko and Ponomarev, *Soviet Foreign Policy*, Volume 2, pp. 262, 498; Ul'yanovsky, *Present Day Problems*, p. 16.

48. Yu. Novopashia, 'Vozdeistvie Real'novo Sotsializma na Mirovoi Revolyutsionnyi Protsess: Metodologicheskie Aspekty', *Voprosy Filosofii* (1982), no. 8, p. 6. See also Yu. Andropov, 'Leninizm – Nauka i Iskusstvo Revolyutsionnovo Tvorchestva', *Pravda* (23 Apr. 1976), pp. 1-2.

49. Lenin pressured Roy to alter his statements to the effect that the fate of world communism depended on the victory of communism in the East. Carrere d'Encausse and Schram, *Marxism and Asia*, p. 160.

50. Stalin considered Sultan-Galiev's ideas on the nature of world politics to be to be evidence of a Tartar nationalist deviation. J. Stalin, 'Speech at the 4th Conference of Russian Communist Workers of the National Republics and Regions' (1923) in Stalin, *Marxism and the National and Colonial Question*, p. 178.

51. A. Zhdanov, 'The International Situation', *For a Lasting Peace, For a People's Democracy* (1947), no. 1, p. 2.

52. M. Suslov, 'O Bor'be KPSS za Splochennost' Mezhdunarodnovo Kommunisticheskovo Dvizhenia: Doklad Tov. M.A. Suslova na Plenume KPSS', *Pravda* (3 April 1964), p. 2. See also Ponomarev, 'O Gosudarstve Natsional'noi Demokratii', p. 34: and (Peredovaya), 'Natsional'no-osvoboditel'noe Dvizhenie', p. 15.

53. Cf. (Editorial), 'Vysshii Internatsional'nyi Dolg Stran Sotsializma', *Pravda* (27.x.65), p. 3: and the comparable editorial in *IA* (1966), no. 4, p. 5. For a later argument, perhaps with a similar motivation to justify Soviet preoccupation with internal development, see Novopashin, 'Vlianie Real'novo Sotsializma', p. 7.

54. For example, Brutents, *National Liberation Revolutions Today*, Part 1, p. 15; and Ul'yanovsky, *Present Day Problems*, p. 12.

55. E. Bagramov, 'Internatsional'noe i Natsional'noe v Mirovom Obshchestvennom Razvitii' *Kommunist* (1975), no. 9, p. 94.

56. A. Litman, 'Ob Opredelenii Ponyatia i Klassifikatsii Tipov Natsionalizma v Osvobodivshikhsya Stranakh', *NAiA* (1975), no. 1, p. 48.

57. A. Aliev, 'Natsionalizm i Natsii Perekhodnovo Tipa', *NAiA* (1975), no. 1, p. 56. For an earlier comment along similar lines See V. Tyagunenko, 'Zaklyuchitel'noe Slovo', *MEiMO* (1964), no. 6, p. 77.

58. Brutents, *National Liberation Revolutions Today*, Part 1, p. 45.

59. For representative views along these lines, see Mukhitdinov, 'Prenia', p. 8; G. Mirskii, 'Sotsializm, Imperializm, i Afro-Aziatskaya Solidarnost", p. 2: A. Maslennikov and A. Trepetov, 'Konstruktivnaya Delovaya Diskussia', *Pravda* (8 Sept. 1979), p. 5; Gromyko and Ponomarev, *Soviet Foreign Policy*, Vol. 2, pp. 629-30; V. Ovchinnikov, 'Ot Managua k Deli', *Pravda* (28 Jan. 1983), p. 4.

60. Ibid., p. 4.

61. Cf. Mirskii, 'Sotsializm, Imperializm, i Afro-Aziatskaya Solidarnost", p. 2; K. Ivanov, 'The National Liberation Movement and the Non-capitalist Path of Development', *IA* (1964), no. 12, p. 10; K. Brutents, 'Epokha Sotsializma i Natsional'no-osvoboditel'noe Dvizhenie', *Kommunist* (1967), no. 18, p. 99; V. Kudryavtsev, 'Let's Be Objective', *New Times* (1969), no. 31, pp. 22-4; Yu. Popov, 'O Prirode Melkoburzhuaznoi Ideologii v Stranakh Afriki', *NAiA* (1971), no. 5, pp. 42-3; B. Ponomarev, 'Aktual'nye Problemy Teorii Mirovovo Revolyut-sionnovo Protsessa', *Kommunist* (1971), no. 15, p. 70; Bagramov, 'Internat-sional'noe i Natsional'noe v Mirovom Obshchestvennom Razvitii', p. 94; L. Tamarin, 'Raschoty i Proschoty Imperialistov v Afrike', *Kommunist* (1976), no. 18, pp. 99-100; P. Demchenko, 'Mnenie', *Pravda* (19.viii. 76), p. 5; Brutents, *National Liberation Revolutions Today*, Part 1, p. 15; Gromyko and Ponomarev, *Soviet Foreign Policy*, Vol. 2, p. 629; E. Primakov, 'The Place of the Newly Independent Countries in the World Economy: Some Problems', *MEiMO* (1982), no. 3, pp. 16-33 in *CDSP* XXXIV (1982), no. 25, p. 14.

62. O. Ogunbadejo, 'Soviet Policies in Africa', *African Affairs* LXXIX (1980), no. 316, p. 324.

63. J. Stalin, *Fundamentals of Leninism*, NY, International Publishers, 1974, p. 85.

64. ECCI, 'Resolution of the 7th Plenum on the Chinese Situation' (1926) in Degras, *Documents*, Vol. 2, p. 341. See also ECCI, 'Resolution of the 12th Plenum on the War in the Far East' (1932) in ibid., Vol. 3, p. 243.

65. E. Zhukov, 'Voprosy Natsional'no-kolonial'noi Bor'by', p. 57.

66. E. Zhukov, 'Raspad Kolonial'noi Sistemy', *Partiinaya Zhizn'* (1956), no. 16, p. 45.

67. CPSU, 'Programma', p. 4;

68. I. Potekhin, 'Panafrikanizm i Bor'ba Dvukh Ideologii', *Kommunist* (1964), no. 1, pp. 108, 109.

69. Mirskii, 'Sotsializm, Imperializm, i Afro-Aziatskaya Solidarnost", p. 2.

70. Cf. G. Akopyan, 'O Dvukh Tendentsiakh Natsionalizma Ugnetyonnykh i Razvivayushchikhsya Stran', *NAiA* (1970), no. 5, pp. 3, 4, 6; Ponomarev, 'Aktual'nye Problemy Teorii', p. 70; N. Simonia, 'Natsionalizm i Politichaskaya Bor'ba v Osvobodivshikhsya Stranakh' (I), *MEiMO* (1972), no. 1, p. 95; G. Akopov, 'Teoreticheskii Analiz Sovremennovo Natsionalizma', *Kommunist* (1974), no. 13, pp. 121. 123.

71. Ul'yanovsky (*Present Day Problems in Asia and Africa*, p. 34) accounts for the occasional breakdown of national democracy in these terms.

72. Aliev, 'Natsionalizm i Natsii Perekhodnovo Tipa', p. 56.

73. Zhukov, 'Raspad Kolonial'noi Sistemy', pp. 45-6.

74. CPSU, 'Programma', p. 5.

75. E. Zhukov, 'Natsional'no-osvoboditel'noe Dvizhenie Narodov Azii i Afriki', *Kommunist* (1969), no. 4, p. 32; G. Kim and A. Kaufman, 'Ob Ideo-logicheskikh Techeniakh v Stranakh "Tret'evo Mira" ', *NAiA* (1971), no. 5, pp. 45, 46; A. Reznikov, 'Iz Istorii Podgotovki V.I. Leninym Reshenii II Kon-gressa Kominterna po Natsional'no-kolonial'nomu Voprosu', *NAiA* (1971), no. 2, p. 41; Simonia, 'Natsionalizm i Politicheskaya Bor'ba'(I), p. 91, and (II), *MEiMO* (1972), no. 2, p. 101; Litman, 'Ob Opredelenii Ponyatia, pp. 45, 48.

76. Ul'yanovsky, *Present Day Problems*, pp. 48, 49.

77. Ibid., p. 50

78. Ibid., p. 50.

79. Khrushchev, *Khrushchev Remembers*, pp. 502-3.

80. Lenin, Draft Theses on the National and Colonial Question', p. 149.

81. J. Stalin, 'Address to the University of the Toilers of the East' (1924) in

Stalin, *Marxism and the National and Colonial Question*, pp. 216-17.

82. 6th Comintern Congress, 'Programme', p. 505.

83. ECCI, 'Theses of the 13th Plenum' (1933)in Degras, *Documents*, Vol. 3, p. 305.

84. The Peick report, as cited in S.M. Goldstein, 'The Chinese Revolution and the Colonial Areas', *CQ* (1978), no. 75, p. 600.

85. Viz., his attitude towards 'advocates of bourgeois democracy and 'socialist parties' in 'The International Situation', pp. 3, 4.

86. Zhukov, 'The Colonial Question', pp. 379-80; and R. Kanet, 'The Soviet Union and the Colonial Question' in Kanet, *The Soviet Union and the Developing Nations*, p. 19.

87. Astafiev, 'From Semi-colony to People's Democracy' in *Krizis Kolonial'noi Sistemy: Natsional'no-osvoboditel'naya Voina Narodov Azii*, Moscow, Izdatel'stvo Akademii Nauk, 1949. In Carrere d'Encausse and Schram, *Marxism and Asia*, p. 268.

88. E. Zhukov, 'On the Character and Attributes of People's Democracy in the Countries of the Orient' (1952), *Izvestia Adademii Nauk: Seria Istorii i Filosofii* IX (1952), no. 1. In *CDSP* IV (1952), no. 20, p. 3.

89. Khrushchev, 'Otchotnyi Doklad XX S'ezdu', p. 4.

90. As cited in D. Zagoria, *The Sino-Soviet Conflict, 1956-1961*, Princeton, Princeton University Press, 1962, p. 52.

91. 'Deklaratsia Soveshchania Kommunisticheskikh i Rabochikh Partii', p. 4.

92. CPSU, 'Programma', p. 4.

93. Cf. for example, A. Iskenderov, 'Rabochii Klass i Natsional'no-osvoboditel' noe Dvizhenie', *AiAS* (1962), no. 5, p. 8; and V. Dimitriev, 'Kontinent Bor'by i Nadezhdy', *AiAS* (1963), no. 4, p. 13.

94. Potekhin, 'Panafrikanizm', p. 111.

95. Ibid., p. 112.

96. N. Khrushchev, 'Otvety na Voprosy Redaktsii Gazet "Ganien Taims", "Alzhei Repyubliken", "Pepl' ", i "Botataun" ', *Pravda* (22 Dec. 1963), pp. 1-2.

97. Legvold, *Soviet Policy in West Africa*, pp. 186-94, gives an informative account of these developments.

98. Uri Ra'anan, 'Moscow and the "Third World" ', *Problems of Communism* XIV (1964), no. 1, p. 30.

99. Cf. M. Kremnyov, 'The UAR – Its Progress and Problems', *World Marxist Review* (1964), no. 7, p. 91; Potekhin's 1964 articled cited in notes 49, 75, and 76 of this chapter; Y. Guzevaty, ' "Third Way" or Genuine Freedom', *IA* (1963), no. 4, pp. 47, 48; Ogurtsov, 'Razvivayushchiesya Strany i Sotsial'nyi Progress', p. 3.

100. Cf. G. Mirsky, 'The Proletariat and National Liberation', *New Times* (1964), no. 18, pp. 8-9; V. Tyagunenko, cited in Carrere d'Encausse and Schram, *Marxism and Asia*, p. 343; and 'Diskussia: Sotsializm, Kapitalizm, Slaborazvitye Strany', *MEiMO* (1964), no. 4, pp. 116-31 and no. 6, pp. 62-81, and in particular pp. 79-80.

101. E. Primakov, 'Krepit' Edinstvo Sil, Boryusnchikhsya protiv Kolonializma', *Pravda* (12 June 1965), p. 3; R. Ul'yanovsky, 'Sotsializm i Natsional'no-osvoboditel'naya Bor'ba', *Pravda* (15 Apr. 1966), p. 4; Simonia, 'O Kharaktere Natsional'no-osvoboditel'noi Revolyutsii', pp. 9, 11-12, 16; and especially K. Brutents, 'Epokha Sotsializma i Natsional'no-osvoboditel'-naya Revolyutsia', *Kommunist* (1967), no. 18, pp. 96-7.

102. G. Kim and A. Kaufman, 'Ob Ideologicheskikh Techeniakh', p. 43; Bagramov, 'Internatsional'noe i Natsional'noe', p. 96; Yu Popov, 'Formirovanie Obshchestvennoi Mysly v Stranakh Afriki', *NAiA* (1970), no. 1, p. 36; A. Kiva, 'Africa: The National Liberation Movement Today', *IA* (1972), no. 8, p. 41;

V. Bushuyev, 'The National Liberation Movement and Neo-colonialism', *IA* (1975), no. 3, pp. 113-14; Brutents, *National Liberation Revolutions Today*, Part 1, p. 116.

103. Popov, 'Formirovanie Obshchestvennoi Mysly', p. 33; Yu. Popov, 'O Prirode Melkoburzhuaznoi Ideologii', pp. 39, 41; Ul'yanovsky, 'Sovremennyi Etap Natsional'no-osvoboditel'novo Dvizhenia i Krest'yanstvo (I)' *MEiMO* (1971), no. 5, pp. 98-9.

104. Kiva, 'Africa: The National Liberation Movement Today', p. 41; Bushuyev, 'The National Liberation Movement', pp. 113-14.

105. V. Zagladin, 'Internationalizm – Znamya Kommunistov', *Pravda* (20 Apr. 1976), p. 3; Brutents, *National Liberation Revolutions Today*, Part 1, p. 105.

106. Popov, 'Formirovanie Obshchestvennoi Mysly', pp. 36-8; Ul'yanovsky, 'Sovremennyi Etap', p. 98; Ul'yanovsky, *Present Day Problems*, pp. 32-3.

107. V. Li, 'The Role of the National Liberation Movement in the Anti-imperialist Struggle', *IA* (1971), no. 12, p. 71; A. Kaufman, 'O Roli Rabochevo Klassa i Evo Partii v Stranakh Sotsialisticheskoi Orientatsii', *NAiA* (1976), no. 4, p. 8.

108. Aliev, 'Oktyabr'skaya Revolyutsia i Natsional'no-osvoboditel'oe Dvizhenie', p. 33.

109. Indeed, one might well ask whether this affirmation of faith was not at least in part an attempt to secure such assistance.

110. For example, Brutents, *National Liberation Revolutions Today*, p. 142.

111. M. Iovchuk, 'Internatsionalizm Sotsialisticheskoi Kultury', *Voprosy Filosofii* (1976), no. 12, pp. 21-2. The author was rector of the Social Sciences Academy under the Central Committee of the CPSU. See also V.Zimyanin, 'Leninizm – Revolyutsionnoe Znamya Nashei Epokhi', *Pravda* (23 Apr. 1977), pp. 1-2.

112. A. Gromyko, 'Socialist Orientation in Africa', *IA* (1979), no. 9, p. 100.

113. (Editorial), 'K Shestomy Plenumu Ts. K. KPK', *Pravda* (5 July 1981), p. 5.

114. V. Medvedev ('Razvitoi Sotsializm: Ekonomika, Politika, Ideologia', *Pravda* (13 July 1979), pp. 2-3) argued that:

> The degree to which objective laws and possibilities are realized depends on the discovery of optimal solutions, but society is not capable of transcending the limits of these possibilities. Attempts to liberate oneself from economc necessity unavoidably lead to subjectivism and voluntarism, that is to say, to a disregard of real conditions and urgent requirements and tasks. Its most extremely deformed manifestation is found in the theory and practice of maoism, in its anti-marxist slogan 'politics is the commanding force'.

See also S. Salychev, 'Faktory Revolyutsii', *Pravda* (18 Sept. 1980), p. 2, where reliance on 'narrow groups of "revolutionary heroes" ' rather than on the working class as the decisive force in revolution is dismissed as 'left wing revisionism'. This makes a telling comparison with the ideas of Guevara and Debray as set out in the previous chapter. See finally Z. Mirsky, 'Maoist Ideology: Behind the Facade', *New Times* (1975), no. 7, pp. 19-20.

115. Soviet writers have generally not provided very convincing definitions of these social groups in terms of their role in the relations of production. This is not surprising, given that class categories developed for description and analysis of developed European societies are difficult to apply in precapitalist conditions at low levels of 'class differentiation'. In discussions prior to the mid-1960s, the 'petty bourgeoisie' was often subsumed within the 'national bourgeosie'. The latter appeared to include anybody with a nationalist or anti-imperialist

orientation and who was not a worker or a peasant. To judge from recent Soviet literature, however (cf. Brutents, *National Liberation Revolutions Today*, Part 1, pp. 93-106), the national bourgeoisie has come to be limited to indigenous entrepreneurs as distinct from the 'comprador bourgeoisie', which is integrated into foreign capitalist enterprise. The petty bourgeoisie and 'middle' or 'intermediate' sections include the 'civilian and miltary intelligentsia, the civil servants and employees, the small and petty traders, artisans, handicraftsmen, etc.' (Ibid., p. 107.)

116. In the first of these periods, Soviet attitudes were determined externally largely by the falling out with the KMT and internally by the campaign to build socialism in one country. In the latter, the dominant factors were on the one hand the collapse of the Grand Alliance into the Cold War and on thé other the post-war tightening of internal Soviet politics associated with reconstruction.

117..7th Congress, 'Resolution on the Danger of a New World War' (1935), Degras, *Documents*, Vol. 3, p. 377.

118. Cf. A; Guber, cited in R. McVey, *The Soviet View of the Indonesian Revolution*, Ithaca, Cornell South East Asia Program, 1957, p. 14; and E. Varga, cited in Kanet, 'The Soviet Union and the Colonial Question', p. 17; and in McVey, *The Soviet View*, pp. 5-7.

119. Djilas, *Conversations with Stalin*, pp. 164-5.

120. E. Zhukov, 'Velikaya Oktyabr'skaya Revolyutsia i Kolonial'nyi Vostok', *Bol'shevik* (1946), no. 20. pp. 38-47. Elsewhere, V. Balabushevich, a Soviet specialist on India, raised doubts about the capacity of the Indian National Congress to lead India to independence ('Bor'ba Indii za Nezavisimost', *Mirovoe Khozyaistvo i Mirovaya Politika* (1946), no. 9, p. 52).

121. Cf. F. Barghoorn, 'The Varga Discussion and Its Significance', *American Slavic and East European Review* VII (1948), no. 2, pp. 214-36.

122. E. Zhukov, 'Obostrenie Krizisa Kolonial'noi Sistemy', *Bol'shevik* (1947), no. 23, pp. 54-5. See also Balabushevich, 'Novyi Etap', p. 45; and Maslennikov, 'O Rukovodyashchei Roli Rabochevo Klassa', pp. 67-8, 72.

123. R. Kanet, 'Soviet Attitudes toward the Developing Nations' in Kanet, *The Soviet Union and the Developing Nations*, pp. 28, 29.

124. Cf. H. Carrere d'Encausse and S. Schram, *L'URSS et la Chine devant les Revolutions dans les Societes Pre-industrielles*, Paris, Armand Colin, 1970, p. 48; Zhukov, 'Raspad Kolonial'noi Sistemy', pp. 45-6, 288-9; 'Editorial', *Sovetskoe Vostokovedenie* (1956), no. 1, as quoted in Carrere d'Encausse and Schram, *Marxism and Asia*, pp. 286-7; Zhukov, 'The October Revolution' (1957), p. 41; D. Yellon, 'Shifts in Soviet Policy towards Developing Countries, 1964-1968' in R. Duncan, ed., *Soviet Policy in Developing Countries*, Waltham, Gin-Blaisdell, 1969, p. 226.

125. Khrushchev, 'Otchotnyi Doklad XX S'ezdu', p. 4. See also 'Deklaratsia Soveshchania Kommunisticheskikh i Rabochikh Partii', p. 4, where the dictatorship of the proletariat is mentioned as one of several universally applicable principles of the transition to socialism.

126. Cf. *World Marxist Review* (1959), no. 8. See also A. Klinghoffer, 'The Soviet Union and Africa' in R. Kanet, *The Soviet Union and the Developing Nations*, p. 56. Some analysts have pointed to the emergence of a 'left' opposition within the CPSU to uncritical gradualism *vis-à-vis* the national bourgeoisie as an additional factor in this shift (cf. Dawisha, *Soviet Policy towards Egypt*, pp. 24-6).

127. 'Zayavlenie Soveshchania Kommunisticheskikh i Rabochikh Partii', p. 4. See also Ponomarev, 'O Gosudarstve Natsional'noi Demokratii', pp. 41-6; Tyagunenko, 'Zaklyuchitel'noe Slovo', p. 78; W. Shinn, 'The National Democratic State', *World Politics* XV (1963), no. 3; and R. Lowenthal, 'On National

Democracy', *Survey* (1963), no. 47.

128. CPSU, 'Programma', p. 4; N. Khrushchev, 'O Programme KPSS: Doklad Tov. N.S. Khrushcheva', *Pravda* (19 Oct. 1961), p. 7; and A. Iskenderov, 'Rabochii Klass i Natsional'no-osvoboditel'noe Dvizhenie', *AiAS* (1962), no. 5, p. 6.

129. For an account of these events, see Attwood, *The Reds and the Blacks*, pp. 59-66.

130. Cf. R. Freedman, *Soviet Policy toward the Middle East since 1970*, NY, Praeger, 1982, p. 16.

131. N. Khrushchev, 'Rech' Tov. N.S. Khrushcheva', *Pravda* (20. v. 62). p. 2.

132. N. Khrushchev, 'Otvety na Voprosy', p. 1. The interview was published simultaneously in *Izvestia* and later in the *World Marxist Review*.

133. Cf. A. Sobolev, 'National Democracy – The Way to Social Progress', *World Marxist Review* VI (1963), no. 2, p. 44. The superficial parallel with the passage in the *Communist Manifesto* (p. 44) referring to a portion of the bourgeoisie 'going over' to the proletariat is striking, though the analogy is tenuous. The historical conditions in which Marx envisaged such a development differ radically from those obtaining in the 'national democracies'.

134. Mirskii, 'The Proletariat and National Liberation', pp. 8-9. See also Sobolev, 'National Democracy', p. 44.

135. Cf. the reservations aired at a IMEMO-sponsored conference in the spring of 1964, as reported in 'Diskussia: Sotsializm, Kapitalizm, Slaborazvitye Strany', *MEiMO* (1964), no. 4, pp. 116-31, and no. 6, pp. 62-81. Suslov, in major speeches in February and May of 1964, omitted any mention of these ideological innovations and in the latter speech failed to mention Khrushchev's contemporaneous visit to Egypt, during which the premier recognized the socialist character of Nasser's domestic policies. Ponomarev, closely linked to Suslov, in a mid-1964 *Pravda* article also ignored the doctrinal innovations, while V. Rumyantsev published several artices by Third World communists critical of the Soviet position on revolutionary democrats in the *World Marxist Review* (Legvold, *Soviet Policy in West Africa*, pp. 198-201).

136. G. Kim and A. Kaufman, 'Non-capitalist Development: Achievements and Difficulties', *IA* (1967), no. 12, pp. 72, 73; K. Brutents, 'African Revolution: Gains and Problems', *IA* (1967), no. 1, pp. 25, 27-8; A. Sobolev, 'Problems of Social Progress', *World Marxist Review* X (1967), no. 1, p. 11; R. Ul'yanovsky, 'Osvoboditel'naya Bor'ba Narodov Afriki', *Kommunist* (1969), no. 11, pp. 38, 42.

137. Ul'yanovsky, R., 'Sotsializm i Natsional'no-osvobodietl'naya Revolyutsia', p. 4.

138. Simonia, 'O Kharaktere Natsional'no-osvoboditel'noi Revolyutsii', p. 12; K. Bogdanov and V. Rumyantsev, 'Nasushchnye Voprosy Revolyutsionovo Dvizhenia v Afrike', *Kommunist* (1967), no. 3, p. 86; Brutents, 'African Revolu- tion', p. 27.

139. Bogdanov and Rumyantsev, 'Nasushchnye Voprosy', p. 89; Ul'yanovsky, 'Osvoboditel'naya Bor'ba', p. 43; and H. Desfosses-Cohn, *Soviet Policy towards Black Africa: The Focus on National Integration*, NY, Praeger, 1972, pp. 152-9.

140. Lufti al-Kholi, 'Leninizm i Korennye Problemy Natsional'no-osvoboditel' novo Dvizhenia', *NAiA* (1970) no. 2, pp. 27-8. One may surmise that al-Kholi, an Egyptian marxist, was reiterating the official position on the Nasser regime in Egypt. See also Popov, 'O Prirode Melkoburzhuaznoi Ideologii', p. 39.

141. Cf. V. Khoros, ' "Narodnichestvo" na Sovremennom Etape Natsional'- no-osvoboditel'noi Revolyutsii', *NAiA* (1973), no. 3, p. 13; G. Kim and A. Kaufman, 'XXV S'ezd KPSS i Problemy Natsional'no-osvoboditel'noi Revo- lyutsii', *NAiA* (1976), no. 3, p. 11.

142. Khoros, ' "Narodnichestvo" ', p. 13. See also Ul'yanovsky, cited in

Freedman, *Soviet Policy toward the Middle East*, p. 66.

143. R. Ul'yanovsky, 'Nekotorye Voprosy Nekapitalisticheskogo Razvitia', *Kommunist* (1971), no. 4, p. 9. See also Brezhnev's comment on the definitive role of the working class in 'Za Ukreplenie Splochennosti Kommunistov za Novyi Pod'yom Antiimperialisticheskoi Bor'by', *Pravda* (8 June 1969), p. 3; A. Kaufman, 'Voprosy Teorii Natsional'no-osvoboditel'noi Revolyutsii', *NAiA* (1975), no. 1, p. 65; and Khoros, ' "Narodnichestvo" ', p. 13.

144. Cf., for example, Irkhin, 'Avangardnye Revolyutsionnye Partii', pp. 56-7.

145. Brutents, *National Liberation Revolutions Today*, Part 1, pp. 84-5.

146. Ibid., pp. 120-5.

147. Ibid., p. 124.

148. Ul'yanovsky, *Present Day Problems*, pp. 18, 19. Ulyanovsky equated the concept of non-capitalist development with that of socialist orientation, as did Brutents (*National Liberation Revolutions Today*, Part 1, p. 17). One wonders, therefore, about the significance of statements by Western writers (for example, S. Bialer, *Stalin's Successors*, NY, Columbia University Press, 1980, p. 270; and M. Katz *The Third World in Soviet Military Thought*, London, Croom Helm, 1982, pp. 106, 107) concerning the purported demise of the concept of non-capitalist development. Bialer argues that it disappeared in 1976 because of a Soviet shift towards more general and flexible criteria in policy-making *vis-à-vis* the Third World. Oddly, Katz cites Bialer to the effect that the Soviets abandoned 'non-capitalist development' because of a preference for narrower, more orthodox formulae (for example, 'socialist development'). This appears to be the opposite of the point that Bialer was making. The fact that it is not difficult to find continued reference to non-capitalist development in the Soviet literature (as with Brutents and Ul'yanovsky as cited above and see also G. Kim, 'Sovetskii Soyuz i Natsional'no-osvoboditel'noe Dvizhenie', *MEiMO* (1981), no. 9, as translated in *CDSP* XXIV (1982), no. 41, p. 9) casts doubt on both their statements, though Katz's more general point concerning a return to more orthodox positions in the period between the 25th and 26th Congresses has much to recommend it.

149. On Soviet-Arab friction over the activities of local communists, see Freedman, *Soviet Policy toward the Middle East*, pp. 3, 15, 16, 34, 60-3, 85, 125, 294, 331, 359.

150. Ibid., p. 441.

151. 7th Comintern Congress, 'Resolution on Fascism' (1935), in Degras, *Documents*, Vol. 3, p. 367.

152. K. Brutents, 'Imperializm i Osvobodivshiesya Strany', p. 3. See also V. Kudryavtsev, 'V Ch'ikh Interesakh?', *Izvestia* (26 Feb. 1977). p. 4.

153. Cf., for example, CPSU, 'Programma', p. 4; Popov, 'O Prirode Melkoburzhuaznoi Ideologii', pp. 39, 41; Ul'yanovsky, *Present Day Problems*, p. 211.

154. Ibid., pp. 204-5.

155. The call for the independence of the communist party within the national front was again present not only in periods of hostility toward the national and petty bourgeoisie, but also in times of relatively close collaboration, as in that of the CCP-KMT united front in 1923-1927, in the mid and late 1950s (cf. Zhukov, 'The October Revolution', p. 43), in the early 1960s (cf. the stress in the 'Zayavlenie Soveshchania Kommunisticheskikh Partii', p. 3, on the need for communists to struggle against reactionary tendencies among bourgeois nationalists in order to carry out resolutely the social aspects of the national liberation revolution), and in the mid-1970s in the aftermath of the failed experiment of 'liquidationism' in the Arab world (cf. A. Kaufman, 'O Roli Rabochevo

196   *The Soviet Union and National Liberation*

Klassa i Evo Partii v Stranakh Sotsialisticheskoi Orientatsii', *NAiA* (1976), no. 4, p. 15).

156. K. Zarodov, *Sotsializm, Mir, Revolyutsia: Nekotorye Voprosy Teorii i Praktiki Mezhdurnarodnykh Otnoshenii*, Moscow, Politizdat, 1977, p. 206.

157. Cf., for example, ECCI, 'Resolution on the Chinese Question' (1926) in Degras, *Documents*, Vol. 2, p. 278; 6th Comintern Congress, 'Theses on the Revolutionary Movement in the Colonial and Semi-colonial Countries' (1928) in ibid., p. 541; 'Zayavlenie Soveshchania Kommunisticheskikh Partii', p. 3; Brutents, 'African Revolution', pp. 27-8; Lufti al-Kholi, 'Leninizm', p. 34; Brutents, *National Liberation Revolutions Today*, Part 1, pp. 87-9; Ul'yanovsky, *Present Day Problems*, pp. 24, 25.

158. From the 1960s and 1970s see, for instance, Brutents, 'African Revolution', p. 21; Kunaev, 'V.I. Lenin', p. 57; Ul'yanovsky, *Present Day Problems*, pp. 25-6, 229; Brutents, *National Liberation Revolutions Today*, Part 1, pp. 91, 92.

159. For example, Ul'yanovsky, *Present Day Problems*, p. 26.

160. Popov, 'Formirovanie Obshchestvennoi Mysly', pp. 32-3; Popov, 'O Prirode Melkoburzhuaznoi Ideologii', pp. 39, 41; Ul'yanovsky, 'Sovremennyi Etap', pp. 98, 99; Ul'yanovsky, *Present Day Problems*, p. 26.

161. N. Khrushchev, *Khrushchev Remembers*, p. 494. For criticism of Latin American guerrilla movements along similar lines, see M.F. Kudachkin (chief of the Latin American section of the CPSU Central Committee), cited in C. Blasier, *The Giant's Rival*, pp. 84-5.

162. See O. Kuusinen, 'Rech' na Fevral'skom (1964 g.) Plenume KPSS', *Pravda* (19 May, 1964), p. 3. pp. 333-4. See also Z. Mirsky, 'Maoist Ideology', p. 20.

163. For example, the ECCI's admonition of 1922 to the Indian National Congress that only a violent revolution could overthrow British rule (cited in Degras, *Documents*, Vol. 2, p. 12); Stalin's 'Address to the Students of the KUTV' (1925), in Stalin, *Marxism and the National and Colonial Question*, p. 215; 6th Comintern Congress, 'Programme', p. 492; 7th Comintern Congress, 'Resolution on Fascism', p. 368; and Zhukov's assertion that the October Revolution was the most appropriate model for anti-colonial revolution (Zhukov, 'Velikaya Oktyabrskaya Revolyutsia', pp. 38-47).

164. Cf. Khrushchev's stress in his 20th Congress speech ('Otchotnyi Doklad XX S'ezdu', p. 4) on the possibility of peaceful transformation to socialism. See also A. Mikoyan, 'Rech' A.I. Mikoyana', *Pravda* (18 Feb. 1956), p. 5; O. Kuusinen, 'Rech' Tov. O.V. Kuusinena', *Pravda*, 20 Feb. 1956; M. Suslov , 'Rech' Tov. M.A. Suslova', *Pravda* (17 Feb. 1956), p. 8; and D. Shepilov, 'Rech' Tov. D.T. Shepilova', *Pravda* (17 Feb. 1956), p. 4.

165. Khrushchev, 'Otchotnyi Doklad XX S'ezdu', p. 4; Khrushchev, 'Otvety na Voprosy', p. 2. A later commentator has expressed this point more generally: 'The fact that it is precisely counter-revolution that is the initiator and principal user of violence is of paramount importance for explaining the conditions of peaceful or non-peaceful progress towards socialism.' Salychev, 'Faktory Revolyutsii', p. 2.

166. For example, M. Suslov, 'O Bor'be KPSS za Splochennosti', pp. 3-4; Mirsky, 'Maoist Ideology', p. 21.

167. On this point, see Colin Legum, 'Angola and the Horn of Africa', in S. Kaplan, ed., *Diplomacy of Power: Soviet Armed Force as a Political Instrument*, Washington, Brookings, 1981, pp. 578, 592-3, 601.

168. On this factor with respect to the aftermath of Khrushchev's ousting, see A. Kosygin, 'O Gosudarstvennom Plane Razvitia Narodnovo Khozyaistvo SSSR na 1965 God', *Pravda* (10 Dec. 1964), p. 4. As Kosygin put it: 'In the area of

foreign policy, our government sees its chief task to be the preservation of peaceful conditions for the construction of socialism and communism, the prevention of a new world war.'

169. For a discussion of this concept, see V. Aspaturian, 'Soviet Global Power and the Correlation of Forces', *Problems of Communism* XXIX (1980), no. 3.

170. See R. Menon, 'Military Power, Intervention, and Soviet Policy in the Third World' in Kanet, *Soviet Policy in the 1980s*, pp. 263-84.

171. This evolution is ably chronicled in Katz, *The Third World in Soviet Military Thought, passim.*

# 6 AMERICAN CONCEPTIONS OF POLITICAL AND SOCIAL CHANGE IN THE THIRD WORLD

This chapter compares certain aspects of Western liberal thought concerning Third World politics with the body of doctrine considered in Chapters 4 and 5. The terms 'Western' and 'liberal' comprehend a wide variety of perspectives on this and on many other problems. Not all of these are mutually consistent. Any attempt to distil a single doctrine from them risks over-simplification and inaccuracy. Partly for this reason, this chapter focuses on *American* liberal thought on the subject. In terms of the brief for this book, this is justifiable since the US is after all the main competitor of the USSR in the quest for influence in the Third World.

Whilst it is perhaps incautious to generalize about 'American liberalism', there appear to be a number of aspects of American thought [with respect to social and political change in the Third World and more broadly, with respect to socio-political change *per se*] which are widely shared in both the policy-making and academic worlds and which differ dramatically from both Soviet and Third World thinking on the same subject.

The discussion of Soviet and American perspectives on political and social change in the non-European world is intended to shed light on whether either of the superpowers enjoys an ideological advantage in the quest for influence in the Third World as a result of an affinity between their thinking and that of radical nationalists. Few would argue that American ideas on this subject and their expression in the policy and practice of successive administrations suggest any substantial similarity of perspective between Third World national liberation movements and radical regimes on the one hand and the USA on the other.[1] As such, an exhaustive analysis intended to explore the parameters of such an affinity would be superfluous. The discussion below is intended merely as a counterpoint to the preceding analysis. It relies principally on secondary sources and is summary in form.

The last chapter suggested that there were considerable differences between Soviet and Third World approaches to national liberation. Yet both share a basic definition of national liberation and a similar vocabulary of concepts and categories around which to structure discussion and argument about political and social processes in the Third

World. One was left with the impression that Soviet and radical Third World writers shared considerable common ground on just what the issues were and on how they should be broached.

Comparison of liberal American and radical Third World discussions, on the other hand yields no such impression. Instead, it appears that the two are talking past each other, using different languages, sharing little if any definitional and analytical common ground. There is no real attempt in the American literature to give substance to and to employ in analysis the term 'national liberation'. Where it appears, usually in the phrases 'national liberation movements' or 'wars of national liberation', it refers to left wing, pro-Soviet, often terroristic, and usually illegitimate (in American eyes) anti-American non-governmental actors. Its evaluative content is generally negative.[2]

With respect to the objectives of national liberation movements, the United States has generally supported the self-determination of territories and peoples under colonial rule, from Roosevelt's disagreements with Churchill on the applicability of the Atlantic Charter to extra-European colonial possessions onwards. The American perspective on self-determination differs from the Soviet one, in that self-determination is viewed as a universal right of subject peoples[3] (though there is little clarity on just what groups this right pertains to), rather than as a tactical expedient which may be supported only when it furthers American interests.[4]

Beyond this, dominant American perspectives on Third World politics have displayed little sympathy for, and often considerable resistance to objectives basic to radical Third World conceptions of the national liberation process.[5] Much of the literature on economic development, for example, assumes or specifies that economic independence from the international capitalist economy and self-reliance are recipes for sustained underdevelopment and low growth, and hence, manifestly run counter to the interests of the new states.[6] Openness favours rapid development. Liberal trade theory assumes that the interests of all states are maximized individually and collectively by their integration into a global trading economy based on comparative advantage.[7] One can detect in some late 1960s and early 1970s discussions of interdependence a similar preference for economic interpenetration and integration as part of an overall global transcendence of the nation states system and creation of a world community, free from poverty and war.[8]

In practice, American and other Western private interests have sought to assure reliable access to primary goods and to secure outlets for surplus capital in the form of direct and indirect investments. These efforts have generally been supported by the American, Japanese, and West European governments. The American government has, at various times and to varying degrees, resisted and retaliated against attempts by developing and other states to achieve economic independence through nationalization or stricter control of foreign interests.[9]

American liberal thought, and the policies in which to varying degrees it has been embodied, display even less acceptance of the social revolutionary aspect of the concept of national liberation. Although American government and mainstream academic thinking have on occasion reflected support for social *reform* (such as land reform programmes) to rectify serious social inequities, this has stopped well short of acceptance of the desirability of revolution, in the sense of a forcible expropriation and redistribution of private property without compensation, the removal from political power of traditional ruling elites and their replacement by forces purportedly more representaive of the interests of the masses. Robert Packenham refers in this context to a widespread American premise that 'radicalism and revolution are bad'. As a result of the exceptional character of the American historical experience (and in particular the weakness of social stratification and the abundance of resources), policy-makers and academics have displayed 'little appreciation of the appropriateness under certain circumstances (circumstances much less rare in poor countries than in the United States) of radical and revolutionary change'.[10] Internally generated social revolution has frequently been dismissed as an externally (usually Soviet) inspired challenge to American interests and has been resisted as such. Contemporary American leadership attitudes towards Central America are a case in point, as is the history of American opposition to leftist reformism in the Caribbean region. President Reagan's remark 'Let us not delude ourselves. The Soviet Union underlies all the unrest that is going on. If they weren't engaged in this game of dominoes, there wouldn't be any hot spots in the world.'[11] is only one of the latest manifestations of this very durable equation.[12]

Moreover, the expropriation and socialization of private property which is often a prominent aspect of social revolution runs against the common American premise that free enterprise is the most efficient motor of economic growth.[13] Finally, with regard to socialism itself, there would appear to be in the American political tradition a sustained lack of interest in and sympathy for socialist ideas, coupled ironically with an occasional intense fear of the threat posed by socialism or communism to liberal American values.[14]

Such premises render it difficult for the United States to cultivate radical groups in the Third World, as such groups are usually dismissed *ab initio* as 'lost', and as contacts with them are difficult to justify to domestic constituencies sharing these predispositions. In this sense, it is probably true that Third World radicalism works to the detriment of American positions in Asia, Africa and Latin America. This is true partly because the Soviet Union has been consistently supportive in doctrine, and often in material terms, of radical movements in the Third World. It also results from a tendency in the Third World to associate the United States with Western colonialism and 'neocolonialism'. But it also follows from the fact that the United States has been and has been perceived to be anti-radical.

With regard finally to the cultural aspect of the process of national liberation, dominant American attitudes display neither strong sympathy nor antipathy. While the rejection of Western norms and symbols may be viewed as obscurantist, atavistic, immature, or foolish, it is not a challenge to the legitimacy of Western systems of government. The authority of these governments is far less grounded in the purported universality of their ideology than is that of the Soviet regime. Hence, the imperative to resist this form of particularism is far less strong.

The issues of the nature and makeup of the world revolutionary process, and the role of the national liberation movement within it, are not prominent elements of mainstream Western thought concerning political and social change in the Third World. The United States is not committed in any important way to such a revolution or to the socialist millenium it is to bring into being and does not claim a role within it. As such, there is little point in expending effort on elucidating the structure and processes of the world revolutionary movement. To the extent that such a process is recognized, it tends to be viewed as anti-Western, Soviet-dominated, and destructive of international order, as are particular manifestations of it in the Third World.

Similar remarks may be made about the question of the universal and particular in theories of revolution and the transition to and state of socialism. Given that the United States is not a socialist country the legitimacy of whose government is to a degree dependent on a claim to possession of universally valid social and political truths, and is by no means committed to a global transition to socialism, the question is not significant from an analytical point of view.

The American agenda is different. To the extent that American policy-makers and scholars promote a universal model for Third World political structures, it has been one drawn from the liberal democratic parliamentary tradition. Essentially, they have taken the view that emulation of American and/or Western European governmental structures and acceptance of the democratic ideology which underlies them best serve the interests of the peoples of the Third World[15] and the global interest as well.[16] The creation of democratic institutions takes precedence over social change. Hence, one saw American advisers demanding democratic reform from Chiang Kai-shek in the aftermath of the Second World War when he was involved in a nationwide civil war against the CCP.[17] American advisers likewise pressured various Vietnamese leaders from Ngo Dienh Diem to Nguyen Van Thieu to hold free elections and to democratize the South Vietnamese political process during the Vietnam War. The current administration is insists on 'progress towards democracy' in Nicaragua as a prerequisite for improvement in Nicaraguan-American relations. Its officials aver that: 'In the last analysis, our interests and those of the Salvadoran people are exactly congruent, for we all see a peaceful and democratic El Salvador.'[18] In the same issue of the newspaper from which the above quotation is taken as an example of conservative Republican views, we see the liberal columnist Anthony Lewis arguing, from the opposite end of the political spectrum, that the recent democratization of Argentina proves that: '[The US] is most effective abroad when its diplomacy coincides with its ideals. Of all people, we should be arguing for the values that President Alfonsin embraces: freedom under laws.'[19]

To judge from the practice of American foreign policy since the Second World War, the objective of democracy is, however, supplemented by those of order and stability and of the limitation of what is perceived to be communist expansionism.[20] These objectives respond to the beliefs not only that stability is a prerequisite for the emergence of democratic institutions and that once a state 'goes communist' it is extremely difficult to resurrect,[21] but also that the expansion of radical leftist influence in the Third World increases Soviet power and hence is inimical to the security interests of the United States and the West.[22]

Where the choice is seen as one between an authoritarianism of the left and one of the right, the latter is fairly consistently preferred, even where it involves substantial and systematic infringement of civil and political rights.[23] This translates frequently into opposition to the left-wing nationalism of many of the groups considered in Chapter 4, and to support for the indigenous social and political forces against which such movements direct their efforts.[24] The American involvement in Vietnam and, currently, in Central America are cases in point, as are American opposition to rebel forces in the Greek Civil War, their counter-insurgency assistance to Haile Selassie's regime in Ethiopia and to various military regimes in Latin America in the mid-1960s, and the tilt towards white rule in Southern Africa in the early years of the 1970s.[25] It is reasonable to assume that this opposition is one reason that leftist movements in the Third World turn elsewhere, and particularly to the USSR, for support. Again, therefore, it is not only Soviet support — verbal and substantive — for national liberation movements, but also American opposition to them which favours close ties between such movements and the USSR.

Turning to the question of the role of various social forces in the national liberation movement and in the new states, there has been during the period of decolonization since the Second World War fairly consistent American opposition to left wing and particularly communist leadership both of the struggle for independence and of the new states created by this struggle. This opposition found its expression most clearly in American behaviour in Vietnam since the Second World War, in the response to Nasser and Castro, and in the US attitude towards the MPLA in Angola and to the Dergue in Ethiopia. Although the question of who should not lead the struggle for liberation was covered, there was far less attention to who should lead. There would seem, however, to be a fairly consistent bias in policy and doctrine in favour of moderates rather than radicals, reformers rather than revolutionaries and economic liberals rather than those advocating restrictive economic policies in the Third World.

Perhaps more important, however, is the prevailing American conception of political structure and process in Third World states. It was noted in Chapter 4 that Third World writers and leaders emphasized the need for the monolithic unity of the people, for the nation to speak with one voice, and to develop a single collective identity *vis-à-vis* the rest of the world. This reflects the dominance in international politics of the idea of the *nation*-state as the basic component part of the system. The prevalence of single party states in the Third World, a tendency to identify state and nation with a specific leader, an intolerance of opposition to government policy, and an emphasis on community or national, rather than individual rights reflect this monolithic conception of the national community. Such perspectives may be explained partially as efforts to stabilize the rule of particular leaders or elites and to free them of constraints on their behaviour *vis-à-vis* opponents of their rule by rendering opposition illegitimate. But they are also attempts to cope with the weakness of political institutions in new states, with the 'problems of creating effective authority in modernizing countries', and the need to accumulate power in order to govern effectively.[26]

It has already been noted that marxist-leninist theories of party and political organization held considerable attraction to radical nationalists in the Third World, precisely because they were deemed applicable to the problem of concentrating power and managing participation. What Samuel Huntington sees as the *challenge* of communist theories of party organization and government structure[27] was seen by many radical movements as a promising *solution* to these problems.

By contrast, the democratic pluralism which has characterized American political development and American doctrine and policy with regard to new states has little attraction. Both Packenham and Huntington have noted that Americans pay greater attention to how power is distributed than to how to increase the amount of power in a given society: 'When an American thinks about the problem of government-building, he directs himself not to the creation of authority but rather to the limitation of authority and the division of power.'[28] Americans tend to oppose the concentration of power, even though such accumulation generally facilitates its accumulation, a precondition for effective governance. This tendency, Packenham argues, has manifested itself in American doctrine and policy since 1949 in an emphasis on 'elections, pluralistic voluntary organizations, more autonomous and powerful legislatures, competitive parties, greater popular participation in decision-making, and other devices excellently conceived to distribute power and limit authority'.[29]

A further manifestation of this American preoccupation with the limitation of governmental power is an occasionally profound concern for human rights evident, for example, in the pressure exerted by the Carter Administration on Latin American regimes and on Iran as a result of human rights violations, and in the recent congressional insistence that the Reagan Administration certify the human rights record of the Salvadoran regime at six-month intervals in order to obtain the release of economic and military assistance appropriations for that country. This stress on *individual* rights contrasts rather strongly with the focus on collective and community rights in the Third World and is frequently seen as interference in internal affairs.

Turning finally to the question of armed struggle, there is evident in American thinking concerning Third World politics a distinct preference for peaceful change where change is deemed necessary and a pronounced opposition to movements seeking violently to overthrow the *status quo*. While this pertains most clearly to what could be characterized as the later stages of the struggle for liberation — that is, to struggles mounted against sovereign governments with a view to promoting radical social change[30] — one can maintain with reasonable confidence that even in the struggle for political self-determination, Americans generally prefer that such struggle be conducted peacefully and within the bounds of accepted constitutional practice. Packenham accounts for the difficulty which Americans have in appreciating the positive role that revolutionary violence may have in certain circumstances to the limited character of American historical experience.[31] Coupled with this more or less instinctive aversion to revolutionary violence is a tendency to equate it with Soviet expansionism (as recently in Central America) and, therefore, to oppose it on security grounds.[32] A third, and somewhat more discriminating source of this antipathy to violence is the view that, in the words of National Security Study Memorandum 39, violence leads to 'increased opportunities for the communists'.[33]

To summarize, American thought concerning political development differs from that of radical nationalists in Asia, Africa and Latin America in its lack of sympathy for the economic and many of the social aspects of national liberation, its rejection of the objective of socialism and opposition to movements espousing it, its aversion to the notion of a world revolutionary process directed against imperialism, its preference for moderate rather than radical leadership in the Third World, and its hostility to violent struggle *per se*. It suffices to note that American and Third World radical nationalist perspectives on political and social change in Asia, Africa and Latin America have little in common, other than (and this is an important exception) a shared recognition of the transcendent right to national self-determination. American like Soviet, ideas on political development display considerable ethnocentrism in the projection of their own normative perspectives and historical experiences in quite different socio-political conditions where these are inappropriate and often unwelcome. They conflict with Third World thought, however, in fundamentally different ways. If one conceives of Third World perspectives on national liberation as a diad embracing nationalist particularism and social revolution, the Soviet perspective emphasizes the social revolutionary aspect while resisting the nationalist one. Americans have far less difficulty with the nationalist animus of doctrines of national liberation (at least in its political manifestations), but resist the aspiration to social revolution.

## Notes

1. Indeed, it is far more common to see the opposite argued. See, for example, R. Barnet, *Intervention and Revolution: The United States in the Third World*, NY, New American Library, 1968, pp. 23-41.

2. Barnet's paraphrase of perceptions of revolutionary war in the Third World among the American national security community as 'the Communist strategy of wars of national liberation' (ibid., p. 28) continues to have considerable merit.

3. As Richard Hofstadter put it with reference to Woodrow Wilson (and in a manner which recalls J.S. Mill's words cited in Chapter 2): 'National self-determination, the international equivalent of democracy in domestic politics, would embody the principle of consent by the governed.' R. Hofstadter, *The American Political Tradition*, p. 356. See also Eric Goldman's reference to Lyndon Johnson's sharing of the 'traditional American assumption that Americans and the peoples of the rest of the world had in common a bedrock interest in ruling themselves'. E. Goldman, *The Tragedy of Lyndon Johnson*, NY, Knopf, 1969, p. 385.

4. Hoffmann in this context refers to a tradition of American sympathy for anti-colonialism. S. Hoffmann, *Gulliver's Troubles, Or The Setting of American Foreign Policy*, NY, McGraw Hill, 1968, p. 100.

5. Cf. Eqbal Ahmad's comment in R. Pfeffer, ed., *No More Vietnams?*, NY, Harper and Row, 1968, p. 283.

6. A recent embodiment of this perspective on the importance of integration through trade into the international economy to the process of development are the 'outward-oriented' or 'export-led' development strategies advocated by, among others, the World Bank. See J.G. Ruggie, *The Antinomies of Interdependence*, NY, Columbia University Press, 1983, pp. 9-10.

7. Cf., for example, the discussion of the gains from trade and the case for free trade in H.G. Grubel, *International Economics*, Homewood, Richard Irwin, 1977, pp. 37-41. Contemporary liberal trade theory has its roots in the works of the Swedish economists Heckscher and Olin, in that of Ricardo, who first laid out the two country model of comparative advantage (see Grubel, *International Economics*, pp. 12-21 for a discussion of comparative advantage in classical trade theory) and ultimately in that of Adam Smith, who argued, effectively, that welfare was maximized by allowing markets to operate without constraint. Ruggie (*Antinomies of Interdependence*, pp. 5-7) juxtaposes the tradition represented by Ricardo to that of Friedrich List who, as was noted in Chapter 2, held that the safety and prosperity of less developed nations would be maximized through temporary restraint on trade. It would appear from Chapter 4 that the Listian tradition predominates in the Third World radical literature.

8. This is implicit in much of what Keohane and Nye have called the 'new rhetoric of interdependence'. R. Keohane and J. Nye, *Power and Interdependence*, Boston, Little and Brown, 1977, pp. 7-8.

9. One could cite here the Hickenlooper Amendment which required the cutoff of American aid to any country which nationalized American property without 'fair' compensation, or, for that matter, diplomatic pressure on Canada in the 1970s to weaken its foreign investment review procedures.

10. R. Packenham, *Liberal America and the Third World*, Princeton, Princeton University Press, 1973, pp. 6, 20, 107, 133-4. The Vietnam experience, however, encouraged some rethinking of these postulates, particularly among American

liberals. This was perhaps most evident in the failure of the United States to intervene to prevent the collapse of the Somoza regime in Nicaragua in 1979. One might conclude from this that dominant American perspectives on radical change in the Third World were displaying increasing sophistication, the product of a process of learning by trial and error. Recent American behaviour in Central America, however, draws this optimistic conclusion into doubt.

11. As cited in A. Schlesinger, 'Foreign Policy and the American Character', *Foreign Affairs*, fall 1983, p. 5.

12. In this vein, one could cite Dulles' June 1954 statement regarding Guatemala that:

> Dramatic events expose the evil purpose of the Kremlin to destroy the inter-American system . . . The intrusion of Soviet despotism was, of course, a direct challenge to the Monroe Doctrine . . . The Communists seized on [the Guatemalan Revolution] not as an opportunity for real reforms but as a chance to gain political power. The master plan of international communism is to gain a solid base in this hemisphere [which] can be used to extend communist penetration . . .

(As cited in C. Blasier, *The Hovering Giant: US Responses to Revolutionary Change in Latin America*, Pittsburgh, University of Pittsburgh Press, 1976, p. 171.

13. Cf. Hoffmann's characterization of mainstream American thinking on economic development (*Gulliver's Troubles*, p. 120).

14. L. Hartz, *The Liberal Tradition in America*, NY, Harcourt, Brace and Winston, 1955, pp. 6, 298, 300.

15. See, for example, W.W. Rostow, *The Stages of Economic Growth: A Non-communist Manifesto*, Cambridge, Cambridge University Press, 1961, pp. 164-5. See also Turner, *Catholicism and Political Development*, pp. 4-6. Tom Wicker, in a recent column on American aid policy in Central America, has referred in this context to the 'same old American assumption' that 'the goal of all societies is to achieve democracy and freedom, as in Wisconsin or Kansas' ('Marshall Plan Again?', *New York Times*, 9. i. 84, p. 19). This is reminiscent of Goldman's remark (*Tragedy of Johnson*, p. 385) that:

> Over the generations, Democrats and Republicans, liberals and conservatives, have tended to assume an international trend, a trend so certain in their minds that it took on the cast of a law of history. Human beings everywhere, the law ran, sought peace and democracy, wanted to get ahead to a farm of their own or a house on the right side of the tracks. Consequently, the real history of man was a long slow swing toward a world consisting actively of middle class democracies.

16. As with Woodrow Wilson's notion that a democratic world would be one free from war and the threat of war. As Kenneth Waltz put it: 'Mazzini had assumed that a self-determined state would be a democratic one; Woodrow Wilson explicitly makes the assumption a precondition of world peace.' K. Waltz, *Man, The State, and War*, NY, Columbia University Press, 1959, p. 144.

17. Ulam, *Expansion and Coexistence*, pp. 479-80.

18. Elliot Abrams (Assistant Secretary of State), 'On Aid to Salvador', *New York Times*, 26 Jan. 1984, p. 25. See also R. Reagan, 'Prepared Text of Reagan Speech on Central American Policies', *New York Times* (10 May 1984), p. 6.

19. A. Lewis, 'Lessons from Argentina', in ibid., p. 25.

20. Hence, Jerome Slater, for example, characterizes the ultimate American

objectives in their relations with the Dominican Republic as the prevention of the establishment of a 'radical, Castroite regime' there and the creation of a stable, democratic, and strongly anti-communist Dominican government. J. Slater, 'The Dominican Republic, 1961-1966' in B. Blechman and S. Kaplan, eds., *Force without War: US Armed Forces as a Political Instrument*, Washington, Brookings, 1978, p. 289. Hoffmann in the late 1960s noted the tendency of United States Agency for International Development (USAID) officials to define political development as 'anti-communist, pro-American political stability' (*Gulliver's Troubles*, p. 190). He accounts for this preoccupation with stability in the following terms:

> A national experience of constitutional continuity that has instilled in us a nostalgia for tranquility, faith in the highly debatable proposition that a stable polity is a healthy one, skills that are most effective when the social system in which they are applied is uncontested have made of political stability the Grail of American foreign policy.

(Ibid., p. 201.)

21. On this point, see, for example, Hosmer and Wolfe, *Soviet Policy toward Third World Conflict*, p. 177.

22. Such reasoning appears to be implicit in much of the recent Kissinger Commission report on Central America (*New York Times*, 12. i. 84, pp. 6-7). See also R. Reagan, as cited in the *New York Times* (10 May 1984), p. 6. See also the comments of Cole Blasier (*The Giant's Rival*, pp. 153-5) on the American tendency to confuse indigenous leftist nationalism with pro-Soviet communism.

23. On these points, see Eqbal Ahmad's comments on the 'paranoid strain in American politics' in Pfeffer, *No More Vietnams?*, p. 14. See also Packenham, *Liberal America*, p. 146, on the preference for right over left authoritarianism during the Johnson years.

24. It is not being maintained here that dislike of radical change, opposition to revolution, and the tendency to link rebel movements to 'international communism' were the sole causes of such actions, but only that these ideological predispositions were factors contributing to them.

25. On the Southern African dimension, see G. Bender, 'Kissinger in Angola: Anatomy of a Failure' in R. Lemarchand, ed., *American Policy in Southern Africa: The Stakes and the Stances*, Washington, University Press of America, 1981, *passim.*, and particularly p. 68.

26. S. Huntington, *Political Order in Changing Societies*, New Haven, Yale University Press, 1968, p. 7.

27. Ibid., p. 8.

28. Ibid., p. 7.

29. Packenham, *Liberal America*, pp. 153-5. A good recent example is the Kissinger report on Central America, which states that:

> The vitality of the inter-American system lies now more than ever before in accepting a firm commitment to political pluralism, freedom of expression, respect for human rights, the maintenance of an independent and effective system of justice and the right of people to choose their destiny in free elections.

As cited in *New York Times*, 12 Jan. 1984, p.6.

30. Packenham asserts in this context that: 'If the record of American foreign policy and doctrines toward revolutionary regimes in power is somewhat mixed, it seems to have been universally negative toward those nongovernmental groups who attempt to change the system "by any means necessary".' (*Liberal America*

*and the Third World*, p. 142.) See also Hoffman, *Gulliver's Troubles*, p. 201. In fairness, one should note, however, that American attitudes towards the armed struggles of the Indonesian independence movement in the late 1940s and towards the Algerian FLN in the Kennedy years are to some extent exceptions to this generalization.

31. Ibid., p. 138; and Barnet, *Intervention and Revolution*, p. 33. See also Blasier, *The Giant's Rival*, p. 156.

32. For example, the Kissinger report on Central America, as cited in the *New York Times*, 12 Jan. 1984, pp. 6-8.

33. As cited in G. Bender, 'Kissinger in Angola', p. 68.

# 7 CONCLUSION

Recalling the questions posed in Chapter 1, it appears first of all that, despite the great cultural and historical diversity of the Third World, there exists an idea of national liberation which is widely shared by radical nationalist movements in Asia, Africa, and Latin America. National liberation involves political independence, freedom from external economic control, the elimination of indigenous oppression through a process of 'anti-feudal' and 'anti-capitalist' social revolution, and the creation of a new national culture through the uprooting of alien cultural influences which facilitate foreign domination.

This idea has found expression not only in statements of doctrine, but to varying degrees in policy. To cite a few examples, widespread nationalization of foreign property, the quest for a restructuring of North-South economic relations, frequent attempts to socialize the means of production, and various programmes of cultural purification or re-education all reflect receptiveness to different aspects of this idea of national liberation. The maximalist character of the social, economic, and cultural programmes which follow from such a conception of national liberation, coupled with the paucity in most cases of the means to achieve them, favours the concentration of power and a statist approach to the problems of economic, social, and cultural development in countries created or seized by radical movements. It is probably true that the ambitious socio-economic policies which have derived from the commitment to this conception of national liberation have resulted in considerable inefficiency, waste, and hardship in countries such as Tanzania, Mozambique, Angola, Guinea and Cuba, among others, though it is by no means clear that alternative approaches to development would have brought better results.

This four-faceted conception of national liberation draws upon several traditions in Western thought. In its stress on the right of a national (putative if not actual) community to direct its own affairs, it reflects a liberal conception of national self-determination. In its aspiration to economic independence, it is beholden to the economic nationalism which originated with Hamilton and List, who argued that a degree of dissociation from the international trading economy was a necessary condition for the economic development of states which were latecomers to the game, and (in List's case) that a strong national economy was a *sine qua non* of real independence. In its emphasis on control of economic activity within the country, the contemporary motion of economic independence also draws upon developments in the theory of imperialism and particularly on the work of Hobson and Lenin.

The notion of a social revolution aimed at the elimination of indigenous as well as foreign exploitation betrays the influence of marxist thought concerning the nature of oppression in presocialist societies, and, conversely, that of freedom. Finally, the cultural dimension of the idea of national liberation, in its stress on separate and distinct cultural development and in its frequent appeal to pre-colonial national traditions, recalls the nineteenth-century cultural nationalism of Herder, which subsequently inspired national movements among subject nationalities or proto-nationalities in the Austro-Hungarian and Russian Empires. The second dimension of the idea of cultural liberation — that of fostering through education and indoctrination the subjective prerequisites for the creation of a socialist society — draws again on marxist and leninist perspectives on the importance of consciousness in revolutionary change.

The idea of national liberation, while drawing upon these various intellectual traditions, is distinct from them. It goes beyond national self-determination as we normally understand it, in that it embraces not only the achievement of political sovereignty, but also the quest for economic autonomy, social revolution and socialism, as well as a struggle to establish, preserve and strengthen a distinctive national culture. It differs from nationalism, as the concept might have been understood by late-nineteenth-century Western writers in complementing political and cultural demands with economic ones, and by synthesizing this amalgam with a commitment to anti-feudal *and* anti-capitalist social revolution. This latter commitment sets it apart from the Listian variant of nationalism as well. It is distinct from marxism in its fundamental commitment to national identity. One might say that the national liberation revolution is national not only in form but also in essence. Class identity is secondary.

While the above are the intellectual roots of the idea of national liberation, these elements of European thought were attractive because they explained and purported to provide solutions for problems faced by new elites in societies experiencing Western domination. These elites were by and large denied a significant role in determining their own affairs and those of the people they sought to represent. The economic activity of the societies from which they emerged, to the extent that

these societies had moved beyond the level of subsistence, was dominated by, and generally directed in such a way as to benefit, metropolitan interests. The coming to power of educated elites spawned by
the colonial system was blocked not only by foreign rule, but by the
continuing presence of traditional hierarchies in many Third World
societies. Colonial rule was to some extent sustained by a general
acceptance of the cultural superiority of Western civilization. These
circumstances favoured the emergence of an idea of national liberation
embracing political, economic, social and cultural objectives.

Beyond this basic idea of national liberation, the analysis in Chapter
4 suggests that Third World radical nationalist doctrines of liberation
share a number of other significant attributes, many of which reflect
the basic tension between transnational universalism and national
particularism which is evident in the idea of national liberation itself.
Although these movements generally recognize that the struggle in
which they were engaged was an international one directed against a
common enemy, they accept no hierarchy in the world revolutionary
movement which would subordinate them to outsiders. In policy, they
display little tendency to subordinate particular interests to general
ones. Loyalties appear to be hierarchically ordered, with the national
interest ranking highest, regional and Third World commitments
second, and global revolutionary ones last.[1]

In the realm of theory-building, although many Third World writers
accept the necessity of learning from the revolutionary experience of
others, Third World doctrines display a persistent tendency to dimin-
ish or reject the applicability of foreign models in national revolutionary situations. They tend to emphasize instead the importance of
national conditions in the development of revolutionary theory. Particularism in practice matches particularism in theory. This reflects a
pragmatic concern not to be distracted by concepts developed in conditions very different from those faced by the movement in question (for
example, the hegemony of the urban working class). Yet it is also part
and parcel of the concern to preserve and strengthen national
autonomy. The insistence on the overriding importance of local
conditions in the development of doctrine amounts to a refusal to
accept dogmas developed elsewhere, and to an assertion of the relevance of national character and culture (cf., for example, Mao Tse-
tung's discussion of the 'sinification' of marxism) to revolutionary
doctrine.

Several modifications of doctrine are particularly common among
radical nationalist movements. Among these is an emphasis on the

importance of will and consciousness in the struggle, and a corresponding playing down of objective preconditions of revolution and socialist development. Related to this is a stress on the leading role of 'petty bourgeois' intellectuals, a focus on rural struggle and on the decisive role of the peasantry, and a parallel tendency in practice to ignore the urban working class (where it exists).

With regard to the tension between national and class identity, varying degrees of discomfort with class struggle are evident, ranging from outright hostility to division within the nation along class lines to the insistence that class struggle should be tempered by (and subordinate to) a concern to maintain national unity. Where class struggle was deemed to be necessary, it was seen not so much as a conflict between large groups within the nation as one between the nation and a small group of exploiters who had abandoned the nation and compromised with imperialism. Moreover, where such a struggle was accepted, in general it involved not so much the exclusion and liquidation of 'exploiting classes' as it did winning them over through re-education or, for that matter, through an appeal to national loyalty. There are, of course, exceptions to this generalization. The Kampuchean case comes quickly to mind. But it is not being claimed that these patterns are universal, only that they are common. Finally, there was evident a general belief that violence was not only justified but necessary in the struggle for liberation. Beyond this, Third World radical writers have often attributed additional benefits (psychological liberation, unification and mobilization of the population, leadership selection, etc.) to the use of violence.

With the exception perhaps of these perspectives on violence, the above radical positions are broadly similar to those of the wider community of Asian, African and Latin American nationalists.

If one compares this body of thought to Soviet and American analyses of and commitments to social and political change in the Third World, it would appear that Soviet doctrine displays a considerably greater affinity with radical nationalism than does American thinking. Soviet writers share a vision of national liberation which embraces political and economic independence and social revolution, leading ultimately to socialism. Both Soviet and Third World writers accept the need for a concentration of power in the national revolution. Both accept the use of violence in order to achieve the political and social objectives of national liberation. Both the Soviets and Third World radicals perceive themselves to be involved in a revolutionary struggle of global dimensions against 'imperialism'. In practice, moreover, the USSR, as a new arrival in Third World politics, can only expand its own influence in Asia, Africa and Latin America to the extent that Western influence is displaced. In this sense, ideology is matched by interest in favouring support for Third World anti-Western agitation. Partly because of its doctrinal commitment to national liberation, partly because of its lack of a history of non-contiguous colonialism, and also because it has frequently assisted particular movements struggling against colonialism or what is considered to be neocolonialism, the Soviet Union has been widely perceived in the Third World to be a friend of national liberation.

By contrast, American doctrine shares with radical Third World writing only the commitment to national self-determination. There is evident in American thought and, to some extent, practice a principled opposition to the notions of economic independence, and, even more clearly, of social revolution, particularly where the latter involves violence. The United States is generally unsympathetic to attempts by Third World radical movements to consolidate their power, considering this inconsistent with the democratic ideals which it considers universal in application. As a result of these positions, of the tendency to identify the United States with the European colonial tradition (however unfairly), of the prominence of American economic interests in many Third World economies, and of the natural resentment by the poor of the very wealthy, the United States is generally perceived by radical nationalist movements and governments to be an enemy of national revolution and, for that matter, a principal target of global anti-Western struggle. Ayatollah Khomeini's characterization of the United States as the 'Great Satan' is an extreme form of what is a widespread sentiment.

However, one must not overestimate the Soviet advantage in this regard. The analysis of Chapters 4 and 5 suggests that the ideological affinity between the USSR and Third World nationalists is strictly bounded by the particularism, in doctrine and policy, of these movements, by their failure on the whole to recognize Soviet leadership or the primacy of Soviet interests, and by their subordination of international commitments to national and regional interests. Where these coincide with Soviet objectives, there is co-operation. Where they do not, there is conflict with the USSR. It is not surprising that the USSR has over the years had considerable difficulty in sustaining durable and useful patron/client relationships with major Third World actors. Moreover, it is no accident that the most reliable Soviet allies in the Third World (for example, Cuba and Vietnam) are those who are most dependent on the USSR in material terms and those most isolated, largely as a result of American policy, from the United States and its Western allies. This begs the question of just how reliable these states would be from the Soviet perspective if the United States competed more actively for influence over their leaders, rather than giving them up for lost.

On the whole, given the balance between universal and particular in Third World theory and practice of national liberation, neither super-power can expect to draw durable one-sided advantage from the rise of radical nationalism in the Third World. Although in the past, Third World nationalism has been directed largely against the West and has damaged Western interests disproportionately, this is because the Western presence permeated Third World societies. There was no Soviet presence to serve as a focus for nationalist agitation. The case of Egypt in the mid-1970s suggests that where the Soviets develop such a presence, it too becomes a target. Moreover, the fact that the motivations and consequences of the rise of radical nationalism in the Third World have been anti-Western by no means suggests that the USSR necessarily derives positive gains from this rise. Indeed, the success of national liberation movements, by removing the more obvious foci of anti-Western sentiment in the Third World (e.g. South Africa), particularly if accepted with reasonable equanimity by the West, may reduce the Soviet capacity to exploit this anti-Westernism to their advantage.

## Notes

1. In a number of cases, it could with justice be maintained that the national was superseded by the personal. The rest of the ordering, however, would remain valid.

# BIBLIOGRAPHY

## Abbreviations

In the bibliography which follows, a number of names of journals are abbreviated. A key follows:

1. *AiAS* – *Azia i Afrika Sevodnya* (*Asia and Africa Today*).
2. *CQ* – *China Quarterly*.
3. *IA* – *International Affairs* (Moscow).
4. *K* – *Kommunist*.
5. *MEiMO* – *Mirovaya Ekonomika i Mezhdunarodnye Otnoshenia* (*World Economics and International Relations*).
6. *NAiA* – *Narody Azii i Afriki* (*Peoples of Asia and Africa*).
7. *NT* – *New Times*.
8. *NYT* – *New York Times*.
9. *PA* – *Presence Africaine*.
10. *PP* – *People's Power*.
11. *WMR* – *World Marxist Review*.

## Sources

Abbas, F. *Guerre et Revolution d'Algerie*. Paris: Rene Juilliard, 1962

Abrams, E. 'On Aid to Salvador'. *NYT* (26 Jan. 1984).

Akopov, G. 'Teoreticheskii Analiz Sovremennovo Natsionalizma' *K* (1974), no. 13

Akopyan, G. 'O Dvukh Tendentsiakh Natsionalizma v Ugnetyonnykh i Razviva-yushchikhsya Stran'. *NAiA* (1970), no. 5

Alekseev, E. 'Natsional'no-osvoboditel'noe Dvizhenie – Sostavnaya Chast' Miro-vovo Revolyutsionnovo Protsessa'. *AiAS* (1963), no. 12

Aliev, A. 'Natsionalizm i Natsii Perekhodnovo Tipa'. *NAiA* (1975), no. 1

Aliev, G. 'Oktyabr'skaya Revolyutsia i Natsional'no-osvoboditel'noe Dvizhenie'. *K* (1977), no. 9

ANC. *Excerpts from Policy and Programme*. Dar Es Salaam: n.p., 1965

ANC. *ANC – South Africa: A Short History*. London: ANC, 1971

ANC. *Forward to Freedom: Documents on the National Policies of the ANC of South Africa*. Dar Es Salaam: n.p., 1971 (?)

Andropov, Yu. 'Leninizm – Nauka i Iskusstvo Revolyutsionnovo Tvorchestva'. *Pravda* (23 Apr. 1978)

Aspaturian, V. 'Soviet Global Power and the Correlation of Forces'. *Problems of Communism* XXIX (1980), no. 3

Attwood, W. *The Reds and the Blacks*. NY: Harper and Row, 1967

Avineri, S. *Karl Marx on Colonialism and Modernization*. Garden City, NJ: Doubleday, 1968.

Bergramov, E. 'Internatsional'noe i Natsional'noe v Mirovom Obshchestvennom Razvitii'. *K* (1975), no. 9

Balabushevich, V. 'Bor'ba Indii za Nezavisimost". *Mirovoe Khozyaistvo i Mirovaya Politika* (1946), no. 9

Balabushevich, V. 'Novyi Etap Natsional'no-osvoboditel'noi Bor'by Narodov Indii'. *Voprosy Ekonomiki* (1949), no. 8

Barghoorn, F. 'The Varga Discussion and Its Significance'. *American Slavic and East European Review*, VII (1948), no. 2

Barnet, R. *Intervention and Revolution: The United States in the Third World.* NY: New American Library, 1968

Bedeski, R. 'The Tutelary State and National Revolution in Kuomintang Ideology'. *CQ* (1971), no. 46

Bennigsen, A. and Quelquejay, C. *Le Sultangalievisme au Tatarstan*. Paris:Mouton, 1960

Bennigsen, A. and Wimbush, E. *Muslim National Communism in the Soviet Union*. Chicago: Uniersity of Chicago Press, 1979

Benson, M., ed., *The Sun Will Rise*. London: IDAFSA, 1981

Benton, G. 'The "Second Wang Ming Line" (1935-1938), *CQ* (1976), no. 61

Bialer, S. *Stalin's Successors*. NY: Columbia University Press, 1980

Biko, S. *Black Consciousness in South Africa*. NY: Vintage, 1979

Blackburn, R., ed. *Strategy for Revolution*. London: Jonathan Cape, 1970

Blasier, C. *The Hovering Giant: US Responses to Revolutionary Change in Latin America*. Pittsburgh: University of Pittsburgh Press, 1976

Blasier, C. *The Giant's Rival: The USSR and Latin America*. Pittsburgh: University of Pittsburgh Press, 1983

Blechman, B. and Kaplan, S., eds. *Force without War: US Armed Forces as a Political Instrument*. Washington: Brookings, 1978

Bogdanov, K. and Rumyantsev, V. 'Nasushchnye Voprosy Revolyutsionnovo Dvizhenia v Afrike'. *K* (1967), no. 3

Brandt, K. *Stalin's Failure in China*. Cambridge: Harvard University Press, 1958

Brandt, K. *et al. A Documentary History of Chinese Communism*. Cambridge: Harvard University Press, 1952

Braunthal, J. *History of the International*. London: Nelson, 1966

Brezhnev, L. 'Za Ukreplenie Splochennosti Kommunistov za Novyi Pod'yom Antiimperialisticheskoi Bor'by'. *Pravda* (8 June 1969).

Brutents, K. 'African Revolution: Gains and Problems', *IA* (1967), no. 1

Brutents, K. 'Epokha Sotsializma i Natsional'no-osvoboditel'noe Dvizhenie'. *K* (1967), no. 18

Brutents, K. 'Natsional'no-osvoboditel'naya Revolyutsia'. *Bol'shaya Sovetskaya Entsyklopedia* XVII. Moscow: Izdatel'stvo Sovetskoi Entsyklopedii, 1974

Brutents, K. *National Liberation Revolutions Today*. Moscow: Progress, 1977

Brutents, K. 'Imperializm i Osvobodivshiesya Strany'. *Pravda* (10 Feb. 1978)

Bushuyev, V. 'The National Liberation Movement and Neocolonialism'. *IA* (1975), no. 3

Cabral, A. *Return to the Source*. NY: Monthly Review Press, 1973

Cabral, A. *Unity and Struggle*. London: Heinemann, 1980

Carr, E.H. *The Bolshevik Revolution, 1917-1923*, Vol. 3 Harmondsworth: Penguin, 1977

Carrere d'Encausse, H. and Schram, S., eds. *Marxism and Asia*. London: Allen Lane, 1969

Carrere d'Encausse, H. and Schram, S., eds. *L'URSS et la Chine devant la Revolution dans les Societes Pre-industrielles*. Paris: Armand Colin, 1970

Carter, G. and O'meara, P., eds. *Southern Africa: The Continuing Crisis*. Bloomington: Indiana University Press, 1980

Carter, G. *Which Way Is South Africa Going?*. Bloomington: Indiana University Press, 1980

Castro, F. *Cuba's Internationalist Foreign Policy*. NY: Pathfinder, 1981

Chabal, P. 'The Social and Political Thought of Amilcar Cabral: A Reassessment'. *Journal of Modern African Studies* XIX (1981), no. 1

Chaliand, G. *Armed Struggle in Africa*. NY: Monthly Review Press, 1969

Chaliand, G. *Revolution in the Third World*. NY: Vintage, 1977

Ch'en, J. *Mao and the Chinese Revolution*. London: Oxford University Press, 1965

Chilcote, R., ed. *Emerging Nationalism in the Portuguese Colonies*. Stanford: Hoover Institution Press, 1972

Clapham, C. 'The Context of African Political Thought'. *Journal of Modern African Studies*, VIII (1970), no. 1

Cobban, A. *The Nation-state and National Self-determination*. London: Collins, 1969

Cohen, A. *The Communism of Mao Tse-tung*. London: University of Chicago Press, 1964

Communist Party of the Soviet Union. 'Programma KPSS'. *Pravda* (2. xi. 61)

*Conference of Heads of State of the Nonaligned Countries*. Belgrade: n.p., 1961

Dahm, B. *Sukarno and the Struggle for Indonesian Independence*. London: Cornell University Press, 1969

Davidson, B. *In the Eye of the Storm: Angola's People*. NY: Anchor, 1973

Davidson, B. *The Liberation of Guine*. Harmondsworth: Penguin, 1969

Dawisha, K. *Soviet Foreign Policy towards Egypt*. London: Macmillan, 1979

Debray, R. *Revolution in the Revolution?*. NY: Monthly Review Press, 1967

Debray, R. 'Marxism and the National Question'. *New Left Review* (1977), no. 105

Degras, J., ed. *Documents of the Third International*, Vols. 1-3. London: Oxford University Press, 1956-65

Degras, J., ed. *Soviet Documents on Foreign Policy*. NY: Octagon, 1978

'Deklaratsia Soveshchania Kommunisticheskikh i Rabochikh Partii Sotsialisticheskikh Stran'. *Pravda* (22 Nov. 1957)

Desfosses-Cohn, H. *Soviet Policy toward Black Africa: The Focus on National Integration*. NY: Praeger, 1972

Deutscher, I. *Stalin*. Harmondsworth: Penguin, 1977

Dimitriev, V. 'Kontinent Bor'by i Nadezhdy'. *AiAS* (1963), no. 4.

Dirlik, A. 'National Development and Social Revolution in Early Chinese Marxist Thought'. *CQ* (1974), no. 58

Djilas, M. *Conversations with Stalin*. London: Hart-Davis, 1962

Dominguez, J. *Cuba: Order and Revolution*. Cambridge: Harvard Univesity Press, 1978

Dominguez, J. *Insurrection or Loyalty: The Breakdown of the Spanish American Empire*. Cambridge: Harvard University Press, 1980

Dorris, C. 'Peasant Mobilization in North China: Origins of Yenen Communism'. *CQ* (1976), no. 68

Drambyants, G. 'Aktual'nye Problemy Natsional'no-osvoboditel'novo Dvizhenia'. *K* (1968), no. 18

Duncan, R., Ed. *Soviet Policy in Developing Countries*. Walthan: Ginn-Blaisdell, 1969

Emerson, R. *From Empire to Nation*. Cambridge: Harvard University Press, 1962

Engels, F. *The Anti-Duhring*. Chicago: Kerr, 1936

Ergang, R. *Herder and the Foundations of German Nationalism*. NY: Columbia University Press, 1931

Fall, B., ed. *Ho Chi Minh on Revolution*. NY: Praeger, 1967

Fanon, F. *Studies in a Dying Colonialism*. NY: Monthly Review Press, 1965

Fanon, F. *The Wretched of the Earth*. Harmondsworth: Penguin, 1967

Fanon, F. *Towards the African Revolution*. Harmondsworth: Penguin, 1970

Freedman, R. *Soviet Policy toward the Middle East since 1970*. NY. Praeger, 1982

FRELIMO. 'Economic and Social Directives'. *PP* (1977), no. 7/8

Frolich, P. *Rosa Luxemburg: Ideas in Action*. London: Pluto, 1972

Gafurov, B. 'The Soviet Union and the National Liberation Movement'. *IA* (1971), no. 7

Gandhi, M. *All Men Are Brothers*. Paris: UNESCO, 1958

Garvey, A.J., ed. *The Philosophy and Opinions of Marcus Garvey*. London: Frank Cass, 1967

Gendzier, I. *Frantz Fanon: A Critical Study*. London: Wildwood, 1973

Gittings, J. *Survey of the Sino-Soviet Dispute*. London: Oxford University Press, 1968

Gittings, J. 'New Light on Mao – His View of the World'. *CQ* (1974), no. 60

Gittings, J. *The World and China, 1922-1972*. London: Eyre Methuen, 1974

Goldman, E. *The Tragedy of Lyndon Johnson*. NY: Knopf, 1969

Goldstein, S. 'The Chinese Revolution and the Colonial Areas: The View from Yenan'. *CQ* (1978), no. 75

Gott, R. *Rural Guerrillas in Latin America*. Harmondsworth, Penguin, 1973

Gremillion, J., ed. *The Gospel of Peace and Justice*. Maryknoll, NY: Orbis, 1976

Gromyko, A. 'Socialist Orientation in Africa'. *IA* (1979), no. 9

Gromyko, A. 'Soviet Foreign Policy and Africa'. *IA* (1982), no. 2

Gromyko, A. and Ponomarev, B. *Soviet Foreign Policy Today*. Moscow: Progress, 1981

Grubel, H. *International Economics*. Homewood, Ill.: Richard Irwin, 1977

Gurr, T.R. *Why Men Rebel*, Princeton: Princeton University Press, 1970

Gutierrez, G. *A Theology of Liberation*. Maryknoll, NY: Orbis, 1973

Guzevaty, V. ' "Third Way" or Genuine Freedom'. *IA* (1963), no. 4

Hamilton, A. *Hamilton's Works*

Hamrin, C. 'China Reassesses the Superpowers'. *Pacific Affairs* LVI (1983), no. 2

Handyside, R., ed. *Revolution in Guine*. London: Stage 1, 1969

Hartz, L. *The Liberal Tradition in America*. NY: Harcourt, Brace and Winston, 1955

Henze, P. 'Communism and Ethiopia'. *Problems of Communism* XXX (1981), no. 3

Hoffmann, S. *Gulliver's Troubles, Or the Setting of American Foreign Policy*. NY: McGraw Hill, 1968

Hofstadter, R. *The American Political Tradition*. NY: Vintage, 1973

Horne, A. *A Savage War of Peace*. London: Macmillan, 1977

Hosmer, S. and Wolfe, T. *Soviet Policy and Practice toward Third World Conflicts*. Lexington: Heath, 1982

Humbaraci, A. and Muchnik, N. *Portugal's African Wars*. London: Macmillan. 1974

Huntington, S. *Political Order in Changing Societies*. New Haven: Yale University Press, 1968

Iovchuk, M. 'Internatsionalizm Sotsialisticheskoi Kul'tury'. *Voprosy Filosofii* (1976), no. 12

Irkhin, Yu. 'Avangardnye Revolyutsionnye Partii Trudyashchikhsya Osvobodivshikhsya Stran'. *Voprosy Istorii* (1982), no. 4

Iskenderov, A. 'Rabochii Klass i Natsional'no-osvoboditel'noe Dvizhenie'. *AiAS* (1962), no. 5

Ivanov, K. 'Present Day Colonialism and International Relations'. *IA* (1962), no. 4

Ivanov, K. 'The National Liberation Movement and the Non-capitalist Path of Development'. *IA* (1964), no. 12

Jackson, R. and Rosberg, C. 'Why Africa's Weak States Persist: The Empirical and Juridical in Statehood'. *World Politics* XXXV (1982), no. 1

Johnson, C. *Peasant Mobilization and Communist Power*. Stanford: Stanford University Press, 1962

Kanet, R. 'The Comintern and the "Negro Question": Communist Policy in the US and Africa'. *Survey* XIX (1973), no. 4

Kanet, R. *The Soviet Union and the Developing Countries*. Baltimore: Johns Hopkins Press, 1974

Kanet, R. *Soviet Foreign Policy in the 1980s*. NY: Praeger, 1982

Kaplan, S., ed. *Diplomacy of Power: Soviet Armed Force as a Political Instrument*. Washington: Brookings, 1981

Kapur, H. *The Soviet Union and the Emerging Nations*. London: M. Joseph, 1968

Katz, M. *The Third World in Soviet Military Thought*. London: Croom Helm, 1982

Kaufman, A. 'O Roli Rabochevo Klassa i Evo Partii v Stranakh Sotsialisticheskoi Orientatsii'. *NAiA* (1976), no. 4

Kautsky, J. *Moscow and the Communist Party of India*. London: Chapman and Hall, 1956

Kautsky, K. *Socialism and Colonial Policy: An Analysis*. Belfast: Athol, 1975

Kedourie, E. *Nationalism and Nationalist Movements in Asia and Africa*. NY: Meridian, 1970

Keohane, R. and Nye, J. *Power and Interdependence*. Boston: Little and Brown, 1977

Khoros, V. ' "Narodnichestvo" na Sovremennom Etape Natsional'no-osvoboditel'noi Revolyutsii'. *NAiA* (1973), no. 3

Khrushchev, N. 'Speech at Rangoon University' (1955). *IA* (1956), no. 1

Khrushchev, N. 'Otchotnyi Doklad Ts. K. KPSS XX S'ezdu'. *Pravda* (15 Feb. 1956)

Khrushchev, N. 'Vseocherednoi XXI S'ezd KPSS: Doklad Tov. N.S. Krushcheva'. *Pravda* (28 Jan. 1959)

Khrushchev, N. 'Otchot Ts. K. KPSS XXII S'ezdu'. *Pravda* (18 Oct. 1961)

Khrushcev, N. 'O Programme KPSS: Doklad Tov. N.S. Khrushcheva'. *Pravda* (19 Oct. 1961)

Khrushchev, N. 'Rech' Tov. N.S. Khrushcheva'. *Pravda* (20 May 1962)

Khrushchev, N. 'Otvety N.S. Khrushcheva na Voprosy Redaktsii Gazet "Ganien Taims", "Alzhei Repyubliken", "Pepl' ", i "Botataun" '. *Pravda* (22 Dec. 1963)

Khrushchev, N. *Khrushchev Remembers*. Harmondsworth: Penguin, 1977

Kim, G. 'Sovetskii Soyuz i Natsional'no-osvoboditel'noe Dvizhenie'. *MEïMO* (1982), no. 9. Translated in *CDSP* XXXIV (1982), no. 41

Kim, G. and Kaufman, A. 'Non-capitalist Development: Achievements and Difficulties'. *IA* (1967), no. 12

Kim, G. and Kaufman, A. 'Leninskie Printsipy Soyuza Sotsializma s Natsional'no-osvoboditel'nym Dvizheniem'. *NAiA* (1970), no. 2

Kim, G. and Kaufman, A. 'Ob Ideologicheskikh Techeniakh v Stranakh Tret'evo Mira'. *NAiA* (1971), no. 5

Kim, G. and Kaufman, A. 'XXV S'ezd KPSS i Problemy Natsional'no-osvoboditel'-naya Revolyutsia'. *NAiA* (1976), no. 3

Kim, G. and Shastitko, P. 'Nekotorye Problemy Natsional'no-osvoboditel'noi Revolyutsii v Azii i Afrike'. *Voprosy Istorii* (1973), no. 8

Kiva, A. 'The National Liberation Movement Today'. *IA* (1972), no. 8

Kohn, H. *The Idea of Nationalism*. NY: Collier, 1967

Kohn, H. 'Nationalism'. *International Encyclopedia of the Social Sciences*, VII. London: Macmillan, 1968

Kolakowski, L. *Main Currents of Marxism*. London: Oxford University Press, 1978

*Kommunist*. (Peredovaya) – 'Natsional'no-osvoboditel'noe Dvizhenie – Neot'-emlemaya Chast' Mirovovo Revolyutsionnovo Protsessa'. *K* (1962), no. 2

Kozygin, A. 'O Gosudarstvennom Plane Razvitia Narodnovo Khozyaistva SSSR na 1965 God'. *Pravda* (10 Feb. 1964)

Kremnyov, M. 'The UAR – Its Progress and Problems'. *WMR* (1964), no. 7

Kudryavtsev, V. 'Let's Be Objective'. *NT* (1964), no. 31

Kudryavtsev, V. 'V Ch'ikh Interesakh?' *Izvestia* (26 Feb. 1977)

Kunaev, D. 'Leninizm i Natsional'no-osvoboditel'naya Revolyutisa'. *K* (1969), no. 17

Kuusinen, O. 'Rech' O.V. Kuusinena [XX S'ezdu] '. *Pravda* (20 Feb. 1956)

Kuusinen, O. 'Rech' na Fevral'skom Plenume (1964 g.) KPSS'. *Pravda* (19 May 1964)

Langley, J. ed. *Ideologies of Liberation in Black Africa, 1856-1970*. London: Rex Collings, 1969

Legge, J. *Sukarno: A Political Biography*. London: Allen Lane, 1972

Legum, C. *Pan-Africanism: A Short Political Guide*. London: Pall Mall, 1962

Legvold, R. *Soviet Policy in West Africa*. Cambridge: Harvard University Press, 1970

Lemarchand, R., ed. *American Policy in Southern Africa: The Stakes and the Stances*. Washington: University Press of America, 1981

Lenin, V. *Collected Works*. London, Lawrence and Wishart, 1960

Lewis, A. 'Lessons from Argentina'. *NYT* (26 Jan. 1984)

Li, V. 'The Role of the National Liberation Movement in the Anti-imperialist Struggle'. *IA* (1971), no. 12

Liberation Support Movement. *Zimbabwe: The Final Advance*. Oakland: LSM Press, 1978

Lichtheim, G. *The Concept of Ideology and Other Essays*. NY: Random House, 1967

Lin Piao. *Long Live the Victory of People's War*. *Peking Review* (1964), no. 36

List, F. *The National System of Political Economy*. Philadelphia: Lippincott, 1856

Litman, A. 'Ob Opredelenii Ponyatia i Klassifakatsii Tipov Natsionalizma'. *NAiA* (1975), no. 1

London, K. ed. *The Soviet Union in World Politics*. Boulder: Westview, 1980

Lowenthal, R. 'On National Democracy'. *Survey* (1963), no. 47

Lufti al-Kholi. 'Leninzm i Natsional'no-osvoboditel'noe Dvizhenie'. *NAiA* (1970), no. 2

Machel, S. *Sowing the Seeds of Revolution*. London: Committee for Freedom in Mozambique, Angola and Guine-Bissau, 1975

Macridis, R., ed. *Foreign Policy and World Politics*. Englewood Cliffs, NJ: Prentice Hall, 1976

Mallin, J., ed. *'Che' Guevara on Revolution*. Coral Gables: University of Miami Press, 1969

Mandouze, A. *La Revolution Algerienne par les Textes*. Paris: Maspero, 1961

Mannheim, K. *Ideology and Utopia*. London: Routledge and Kegan Paul, 1936

Mao Tse-tung. 'The Great Union of the Popular Masses' (1919). As translated in *CQ* (1971), no. 45

Mao Tse-tung. *Selected Works*. Peking: Foreign Languages Publishing House

Marcum, J. *The Angolan Revolution*. Boston: MIT Press, 1978

Marighela, C. *For the Liberation of Brazil*. Harmondsworth: Penguin, 1971

Martin, D. and Johnson, P. *The Struggle for Zimbabwe*. NY: Monthly Review Press, 1981

Marx, K. *Capital*. Vol.1. Harmondsworth: Penguin, 1976

Marx, K. and Engels, F. *On Colonialism*. Moscow: Progress, 1976

Marx, K. and Engels, F. *Selected Corespondence,1846-1895*. London: Lawrence and Wishart, 1936

Marx, K. and Engels, F. *Selected Works in One Volume*. London: Lawrence and Wishart, 1968

Marx, K. and Engels, F. *Selected Works in Three Volumes*. Moscow: Progress, 1969

Maslennikov, A. and Trepetov, A. 'Konstruktivnaya Delovaya Diskussia'. *Pravda* (8 Sept. 1979)

Maslennikov, V. 'O Rukovodyaschei Roli Rabochevo Klassa v Natsional'no-osvoboditel'nom Dvizhenii'. *Voprosy Ekonomiki* (1949), no. 9

Mast, H. 'Revolution out of Tradition: The Political Ideology of Tai Chi-t'ao'. *Journal of Asian Studies* XXVIII (1974), no. 1

Mazzini, J. *The Duties of Man and Other Essays*. London: Dent and Sons, 1936

Mboya, T. *Freedom and After*. London: Andre Deutsch, 1963

McCann, D. *Christian Realism and Liberation Theology*. Maryknoll, NY: Orbis, 1981

McLane, C. *Soviet Strategies in South East Asia*. Princeton, Princeton University Press, 1966

McVey, R. *The Soviet View of the Indonesian Revolution*. Ithaca: Cornell South

East Asian Studies Program, 1957

Medvedev, V. 'Razvitoi Sotsializm: Ekonomika, Politika, Ideologia'. *Pravda* (13 July 1979)

Meisner, M. 'The Despotism of Concepts: Wittfogel and Marx on China'. *CQ* (1963), no. 16

Meisner, M. *Li Ta-chao and the Foundations of Chinese Marxism*. NY: Atheneum, 1977

Meyer, A. *Leninism*. Cambridge: Harvard University Press, 1957

Migdal, J. *Peasants, Politics and Revolution: Pressures toward Political and Social Change in the Third World*. Princeton: Princeton University Press, 1974

Mikoyan, A. 'Rech' A.I. Mikoyana [XX S'ezdu] '. *Pravda* (18 Feb. 1956)

Mill, J.S. *Three Essays*. London: Oxford University Press, 1975

*MEiMO*. 'Diskussia: Sotsializm, Kapitalizm, Razvivayushchiesya Strany'. *MEiMO* (1964), no. 4 and no. 6

Mirskii, G. 'Sotsializm, Imperializm, i Afro-Aziatskaya Solidarnost', *Izvestia* (16 July 1963).

Mirskii, G. 'The Proletariat and National Liberation'. *NT* (1964), no. 18

Mirskii, Z. 'Maoist Ideology: Behind the Facade'. *NT* (1975), no. 7

Mondlane, E. 'The Movement for Freedom in Mozambique', *PA* (1965), no. 53

Mondlane, E. *The Struggle for Mozambique*. Harmondsworth: Penguin, 1969

Moore, B. *The Social Origins of Dictatorship and Democracy*. Boston: Beacon, 1967

Morison, D. 'Tropical Africa: The New Soviet Outlook'. *Mizan* XII (1971), no. 1

MPLA. 'Declaration'. *PP* (1976), no. 5

MPLA. *Documents of the MPLA Plenary*. London: Mozambique, Angola, Guine-Bissau Information Centre, 1976

MPLA. *Road to Liberation*. Oakland: LSM Press, 1976

MPLA. *Report to the First Congress*. London: Mozambique, Angola, Guine-Bissau Information Centre, 1977

Mukhitdinov, N. 'Prenia po Dokladu Tov. N.S. Khrushcheva'. *Pravda* (31 Jan. 1959)

*Namibia News*. 'Interview with E. Katjivena'. *Namibia News* II (1970), nos. 7-12

Nasser, G. *The Philosopy of the Revolution*. Cairo: Dar-al-Maaref, 1954

Nehru, J. *India and the World*. London: George Allen and Unwin, 1936

Nehru, J. *A Discovery of India*. London: Meridian, 1951

Nehru, J. *An Autobiography*. London: The Bodley Head, 1953

Nettl, J. *Rosa Luxemburg*. London: Oxford University Press, 1966

Nielsen, W. *The Great Powers in Africa*. London: Pall Mall, 1969

Nkrumah, K. *I Speak of Freedom*. London: Heinemann, 1961

Nkrumah, K. *Africa Must Unite*. London: Heinemann, 1963

Nkrumah, K. *Consciencism*. London: Heinemann, 1964

Nkrumah, K. *Neocolonialism: The Last Stage of Imperialism*. London: Nelson, 1965

Nkrumah, K. *A Handbook of Revolutionary Warfare*. NY: International Publishers, 1968

Novopashin, Yu. 'Vozdeistvie Real'novo Sotsializma na Mirovoi Revolyutsionnyi Protsess: Metodologicheskie Aspekty'. *Voprosy Filosofii* (1982), no. 8

Nyangoni, C. and Nyandoro, G., eds. *Zimbabwe Independence Movements, Select Documents*. London: Rex Collings, 1979

Nyerere, J. 'African Unity'. *PA* (1961), no. 39

Nyerere, J. *Uhuru na Umoja: Freedom and Unity*. London: Oxford University Press, 1967

Nyerere, J. *Uhuru na Ujamaa: Freedom and Socialism*. London: Oxford University Press, 1968

Nyerere, J. 'Speech at the University of Ibadan'. *African Currents* (1977), no. 8

Ogunbadejo, O. 'Soviet Policies in Africa'. *African Affairs* LXXIX (1980), no. 316

Ogurtsov, S. 'Razvivayushchiesya Strany i Sotsial'nyi Progress'.*AiAS* (1963), no. 7

Ojha, I. *Soviet and Chinese Conceptions of the National Bourgeoisie in the Developing Areas*. PhD Dissertation, Fletcher School of Law and Diplomacy, 1965

Ottaway, D. and M. *Afrocommunism*. NY: Africana, 1981

Ovchinnikov, V. 'Ot Managua k Deli'. *Pravda* (28 Jan. 1983)

Packenham, R. *Liberal America and the Third World*. Princeton: Princeton University Press, 1973

Padmore, G. *Panafricanism or Communism?* London, Dennis Dobson, 1956

*Peking Review*. Miscellaneous articles and documents, 1957-1976

Pfeffer, R. ed. *No More Vietnams?* NY: Harper and Row, 1968

Ponomarev, B. 'O Gosudarstve Natsional'noi Demokratii'. *K* (1961), no. 8

Ponomarev, B. 'Aktual'nye Problemy Teorii Mirovovo Revolyutsionnovo Protsessa'. *K* (1971), no. 15

Popov, Yu. 'Formirovanie Obshchestvennoi Mysly v Stranakh Afriki'. *NAiA* (1970), no. 1

Popov, Yu. 'O Prirode Melkoburzhuaznoi Ideologii v Stranakh Afriki'. *NAiA* (1971), no. 5

Potekhin, I. 'Panafrikanizm i Bor'ba Dvukh Ideologii'. *K* (1964), no. 1

*Pravda*. 'Vysshii Internatsional'nyk Dolg Stran Sotsializma'. *Pravda* (27 Oct. 1965)

*Pravda*. 'K Shestomu Plenumu Ts. K. KPK'. *Pravda* (5 July 1981)

*Presence Africaine*. 'Our Future'. *PA* (1960-1961), no. 37

Primakov, E. 'Krepit' Edinstvo Sil Boryushchikhsya protiv Kolonializma'. *Pravda* (12 June 1965)

Ra'anan, U. 'Moscow and the "Third World" '. *Problems of Communism* XIV (1965), no. 1

Reznikov, A. 'Lenin i Natsional'no-osvoboditel'noe Dvizhenie'. *K* (1967), no. 7

Reznikov, A. 'Iz Istorii Podgotovki V. I. Leninym Reshenii II Kongressa Kominterna po Natsional'no-kolonial'nomu Voprosu'. *NAiA* (1971), no. 2

Rodinson, M. *Marxism and the Muslim World*. NY: Monthly Review Press, 1981

Rosberg, C. and Callaghy, T. *Socialism in Sub-Saharan Africa: A Reaassessment*. Berkeley: Institute of International Studies, 1979

Rostow, W. *The Stages of Economic Growth: A Non-communist Manifesto*. Cambridge, Cambridge University Press, 1961

Rousseau, J.-J. *The Social Contract*. Harmondsworth: Penguin, 1976

Rubinstein, A., ed. *The Foreign Policy of the Soviet Union*. NY: Random House, 1966

Ruggie, J. *The Antinomies of Interdependence*. NY: Columbia University Press, 1983

Salychev, S. 'Faktory Revolyutsii'. *Pravda* (8 Sept. 1980)

Schichor, Y. *The Middle East in China's Foreign Policy, 1949-1977*. London: Cambridge University Press, 1979

Schriffin, H. *Sun Yat-sen and the Origins of the Chinese Revolution*. Los Angeles: University of California Press, 1970
Schlesinger, A. 'Foreign Policy and the American Character'. *Foreign Affairs* (fall, 1983)
Schram, S. *The Political Thought of Mao Tse-tung*. NY: Praeger, 1969
Schram, S. *Mao Tse-tung*. Harmondsworth: Penguin, 1977
Schram, S. ed. *Mao Tse-tung Unrehearsed*. Harmondsworth: Penguin, 1979
Schurmann, F. *Ideology and Organization in Communist China*, 2nd edn. Berkeley: University of California Press, 1971
Schwartz, B. *Chinese Communism and the Rise of Mao*. Cambridge: Harvard University Press, 1952
Schwartz, B. *Communism and China: Ideology in Flux*. Cambridge: Harvard University Press, 1968
Senghor, L.'L'Esprit de la Civilisation ou Les Lois de la Culture Negro-Africaine'. *PA* (1956), no. 8-10
Senghor, L. 'Negritude and the Concept of Universal Civilization'. *PA* (1959), no. 24
Seton-Watson, H. *Nations and States*. London: Methuen, 1977
Sharabi, H., ed. *Nationalism and Revolution in the Arab World*. NY: Van Nostrand, 1966
Sharabi, H. *Arab Intellectuals and the West: The Formative Years, 1875-1914*. Baltimore: Johns Hopkins Press, 1970
Shari'ati, A. *On the Sociology of Islam*. Berkeley: Mizan, 1979
Shari'ati, A. *Marxism and Other Western Fallacies: An Islamic Critique*. Berkeley: Mizan, 1980
Shepilov, D. 'Rech' Tov. D.T. Shepilova [XX S'ezdu]'. *Pravda* (17 Feb. 1956)
Shinn, W. 'The National Democratic State'. *World Politics* XV (1963), no. 3
Simonia, N. 'O Kharaktere Natsional'no-osvoboditel'noi Revolyutsii'. *NAiA* (1966), no. 6
Simonia, N. 'Natsionalizm i Politicheskaya Bor'ba v Osvobodivshikhsya Stranakh'. *MEiMO* (1972), nos. 1 and 2
Sithole, N. *African Nationalism*. London, Oxford University Press, 1968
Slovo, J. 'Interview with Marcelino Dos Santos'. *African Communist* (1973), no. 55
Slovo, J. 'Interview with Lucio Lara'. *African Communist* (1978), no. 74
Smith, E. *Turkey: The Origins of the Kemalist Movement*. Washington, Judd and Detweiler, 1959
Snow, E. *Red Star over China*. Harmondsworth: Penguin, 1977
Sobolev, A. 'National Democracy: The Way to Social Progress'. *WMR* VI (1963), no. 2
Sobolev, A. 'Problems of Social Progress'. *WMR* X (1967), no. 1
SWAPO. *Namibia: SWAPO Fights for Freedom*. Oakland: LSM Press, 1978
Spectar, I. *The Soviet Union and the Muslim World*. Seattle: University of Washington Press, 1969
Stalin, J. *Marxism and the National and Colonial Question*. London: Lawrence and Wishart, 1942
Stalin, J. *Fundamentals of Leninism* NY: International Publishers, 1974
Strausz-Hupe, R. and Hazard, H., eds. *The Idea of Colonialism*. NY: Praeger, 1958
Sukarno, A. 'Nationalism, Islam, and Marxism' (1926). Ithaca: Cornell Modern

Indonesia Project, 1960

Sun Yat-sen, *A Programme of National Reconstruction for China*. London: Hutchinson, 1927

Sun Yat-sen. *San Min Chu-i*. Taipei: Taipei Publishing Co., 1963

Suslov, M. 'Rech' Tov M.A. Suslova [XX S'ezdu]'. *Pravda* (17 Feb. 1956)

Suslov, M. 'O Bor'be za Splochennost' Mezhdunarodnovo Kommunisticheskovo Dvizhenia: Doklad Tov. M.A. Suslova na Plenume KPSS'. *Pravda* (3 Apr. 1964)

Suslov, M. 'Kommunisticheskoe Dvizhenie v Avangarde Bor'by za Mir, Sotsializm, i Natsional'noe Osvobozhdenie'. *K* (1975), no. 11

Sutan Sjahrir. *Out of Exile*. NY: John Day, 1949

Tamarin, L. 'Raschoty i Proschoty Imperialistov v Afrike'. *K* (1976), no. 18

Tekin Alp. *Le Kemalisme*. Paris: Librairie Felix Alcan, 1937

Toure, S. *Experience Guineene et Unite Africaine*. Paris: Presence Africaine, 1959

Toure, S. 'Le Leader Politique Considere comme le Representant d'une Culture'. *PA* (1959), no. 24-5

Toure, S. *Guinean Revolution and Social Progress*. Cairo: SOP Press, n.d

Toure, S. *The Doctrine and Methods of the P.D.G.* Conakry: n.p., 1963

Truong Chinh, *Primer for Revolt*. NY: Praeger, 1963

Tucker, R. *The Marxian Revolutionary Idea*. NY: Norton, 1970

Turner, F. *Catholicism and Political Development in Latin America*. Chapel Hill: The University of North Carolina Press, 1971

Tyagunenko, V. 'Zaklyuchitel'noe Slovo' in *MEiMO*. 'Diskussia: Sotsializm, Kapitalizm, Slaborazvitye Strany'

Tyagunenko, V. 'Mirovoi Sotsializm i Natsional'no-osvoboditel'naya Revolyutsia'. v Svete Leninizma'. *MEiMO* (1970), no. 5

Tyagunenko, V. 'Mirovoi Sotsializm i Natsional'no-osvoboditel'noi Revolyutsii'. *K* (1973), no. 8

Tyul'panov, V. 'Tendentsii Razvitia "Tret'evo Mira" '. *K* (1975), no. 3

Ulam, A. *Expansion and Coexistence*. NY: Praeger, 1974

Ul'yanovsky, R. 'Sotsializm i Natsional'no-osvoboditel'naya Bor'ba'. *Pravda* (15 Apr. 1966)

Ul'yanovsky, R. 'Osvoboditel'naya Bor'ba Narodov Afriki'. *K* (1969), no. 11

Ul'yanovksy, R. 'Nekotorye Voprosy Nekapitalisticheskovo Razvitia'. *K* (1971), no. 4

Ul'yanovsky, R. 'Sovremennyi Etap National'no-osvoboditel'novo Dvizhenia i Krest'yanstvo'. *MEiMO* (1971), no. 5

Ul'yanovsky, R. 'Natsional'no-osvoboditel'noe Dvizhenie v Bor'be za Ekono-Micheskuyu Nezavisimost'. *K* (1975), no. 14

Ul'yanovsky, R. *Present-Day Problems in Asia and Africa*. Moscow: Progress, 1980

Valkenier, E. 'New Trends in Soviet Economic Relations with the Third World'. *World Politics* XXII (1970), no. 3

Van Slyke, L. *Enemies and Friends: The United Front in Chinese Communist History*. Stanford: Stanford University Press, 1967

Vo Nguyen Giap. *People's War, People's Army* NY: Praeger, 1962

Wallerstein, I. 'The Political Ideology of the P.D.G.'. *PA* (1962), no. 40

Waltz, K. *Man, The State, and War*. NY: Columbia University Press, 1959

Weatherbee, D. *Ideology in Indonesia*. New Haven: Yale South East Asian Studies Program, 1966

Whitaker, J. ed. *The US and Africa: Vital Interests*. NY: New York University Press, 1978

White, S. 'Communism and the East, 1920'. *Slavic Review* XXIII (1974), no. 4

Wicker, T. 'Marshall Plan Again?'. *NYT* (9 Jan. 1984)

Wilson, E. *Russia and Africa*. London: Holmes and Meier, 1974

Wylie, R. 'Mao Tse-tung, Ch'en Po-ta, and the "Sinification of Marxism", 1936-1938'. *CQ* (1979), no. 79

Young, C. *Ideology and Development in Africa*. New Haven: Yale University Press, 1982

Yu, G. *China's Africa Policy – A Study of Tanzania*. London: Praeger, 1975

'Zadachi Bor'by protiv Imperializma na Sovremennom Etape i Edinstvo Deistvii Kommunisticheskikh i Rabochikh Partii, Vsekh Antiimperialisticheskikh Sil'. *Pravda* (18 June 1969)

Zagladin, V. 'Internatsionalizm – Znamya Kommunistov'. *Pravda* (20 Apr. 1976)

Zagoria, D. *The Sino-Soviet Conflict, 1956-1961*. Princeton: Princeton University Press, 1962

Zagoria, D. 'Into the Breach: New Soviet Allies in the Third World'. *Foreign Affairs* (spring, 1979)

Zarodov, K. *Sotsializm, Mir, Revolyutsia: Nekotorye Voprosy Teorii i Praktiki Mezhdunarodnykh Otnoshenii i Klassovoi Bor'by*. Moscow, Politizdat., 1977

'Zayavlenie Soveshchania Predstavitelei Kommunisticheskikh i Rabochikh Partii'. *Pravda* (6 Dec 1960)

Zhdanov, A. 'The International Situation'. *For a Lasting Peace, For a People's Democracy* (1947), no. 1

Zhukov, E. 'Velikaya Oktyabr'skaya Revolyutsia i Kolonial'nyi Vostok', *Bol'shevik* (1947), no. 23

Zhukov, E. 'Voprosy Natsional'no-kolonial'noi Bor'by posle Vtoroi Mirovoi Voiny'. *Voprosy Ekonomiki* (1949), no. 9

Zhukov, E. 'Raspad Kolonial'noi Sistemy Imperializma'. *Partiinaya Zhizn'* (1956), no. 16

Zhukov, E. 'Znamechatel'nyi Faktor Nashevo Vremeni'. *Pravda* (26 Aug. 1960)

Zhukov, E. 'Natsional'no-osvoboditel'noe Dvizhenie Narodov Azii i Afriki'. *K* (1969), no. 4

Zimmerman, W. *Soviet Perspectives on International Relations, 1956-1967*. Princeton: Princeton University Press, 1969

Zimmern, A., ed. *Modern Political Doctrines*. London: Oxford University Press, 1939

Zimyanin, V. 'Leninizm – Revolyutsionnoe Znamya Nashei Epokhi'. *Pravda* (23 Apr. 1977)

# INDEX

Abbas, F. 51, 109, 115n, 117n, 129n
Abrams, E. 207n
Adamolekun, L. 125n, 127n
Afghanistan 4, 83, 132, 137, 141, 152, 158, 175
Africa 52, 60, 66, 67, 75, 80, 103, 113, 125n, 135, 137, 140, 143, 148, 159, 162, 165, 166, 172, 175, 201, 205, 210
African National Congress (ANC) 42, 47, 76, 87, 93, 109, 114n, 116n, 125n
African socialism 95, 162; see also national forms of socialism
Afro-Asian Movement 45, 82, 112, 152, 154, 163; see also Bandung; Nonalignment; Third World solidarity
Afro-Asian People's Solidarity Organization (AAPSO) 67, 76, 127n
Afro-marxism 48
agrarian revolution 49, 51, 89, 101, 115n
Ahmad, E. 206n, 208n
Akopov, G. 190n
Akopyan, G. 190n
al-Kholi, Lufti 194n, 196n
Alekseev, E. 188n
Algeria 2, 43, 51, 68, 87, 92, 105, 110, 129n, 137, 163, 164, 174
Algerian Communist Party 67
alienation 18, 21
Aliev, A. 189n, 190n
Aliev, G. 189n, 192n
Alpers, E. 114n, 116n, 120n, 121n, 127n
American Revolution 42
Aminullah 35, 132
Andropov, Yu. 189n
Angola 4, 44, 53, 69, 77, 87, 116n, 140, 141, 143, 158, 166, 175, 203, 210
anti-feudal revolution 33, 34, 64, 105, 182; see also bourgeois democratic revolution
apartheid 76
Argentina 140, 202

armed struggle; see violence
Asia 17, 18, 20, 25, 28, 35, 66, 67, 80, 108, 113, 136, 137, 148, 159, 161, 169, 172, 180, 201, 205, 210
Asiatic mode of production 18, 22, 23, 117n
Aspaturian, V. 8n, 197n
Attwood, W. 194n
Avineri, S. 23, 38n, 39n

Ba'athist Party 60
Bagramov, E. 189n, 190n, 191n
Bakdash, K. 114n
Baku Congress 66, 132, 142, 187n
Balabushevich, V. 186n, 187n, 193n
Bandung 82, 152
Barghoorn, F. 193n
Barnet, R. 206n, 209n
base areas 89, 105
Batista, F. 52
Bedeski, R. 121n
Belgium 63
Belyayev, I. 162
Ben Bella, A. 51, 130n, 163, 173
Bender, G. 208n
Bennigsen, A. 114n, 123n, 126n
Benton, G. 126n
Bialer, S. 195n
Biko, S. 61, 119n
Black Consciousness Movement 61
Blackburn, R. 116n, 122n
Blasier, C. 114n, 126n, 196n, 207n, 208n
Blechman, B. 208n
Blida 56
Blyden, E. 94, 125n
Bodin, J. 10
Bogdanov, K. 194n
bourgeois democratic revolution 18, 23, 24, 34, 35, 45; see also revolution; stages of revolution; united front
bourgeoisie 18, 21, 22, 23, 28, 30, 31, 34, 35, 38n, 78, 100, 101, 121n, 122n, 149, 150, 153, 154, 169, 170, 176, 178, 179, 185, 187n, 194n; see also national

228